HUMOR
THE PSYCHOLOGY OF
LIVING BUOYANTLY

THE PLENUM SERIES IN SOCIAL/CLINICAL PSYCHOLOGY

Series Editor: C. R. Snyder

University of Kansas
Lawrence, Kansas

HUMOR
THE PSYCHOLOGY OF
LIVING BUOYANTLY

HERBERT M. LEFCOURT
University of Waterloo
Waterloo, Ontario, Canada

KLUWER ACADEMIC / PLENUM PUBLISHERS
NEW YORK, BOSTON, DORDRECHT, LONDON, MOSCOW

Library of Congress Cataloging-in-Publication Data

Lefcourt, Herbert M.
    Humor: the psychology of living buoyantly/Herbert M. Lefcourt
    p. cm. — (The Plenum series in social/clinical psychology)
    Includes bibliographical references (p.) and indexes.
    ISBN 0-306-46407-1
    1. Wit and humor—Psychological aspects. 2. Wit and humor—Therapeutic use. I. Title.
    II. Series.

BF575.L3 L435 2000
152.4'3—dc21
                                                                              00-033112

ISBN: 0-306-46407-1

©2001 Kluwer Academic / Plenum Publishers, New York
233 Spring Street, New York, New York 10013

http://www.wkap.nl/

10 9 8 7 6 5 4 3 2 1

A C.I.P. record for this book is available from the Library of Congress

Printed in the United States of America

PREFACE

Although I have been involved in the psychological study of humor for more than a decade, it was not until I began reading Doris Kearns Goodwin's *Wait Till Next Year* (1997) that I began to connect my research interest in humor with my own personal history. In this autobiographical memoir by the Pulitzer Prize-winning presidential biographer, Goodwin recounts growing up in the suburbs of New York City where she enjoyed the warmth of family and neighbors in what seemed to be an idyllic childhood. Her commitment to and near-obsession with the Brooklyn Dodgers—which gave her much to share with her loving father—resonated with that of my own Dodger's worship, which was central to my existence from the age of about 9 to 18. It was this "religious" commitment that bound our extended family together—my father, cousins, uncles, and me. The women tolerated the male obsession with baseball with some amusement and rarely shared in the enthusiasm. Goodwin's book set in motion memories of funny events that occurred throughout my childhood which undoubtedly contributed to my interest in the study of humor.

Humor and laughter filled the milieu in which I grew up. Family memories are replete with laughter, although I cannot always recall the exact scenarios that resulted in hilarity of such intensity that the milk I was drinking would be forced up into my nose. I can recall, however, a few specific events, such as when, as an innocent six-year-old, I was set up with a "perfect hand" in a card game by my Aunt Lillian—during the moment I had been sent to the kitchen to fetch a platter of treats. The uproarious laughter that erupted with my look of excitement and wide-eyed amazement while I perused that card hand is an indelible memory. Similarly, although more than 50 years have passed since it occurred, the hilarity that exploded when I was about to furtively flush away a bogus dog turd is still fresh in my mind. I had been horrified when my Uncle Dave whispered that I must look in the corner of the living room to spot a fecal disaster. Two days earlier my father had threatened to get rid of our beloved Jasper if the mutt were to have even one more accident in the house. I can just imagine the difficulty the observing adults must have had in stifling their laughter as they watched this benighted child sneak away with the offending turd in my quest to save Jasper from a canine's worst fate. I can also still recall having extended conversations with the "talking brick" that must have convulsed my Aunt Jean as she hid indoors below a windowsill to create magic while I played in the backyard.

Mine was a childhood punctuated with laughter, with family traditions that involved weekly listening to radio's Jack Benny and Fred Allen and watching every Abbott and Costello and every Laurel and Hardy film. Laughter was all around me much of the time—and only recently have I come to realize that it was probably this childhood that fueled my interest in the study of humor.

In this volume, I continue an undertaking that began in my earlier writings concerning stress and those personality characteristics that seem to protect us from it's harmful effects on our health and well-being. Specifically, this book places humor more firmly in the literature concerned with coping processes, the moderation of stressful experiences, and health.

Although I am sanguine about the value of humor in helping people deal with stress, I fear I may "overinflate" the importance of characteristics such as humor as a means of coping with the inevitable difficulties that life presents us. To minimize the likelihood of overinflation I have tried to make it clear that humor is facilitative only at some times and under certain conditions. At other times, personality characteristics such as beliefs about control, the accessibility of social support, and the depths of our commitments may be equal or more prominent psychological tools when we must protect ourselves from succumbing to the effects of particular stressors.

Nevertheless, when remembering my childhood, I recall how humor and laughter helped create feelings of community and closeness. Humor's effects are not ephemeral. Like that of Doris Kearns Goodwin, my childhood was idyllic. Though World War II was a threatening backdrop that cast shadows on everyday life throughout the 1940s, the warmth within a secure and protective web of family, friends, and neighbors, and the laughter and humor in a close and loving family, turned those years into the stuff of nostalgia and grist for this psychologist's mill as I try to comprehend the meaning and effects of humor.

I have taken the liberty of including a number of anecdotes and stories to illustrate "humor in action." Although my biases and talents lie more with demonstrations of empirical research, I have always felt that stories can help to convey the meaning of empirical data, sometimes with greater clarity and (thankfully) less torturous language. In my earlier writings on the locus of control construct, I found numerous literary references to help illuminate the ideas I was presenting. In writing about humor, the problem has been to select the most appropriate stories from the many that could have illustrated points I wanted to make. I hope that my use of both "hard data" and anecdotal reports makes the book useful for the academic and enjoyable at the same time. Humor is a topic worthy of study because of what it tells us about ourselves and our species. But it is also an intrinsically attractive subject because of the amusement we can find in the studies we do and the stories we tell. My hope is that the number of serious researchers who become attracted to the subject of humor will increase, making it a less peripheral subject of study than it is now.

When it comes to acknowledging those who have aided me in the work that has gone into this volume, my greatest gratitude goes to my wife and life partner Barbara Ellen Lefcourt, who has tirelessly edited each portion of this volume and shared with me the breaks in between that refreshed my energy and enthusiasm. Second, I wish to thank the Rockefeller Foundation for allowing me a second residence as a scholar at the Bellagio Study and Conference Center in Bellagio, Italy, where much of this book was finalized. Third, I would like to express my thanks to Dr. Ken Prkachin, who has helped to sharpen my understanding of physiological stress responses. Penultimately, I'd like to thank all of those persons whose stories have served to liven up my theoretical discussions: my students, former strangers whose stories I have come to know, and my children, grandchildren, and other family members with whom much laughter has been shared over the years. Finally, I want to forward my future appreciation to those others who, in sensing the incompleteness of this book, will pick up on the suggested and unfinished contentions and carry on the serious pursuit of understanding what humor contributes to the human condition.

Permission to reprint the selection from Brian Keenan's *An Evil Cradling* was granted by Penguin-Putnam, Inc. The cartoons throughout the book are by Jack Lefcourt, whose comic productions can be seen on the Internet at www.lefcourtland.com.

CONTENTS

Chapter 8

Humor as a Coping Strategy 109

Chapter 9

Humor as a Means of Retaining Social Cohesion and Support 127

Chapter 10

Sense of Humor and Physiological Stress Responses 141

Chapter 11

Sex and Humor: Interactive Predictors of Health? 151

Chapter 12

Summing Up 165

Appendixes

THE CHANGING CONCERNS OF PSYCHOLOGY

If the 20th century had not been so marked by the horrors brought on by two world wars and the threat of a third and "final" war—to say nothing of the skirmishes in between—humor might have been taken as a serious subject for study far earlier than now. Prominent psychological theoreticians such as William James, William McDougall, and Gordon Allport were all curious about the great range of thought processes and behaviors that characterize our species, and they proposed particular personality characteristics that could account for "maturity" and positive states of mind (e.g., "self-regarding sentiment"; "unifying philosophy of life"). Humor, one of those features that seems to be more prevalent among humans than other species, and laughter, which results in aberrant sounds and respiratory activity, were likely to become subjects of investigation for such curiosity-driven psychologists.

Perhaps a signal of the detour from such curiosity driven research in American psychology occurred when Robert S. Woodworth, a notable experimental psychologist at Columbia University, was invited to create a testing device to screen potential draftees into the U.S. Army during World War I. The device was to assess vulnerability to battle fatigue, "shell-shock," or what we now call posttraumatic stress response. This diversion from mainstream experimental psychology, coinciding as it did with an interest in psychopathology that psychoanalytic theoreticians introduced into the United States in the first half of the 20th century, may have helped shape the direction of psychology more toward the care of the "mentally ill" than toward the understanding of "ephemeral" human characteristics, which were not seen to have value in terms of application. The urgency of the U.S. government to deal with mental illnesses manifested by returning World War II veterans further shaped the concerns of psychology. Funding for graduate programs in clinical psychology at universities and the development of Veteran's Administration hospitals across the country where students in clinical psychology were introduced to a variety of exotic psychopathologies, sidelined less urgent interests that were driven more by curiosity than by the need to help. To students in those programs, research into the functioning of memory by experimental psychologists such as Ebbinghouse, for example, might only become of interest if it could illuminate issues such as amnesia following trauma. The abberations of psychosis were far more compelling than were the routine psychological processes of everyday life that might afford pleasure and a sense of well-being.

If interest in processes such as memory, decision making, and cognitive activity was diminished in face of the pressing need to treat persons exhibiting florid forms of psychopathology, then interest in such positive human features as happiness, hope, well-being, euphoria, and humor could easily come to be regarded as trivial. Even if not explicitly labeled as frivolous, the unlikelihood of receiving research grants or rewarding publishing contracts for studying and writing about positive experience in human life no doubt lowered the probability that such positive affect states would be closely examined. Many years have passed since the end of the Second World War, and positive economic conditions have served to allow for the resurfacing of such "frivolous" topics, such as, humor, in fields like psychology.

An early heralding of this resurfacing was evident in the publication of a small book by Marie Jahoda (1958) entitled *Current Concepts of Positive Mental Health*. In this volume, supported by the Joint Commission on Mental Illness and Health of the U.S. Public Health Service, Jahoda grappled with the problems inherent in psychology's entrapment in the "medical model." Health, she argued, could not be defined solely by the absence of illness, which was so characteristic of medical approaches. Rather, she began to address the issue of what humans might aspire to be if they were not thwarted by conditions conducive to the development of psychopathology. In doing so, Jahoda discussed characteristics that were relatively new to psychology at that time and which could serve as crude indices of "positive mental health" and not only indices of the absence of disease.

Attitudes of self-regard, growth, development, self-actualization, personality integration, autonomy, perception of reality, and environmental mastery made up the elements of positive mental health within Jahoda's framework. Questions were raised about how accuracy of self-perception; sense of identity; the investments people made in work, friendships, and love relationships; their plans for shaping their futures; and the integration of internal characteristics or balance of psychic forces could be responsible for resilience in encounters with life's inevitable challenges.

Although the methods used to explore them at that time seem quaint and dated today, many of the constructs Jahoda described are still being used in studies of human well-being. And, Jahoda's contribution raised interest in optimal human functioning in contrast to clinical psychology's predominant obsession with deficits and mental illness

The regard for *optimal states* had not been completely overlooked in psychology. Optimal human functioning had served as a criterion in an earlier experimental literature concerned with motivation and persuasion. Investigators associated with the Yale studies on persuasion spoke of optimal states for influencing people to improve in their self-regulating behaviors. Janis (1965), for example, had discussed the "inverted U" phenomenon in motivational studies in which attitude change toward health-related matters was sought by the investigator. In one study, subjects who were "underaroused" were found unlikely to change attitudes and behavior associated with dental hygiene. Simple information presented without threat seemed to have little impact on habitual behaviors. Likewise, subjects who were shown ghastly pictures of what their mouths could look like with ill-managed dental hygiene were equally unlikely to change their dental habits. These "overaroused" subjects were said to have resorted to defensiveness in the face of highly threatening stimuli. Only those who were exposed to moderate threat, pictures of less repulsive decay than those in the overarousal condition, were found to alter their dental habits.

These findings were replicated in other research studies in which threats were used to induce behavioral change, and the inverted U phenomena that had earlier been referred to in terms of *optimal stimulation* (Leuba, 1955) became well used in attempts to explain how people coped with the effects of different stressors (Janis, 1958). This early concern with optimal stimulation or arousal for moderating human behavior can be seen as an antecedent to the models of coping advanced by Richard Lazarus (1966) and his colleagues (Lazarus & Folkman, 1984), wherein anticipated threats that are appraised as being uncontrollable (nonoptimal arousal) result in emotion-focused responses instead of instrumental responses. To cope instrumentally with the threatening circumstances themselves requires that people feel that they have it in their power to influence those events. If *secondary appraisals* lead the person to see the circumstance as controllable, then the arousal engendered by that event would be less overwhelming, or more optimal.

Despite these interests in the best conditions and states for humans to be in if they are to learn new and better ways of functioning, little progress was evident in the psychological literature concerned with those positive characteristics that could help explain what Jahoda called positive mental health.

One exploration of positive human characteristics was described by Richard Coan (1974) in his book *The Optimal Personality*. Coan expanded on Jahoda's work by presenting empirical evidence about the interrelationships among the constructs she had proposed as indices of positive mental health. However, these investigations served more to encourage interest in optimal functioning than in empirically demonstrating the validity of her proposed characteristics. The last two decades of the 20th century witnessed rapidly growing interest in optimal functioning and explorations undertaken to test its value. Hope, optimism, competence, efficacy, belief in ability to control events, self-regulation, and well-being are commonly accepted terms in the psychological literature today, which will be examined briefly as a prelude to our discussion of humor. However, before we begin this exploration I would like to share something of my own academic odyssey that brought me to the study of humor.

MY PERSONAL ODYSSEY

Throughout my career as a psychologist I have always been drawn more to the investigation of human strengths than to the study of psychopathology. I am more likely to marvel at the courage and competence manifested by individuals in difficult circumstances than to be attracted by examples of deviance and abnormality. Because I find incompetence and bungling commonplace in daily affairs, I never fail to be surprised at evidence of ingenuity, skill, and occasional brilliance as humans deal with seemingly insurmountable obstacles.

In the early 1960s I spent two years as a young psychology intern at the U.S. Public Health Service Hospital in Lexington, Kentucky. Drug addicts from the eastern United States were commonly referred to that institution for treatment, willingly or otherwise. I was often enlisted in assessing the psychological states of incoming patients and was often pleasantly impressed by their intelligence and perspicacity. With some exceptions, they were mostly from the most impoverished urban slums, where one would not expect to routinely find people capable of introspection and philosophical deliberation. Consequently, I became convinced that competence, resilience, and even brilliance could be found anywhere, and would be less of a rarity if people like the patients I was seeing could be helped to succeed in living their lives through the use of social interventions that provided them with opportunities. With such encouragement and support, they could probably find the personal strength to succeed and cease being burdens on the country's health and penal systems.

The larger part of my research career was shaped by these experiences with talented and bright but failed individuals, and my laboratory investigations were often directed at examining the causes of their failures. Many of my research investigations concerned the role of *locus of control* as an explanatory construct deriving from social learning theory (Rotter, 1954) that could account for the failure of people to make efforts to accomplish their chosen goals (Lefcourt, 1982). I contended that if people held external control expectations, disbelieving that their own efforts could attain for them the ends they sought, then they would rarely exert themselves to try to attain their goals. Consequently, they were often doomed to failure in reaching for their desired outcomes. To put it in positive terms, when people hold internal control expectations they are more apt to work at securing valued goals, doing so in the belief that their efforts matter, that they are not simply "tilting at windmills." Given such effort, success, at least, becomes more of a possibility.

While I was enmeshed in the study of control a particular issue often arose in discussions with colleagues and students. It concerned the limitations of internal control as an optimal personality characteristic. Some wondered whether fatalistic (external control–oriented) people would not be at an advantage in situations where little or no control was possible. Or, to put it another way, would people who were accustomed to exerting control in their lives (internal control–oriented) be less capable than fatalistic individuals in dealing with or at least accepting uncontrollable circumstances?

This issue is readily apparent in the famous *serenity prayer* created by Reinhold Niebuhr in 1934, which eventually became the mantra for members of Alcoholics Anonymous. In that prayer, the supplicant instructs himself or herself to struggle when control is possible, accept what is uncontrollable, and be wise enough to know when something is or is not controllable. The idea of accepting what is uncontrollable struck me as potentially being as optimal a response as actively struggling to achieve what is controllable—although we can always wonder about our wisdom in deciding what is or is not controllable. However, even if we acknowledge that accepting of the uncontrollable could be a healthy alternative to continuously beating our heads against the wall in attempts to master insoluble problems, we are faced with the issue of how to recognize acceptance when it occurs. How might "acceptance of the uncontrollable" be manifested? Humor seemed to offer itself as one possible avenue toward the study of acceptance.

As I noted in the preface to an earlier book (Lefcourt & Martin, 1986), humorous incidents occurring at the time of my father's funeral and my reading of Norman Cousins' (1979) *Anatomy of an Illness*, in which humor played an important therapeutic role, had primed my attention to the benefits of humor in aversive circumstances. I described what had seemed a surprising departure from solemnity at my father's funeral. The reuniting of family members from far and wide proved to be an occasion for both mirth and goodwill. This was not at all out of disrespect for the deceased but was almost in his honor. My father had always been ready to make light of the grimmest circumstances, often with a joke or cliché that somehow would fit the occasion and cause others to take it less seriously. The humor displayed at his funeral was very much in character with the way in which he would have jested had he been there to take part. Most importantly, the relatives reveled in that good humor so that everyone left the ceremonies with better feelings toward each other.

In the limousine on the way to the funeral the family members who were closest to the deceased had, by the time the car reached the cemetery, been joking and laughing quite a bit, much to their own surprise. The jokes for the most part derived from my father's interests and concerns. For example, because he had been a devoted gardener who always griped aloud about garden pests while digging grubs from his plant beds, macabre jokes about it being time for the "revenge of the grubs" were typical. Others continued the badinage when the pallbearers entered the chapel prematurely to remove the coffin during a seemingly endless eulogy by a garrulous and obviously annoyed rabbi. "It was Irv who called them in, saying . . .enough already, get me out of here," quipped one of his old friends.

Luckily, I had an opportunity to question the hearse driver about the irreverence during this funeral. As witness to many funerals, he had observed a number of humor-infused ones, estimating them to make up possibly 5%. His final comment, interestingly enough, was that he wished they were all like this; "It seems so much better this way." Here was humor reflecting an acceptance of the inevitable. My father had been in his mid-eighties and at such an age death is simply to be expected. Thus far, there is little we can do to prolong a life beyond this age, so we accept its demise, and in this case at least did so with humor as our tool.

As at my father's funeral and also in Norman Cousins' description of the way he dealt with his life-threatening disease through the use of humor, we see that humor sometimes reflects acceptance of the inevitableness of illness and death. In Norman Cousins' case, humor may have even served to change the course of his disease, a point he came to emphasize in his subsequent books (Cousins, 1983, 1989). My attention to humor as an indication of the acceptance of the uncontrollable has been a focus of my research interests now for close to two decades.

TURNING PSYCHOLOGY TO THE STUDY OF POSITIVE ASSETS

Of the myriad articles that I read as a graduate student, one that was most seminal to my thinking was written by Robert White (1959). White spoke of a drive or motivation for competence and efficacy that, he asserted, allowed for the prediction of a wide range of behaviors. Persons were described not in terms of inadequacy or ineffectiveness but in terms of motivation to excel and prove their capacity for achievement. This refocusing on assets rather than deficits derived in no small degree from the antithesis between Alfred Adler's writings (Ansbacher & Ansbacher, 1956) and those of Freud. For Freud, an absence of tension from ever-present neurotic conflicts that were thought to be universal was the best to which humans could aspire. *Sublimation*, the optimal defense mechanism Freud discussed, simply allowed for the draining away of unsavory desires into more socially acceptable pursuits, none of which could deliver the extreme pleasure afforded by direct and immediate satisfaction of needs. In essence, humans were forever trapped in dissatisfaction and frustration deriving from the conflict between their organic nature and their need to fit in a social group. Adler, on the other hand, spoke of the pleasure to be derived from overcoming inferiorities and pursuing the goals or fictions in one's life with ever-increasing competence. Feeling encouragement from the success of one's efforts would beget confidence, courage, further striving, and as a consequence, the satisfaction of goal accomplishment. To Adler, the struggle to attain superiority was not so much in seeking power over others but in overcoming of feelings of inferiority that are inherent in the state of being a child. This struggle for mastery and superiority was said to be the major motivator of daily behavior by Adler, and White acknowledged his debt to Adler in his discussion of competence motivation (White, 1959). White's conceptualization of competence and his linking of competence with empirical findings from research in psychology offered a scaffolding on which I came to depend in my research on control and effectiveness.

In the early 1960s, research with the locus of control construct became prominent in the psychological literature concerned with personality. Articles by Julian Rotter (1966), myself (Lefcourt, 1966), and others attained citation classic status, and a number of books appeared that helped to popularize the construct (Phares, 1976; Lefcourt, 1976, 1982). Although the control construct was originally proposed and researched in the framework of social learning theory, researchers in personality and social psychology came to study similar phenomena with a somewhat different lexicon and some different assumptions. Susan Kobasa and Sal Maddi used control expectations along with "commitment" and "challenge" as components of what they named *hardiness*, a construct used to predict resistance to the onset of illness following stressful experiences (Kobasa, 1979; Kobasa, Maddi, & Kahn, 1982). In their well-known research, executives who were assessed as "hardy" were less likely to develop serious illnesses during a period when they were anxiously awaiting news about whether they were to be demoted or laid off. Their research became popularized in workshops which industries promoted to help maintain staff morale.

Richard deCharms published his research on *personal causation* (deCharms, 1968), through which he attempted to explain achievement behavior as a function of perceiving oneself as a source rather than an object. Judy Rodin and Ellen Langer discussed perceived personal control (Langer &

Rodin, 1976; Langer, 1983) as a contributing determinant of longevity among the elderly. As well, attribution researchers such as Carol Dweck (1975) wrote about the achievement outcome effects of accepting responsibility for one's evaluative outcomes (internal attributions) as opposed to attributing them to external causes. Attributional predispositions were found to predict children's responses to evaluative outcomes with, internal attributions for success resulting in persistence, while internal attributions for failure often resulted in withdrawal and surrender.

Though there are differences within this family of constructs, each demonstrated the role that beliefs about personal efficacy could play in determining the choices people make and the behaviors they display. Rather than focusing on the deficits deriving from alienation, fatalism, and anomie, these researchers demonstrated how beliefs about one's own abilities to affect the events in one's life could have impacts on achievement-related behavior, persistence in goal-directed activity, social behaviors, and the like.

Other researchers have studied the role that perceived efficacy could offer in helping to solve clinical difficulties. Albert Bandura's work in particular served to popularize the term *efficacy* and to disseminate the construct into clinical psychology lore (Bandura, 1977). Martin Seligman's early research on helplessness (Seligman, 1975) also dealt with the ramifications of control beliefs, though initially his focus was on the depression that resulted from feelings of helplessness. However, early on he too began to explore how the absence of malignant helplessness could serve as a protection against depression. If an animal could have experiences through which he sensed his own efficacy, he would not as likely become crippled in subsequent encounters with stressors (Seligman, Maier, & Geer, 1968), a finding similar to that which had been reported earlier by O. Hobart Mowrer (Mowrer & Viek, 1948).

Concurrent with the development of research about locus of control, Ezra Stotland and Arthur Kobler (Kobler & Stotland, 1964; Stotland, 1969) reported on a fascinating set of observations that illuminated the role that hopefulness could play in human behavior. In their field observations at an innovative new "mental" institution, Kobler and Stotland found that staff morale had direct consequences on the mental health of the patients. When the institution was newly founded and the atmosphere was one of hopefulness and optimism, the morale of staff and patients was equally high. However, when staff conflicts later emerged and demoralization spread throughout the ranks, patients began to lose faith in the efficacy of their therapeutic caretakers. As a consequence, a rash of suicides occurred among the patients, leading the authors to emphasize the role that the loss of hope plays in the ways patients cope with their difficulties. In a second book, Stotland (1969) reviewed the relationships between hope, expectations of control, and other cognate constructs that address the positive characteristics of people and promote resilience in their encounters with subsequent stressful events. The introduction of lay terminology into the psychological literature on positive characteristics facilitating resilience continued a tradition that began when Adler deliberately used readily accessible terms like *courage* and *common sense* to explain human behavior. This tradition continued in psychiatry in the writings of Karl Menninger, whose *Vital Balance* (1963) used terms like *faith* and *hope* to explain how humans could soldier on in adverse circumstances.

Some psychological researchers extended their investigations into the development of resilience in the childhood years. Murphy and Moriarity (1976) examined the coping strategies of children, describing personality characteristics as well as the environmental milieu that resulted in the children being able to deal with life stresses. In their work, some evidence was provided for Seligman's helplessness research in their finding that early traumas that undermined a child's sense of effectiveness led to less successful coping with later stressful experiences. This pursuit of the understanding of resilience also became a primary concern for psychological researchers at the University of Minnesota led by Norman Garmezy (Garmezy, Masten, & Tellegen, 1984; Garmezy & Tellegen, 1984). It was through these investigators that humor entered the literature concerned with resilience.

A number of other psychological researchers have contributed to the burgeoning emphasis on the positive characteristics that allow people to survive under adverse circumstances. Whereas Seligman began his research career focusing on helplessness, his more recent contributions have focused on the learning of optimism and its implications for persistence in striving to overcome obstacles (Seligman, 1991). Some investigators (Scheier & Carver, 1985, 1992) have contributed to this literature with a significant number of inquiries where optimism has been implicated as an important variable in the prediction of health outcomes; some of these will be discussed in a later chapter.

Most germane to our review of this newer emphasis on positive assets that facilitate survival under difficult circumstances is a recently published account of Sir Ernest Shackleton' travails during his Antarctic expedition that began in 1914. *The Endurance* (Alexander, 1998) describes the incredible, hair-raising adventures of these explorers, who became stranded on ice floes with no means of contacting the outside world. It is difficult to comprehend how self-sufficient these early explorers were. They could not depend upon outside resources once they had proceeded beyond the southernmost whaling stations near the tip of South America. Anything they required for survival had to be carried in their boats or on their shoulders. After their ship became locked in by ice and was eventually crushed by moving ice floes, the crew was stranded. Thus began an ordeal that lasted for more than a year and a half. The bravery of these men in the face of one incredible hardship after another makes for such a captivating story that the book became a best-seller almost immediately and, incidentally, kept me up many a night as I vicariously lived through the impossible situations they overcame.

What makes Shackleton's adventure so pertinent to this book is his brilliance in recognizing just what kind of people he wanted to take on his voyage and in engineering the social interactions between crew members to protect them from growing despondent. They all survived the ordeal, which seems miraculous considering the hardships and terror they encountered. As for crew selection, aside from navigation skills and all those abilities necessary for keeping ships afloat, Shackleton sought out people who could play musical instruments, sing, and were willing to perform in regular entertainments such as plays, readings, and the like. From diary descriptions of these entertainments, we learn that there was much laughter as actors parodied each other and stereotyped themselves—the meterologist who played "the mad scientist," for example. Shackleton was continually vigilant about anything that could affect the morale of the crew and isolated anyone who began to show signs of declining morale. One member of his officer crew who had a propensity toward pessimism was kept away from others by being given a desired place in the captain's cabin. If someone became objectionable, Shackleton would provide him with better quarters than those to which he had been accustomed, effectively preventing him spreading malaise among the crew. This also bolstered his own morale.

Whenever certain men were becoming troublesome, Shackleton made sure to take them with him on his various journeys in search of rescue, assuming that he would be better able to cope with them than would the others and thus preventing them from "infecting" their comrades. Consequently, when he ventured out in an open lifeboat on turbulent seas sprouting skyscraper-high waves, Shackleton included in his crew of six men one whom he feared would aggravate those who had to remain behind on Elephant Island keeping a long and arduous vigil. He and this small exploratory crew would spend many months traveling, eventually returning with rescue help. Because a photographer was among them, we can see the men as they underwent each of their many hardships. It is notable that despite their long and intense suffering, most of the pictures convey individuals who appear undaunted. The nightly entertainments continued as long as possible, and the provisions actually held out, supplemented with meat from penguins and seals that were butchered and cooked by their talented cook.

The attention to the crew's basic needs, the maintaining of the crew's morale, and the models of optimism provided by Shackleton and his fellow officers worked what any reader of the chronicles would regard as a miracle. That they all survived required not only luck but planning. The criteria that Shackleton used to choose his crew and the lengths to which he went to maintain their morale provides evidence that the current psychological emphasis on efficacy, control, and optimism, and so on as positive assets that aid survival during stressful events is not new but represents a time-honored tradition and the fruits of human wisdom.

Most recently, Martin Seligman (1998), in his role as president of the American Psychological Association, began advocating that psychology turn its talents toward understanding the sources of resilience and what he has termed *positive psychology*. He sees as the new mission of psychology to move beyond the medical model's focus on mental illness and deficits and follow the direction that was heralded by Jahoda. Seligman speaks of the need to understand the sources of hope, courage, optimism, and the like, which, as noted earlier, have been a growing presence in the psychological literature in recent decades. Still, notably missing from the pantheon of positive characteristics he mentions is humor. Throughout the 20th century a few philosophers and psychologists engaged in discourse about humor, as we shall see in a subsequent chapter. In empirical psychological research, however, studies were sporadic and rarely followed up or replicated. A selection of these studies was presented in the book *Motivation in Humor* edited by Jacob Levine (1969). Because humor has only recently come to be regarded as a legitimate topic of interest it is still not well represented in the psychological literature. The journal, *Humor: International Journal of Humor Research*, which began publication in 1987 supported by the *International Society for Humor Studies*, is an attempt to increase awareness of humor research in a number of disciplines, including psychology.

THE INTRODUCTION OF HUMOR
INTO RESEARCH ON RESILIENCE

In the 1970s one of my graduate students, Carl Sordoni, argued convincingly that humor could be regarded as a coping strategy, that it reflects an ability to rise above challenges to one's self-respect and is an alternative to becoming defensive before such threats. Because I had been examining the role of locus of control as a predictor of coping strategies, the merging of research in control expectancies and humor seemed inevitable. In two articles (Lefcourt, Sordoni, & Sordoni, 1974a; Lefcourt, Antrobus, & Hogg, 1974b) we examined the likelihood that people who felt capable of coping with difficulties (people assessed as having an internal locus of control) would be more apt to display humor in circumstances that could be regarded as irritating or threatening than would their more helpless peers (people assessed as having an external locus of control).

In one study (Lefcourt et al., 1974a) students were led through a series of tedious tasks that assumedly assessed their verbal skills. By the time our subjects engaged in their last task they had been lulled into a near-soporific state. The last task, described as a word association test, began simply enough, with subjects responding to benign words (face, plant, voice and so on) with the first word that occurred to them. Beginning with the 13th word, however, sexual double entendres made their appearance as every third word (rubber, bust, snatch and so on). Our hypothesis was that our internal subjects, being more attentive to information related to their efforts than were externals, would be quicker to manifest some sign that they perceived the "double-cross." That is, we expected an earlier recognition that the task—let alone the whole experiment—was not as it had been represented, that they had been tricked in terms of our purposes, and that they were not daunted by this discovery. In essence, these persons were thought to be less threatened by the growing awareness that they had been duped by our misleading soporific instructions. We assessed "awareness" by examining how long it took them to catch on to the fact that the words were double entendres, indicated by the first excessive time delay in responding. Then we looked at smiles and laughter and the actual responses given as signs that they were not perturbed by their discovery of our duplicitousness. In brief, we found that internals did look less "flappable." They were quicker to respond to the task changes, more likely to smile and laugh, and more apt to respond back with a double entendre, turning the joke back on us. These findings were published in one paper (Lefcourt, Gronnerud, & McDonald, 1973) and expanded on in another (Lefcourt et al., 1974a). In the latter paper, we examined the videotaped responses of subjects, differentiating between what we referred to as superiority, social, and tension-relief laughter. These differences were assessed by the facial expressions accompanying laughter and smiles. Social and tension-relief humor were not thought to be as relevant to beliefs about control as superiority humor. This latter form of humor included "knowing" looks, narrowed eyes, and pursed lips along with laughter. As hypothesized, internals increased and externals decreased in the exhibition of superiority humor as the task progressed. Equivalent changes in social smiling and laughter, and in laughter reflecting tension and unease, were not found. We were able to conclude that persons who believed they were effective in determining the events in their lives were less likely to become disturbed by discovering themselves to be in an embarassing or compromising position. Corroborating these findings, we found that internals were again less challenged than externals in a second double-cross experiment described in Lefcourt (1982) and were able to behave humorously in role-playing situations where failure and embarassment were intrinsic to the roles being performed (e.g., explaining rejection from graduate schools to a friend; Lefcourt et al., 1974b).

In these experiments, redescribed in our book *Humor and Life Stress* (Lefcourt & Martin, 1986), humor was taken to be a sign of resilience in the face of stress, a theme that we returned to a decade later in the study of humor as a stress moderator.

Other investigators have also linked humor to personality characteristics that are portents for the ways in which people deal with stressful experiences. Ann Masten (1986), a member of the University of Minnesota team concerned with the sources and correlates of children's resilience, had children respond to Ziggy cartoons with ratings, expressions of mirth, and explanations of why the cartoon was seen as funny (comprehension). In addition, they were given the opportunity to complete cartoons that were missing captions. These measures, along with IQ, were used to predict competence as assessed by sociometric ratings of teachers and peers. Masten found that humor and competence were positively related. Academic and social competence were associated with humor production, comprehension, and the expression of mirth. Teachers rated children who scored high on the humor measures as being more effective in the classroom, "more attentive, cooperative, responsive, and productive." Peers rated them as more "popular, gregarious, and happy, and as leaders with good ideas of things to do." Although there was some overlap with IQ scores in the prediction of some criteria, humor seemed to carry special weight with regard to social competence, which in turn we would expect to be positively associated with resilience in stressful social situations.

Finally, in a study to be described more fully later, humor as a means of coping has been found to operate in concert with optimism in predicting levels of distress for women following diagnosis and treatment of breast cancer. Carver *et al.* (1993) found their measure of *use of humor* to predict, along with *optimism*, the emotional distress of women over the year that followed their diagnosis of breast cancer. The more optimistic, and the more likely to have indulged in humor about their illness, the less distressed the women seemed to become over that time period. Given that emotional distress is associated with diminished activity of the immune system and the speed of growth of tumors (Sklar & Anisman, 1979, 1981; Visintainer, Volpicelli, & Seligman, 1982), both humor and optimism can be seen to have had possible beneficial effects on the health and well-being of these women. In these three research enterprises, then, each concerning success in dealing with stressful circumstances, humor has been associated with variables that have a positive impact on well-being, internal control, competence, and optimism.

At this point we will turn our attention more fully to humor, concerning ourselves with what it means to be humorous or to be said to have a good sense of humor. Because many investigators who have begun to explore humor empirically have created definitions and assessment tools, there is considerable room for discrepancies and inconsistencies in these discussions. In the following chapter we will see what questions arise when we try to make humor comprehensible that may account for the different ways in which psychologists have conceptualized and gone about researching the subject.

EXPERIENCING HUMOR
IN EVERYDAY LIFE

When introducing students to the psychological literature on humor, I have usually found it both enjoyable and fruitful to begin by having them present personal examples of humor and funniness. Most people are eager to talk about funny events that have occurred in their lives, and though others may not judge the events to be as funny as the person describing them, they usually end up laughing along with the storyteller, if only in response to the storyteller's own laughter. What is being shared in these "show and tell" exercises is an appreciation of our "sense of humor," our readiness to respond with laughter to all sorts of experiences that otherwise could have caused us embarassment and grief.

For approximately a decade I annually conducted an undergraduate seminar on the psychological study of humor. For one assignment students were required to describe a personal experience that was so uproarious to them that they had laughed uncontrollably during its occurrence. Over the years I found that many students could recall these events in minute detail despite the length of time that had elapsed since their occurrence. Subsequently, these events became the target of psychological exercises in which students would attempt to explain their experiences using different theoretical perspectives and hypothetical constructs. Armed initially with two constructs deriving from Arthur Koestler's tome *The Act of Creation* (1964), the students began wading out into the quagmire of interpretation and explanation of humor.

The two constructs that Koestler considered necessary and sufficient to explain humor were based largely on Freud's writings about humor (Freud, 1905). They are *bisociation* and *tension* (or arousal). The former is similar to what many humor scholars refer to as *incongruity*: the simultaneous perceiv-

15

ing of some object from two mutually exclusive frames of reference. For example, when adults behave in a childish manner, we can conceive of them as the respectable adults whom they appear to be while at the same time as selfish, squabbling schoolchildren. Koestler suggested that when incongruous perceptions occur simultaneously they can result in humor if—drawing a metaphor from his libationary habits—there is an added splash of adrenaline. That is, bisociation can lead to humor if the observer experiences some degree of emotional arousal while considering the object of his perception. In simple terms, there must be something threatening or fearsome about the objects of perception. If, for example, the adult who was behaving in a childish way had been making some threats that might have aroused feelings of fear, then the visual image of the adult as a demanding child could result in laughter, especially if the threat has evaporated. This tension-reduction view of humor derived directly from Freud's conservation-of-energy theorizing about humor: laughter allowed for a release of energy that had proved to be unnecessary when what had seemed threatening became innocuous through bisociation.

Armed with these sparse conceptual tools for making sense of humor, students were asked to make an initial sortie toward interpreting the stories that they had told. The following is a story written several years ago by one of the students in my humor seminar, who has since gone on to become a practicing attorney. Upon my initial reading of it, I found it so engaging and well told that I encouraged the young woman to consider tailoring it into a publishable short story. I am pleased to be able to present it here in all its poignancy and humor. Afterward we will consider a range of issues that the story raises with regard to humor. In accordance with the author's wish the names of the people involved have been changed to preserve anonymity.

> Christmastime for my family has always been a festive and joyous occasion. My mother's side of the family always spends Christmas at my aunt's home. Christmas dinner consists of a massive meal, prepared by my grandmother, her two daughters (my mother and her sister), and my uncle's wife. The meal itself is always consumed with a heartiness and gusto that would put a pack of starving wolves to shame. The evening brings a barrage of other family members and friends to my Aunt Annette's home. Children, adults, and grandparents alike join in avid discussions and story telling. By midnight, however, family and friends (which by this point number close to 40 people) gather around my Aunt Annette's dining room table, are divided into teams, and begin to engage in a ritualistic card game that sets husbands against wives and brothers against sisters. A night of laughter and fun ensues.
>
> The Christmas of 1982, however, was much different from all our previous holiday celebrations. It was different for two reasons. First, and most importantly, my mother had died a tragic and unexpected death in June of that year. Second, my cousin Sue's fiancé Erik was present. Although the immediate family

had embraced Erik and welcomed him into "the nest," the extended family, as well as all my Aunt Annette's friends, had not yet met him. So, that Christmas marked the first absence of my mother on a celebrated occasion and brought a new family member amongst us.

Christmas dinner found 13 of us gathered around my Aunt Annette's lavish dining room table. My grandparents (my mother's parents), my Aunt Annette's family (her husband Vito, Sue, and Sue's fiancé Erik), my family (Tony, my brother, my father, and myself), my mother's brother, Uncle Fred and his wife, and lastly my dreaded Great Aunt Gina (my grandfather's sister) sat forlornly around the table picking at the fabulous meal that had been prepared. My grandmother made an imposing impression as she sat dressed in black from head to toe and continually sighed and made comments like, "The stuffing is just not the same without my precious daughter here to add her special touch." Needless to say, no one dared to take a second helping of the turkey stuffing, although we all agreed, at a later date, that it tasted exactly as it always had.

After dinner, we all retired to the living room, which happens to be at the opposite end of the dining room. Coffee and liqueurs were served, and my grandfather stood to make his traditional Christmas toast. His sister, the dreaded Aunt Gina, quickly hushed him and whispered loud enough for all to hear, "Leo, this is no time for a toast. Have a little respect for the dead, she's your own daughter for Christ's sake." My grandmother at this point began to sob and mumble endearing things about her "dear departed" daughter.

Aunt Annette, in the meantime, began preparing trays for the arrival of guests who would undoubtedly come to offer a subdued bit of Christmas cheer. Sue and I were assisting her when she summoned Erik into the kitchen. At this point she warned Erik to be on his best behavior when the guests arrived and not to play the "clown" as he most often did.

Erik is quite a character. He is constantly telling jokes and doing a numerous variety of impersonations. He is a very imposing figure with his athletic build and mischievous green eyes. One point that should be made clear is that Erik had only recently been embraced by the immediate family. He had entered on the heels of my cousin Sue's ex-boyfriend, Rob. Rob was the typical "all-American, apple pie" kind of young man. We had all grown to love his sensitivity and kind-naturedness. It came as quite a shock, therefore, when Sue had dumped her boyfriend of three years and introduced Erik. Erik's good looks struck one up front; his imposing size and slapstick humor were quite an affront to Rob's memory. We eventually accepted Erik as one of our own, however. My aunt's warning was given because she knew that the guests had yet to meet Sue's new fiancé and would immediately reject him if "he made an ass of himself."

When the trays had been prepared, my aunt, Sue, and I proceeded into the living room to await the guests. My grandmother was seated on one end of the large sectional chesterfield and my great aunt had taken up the other side with her massive bulk. She too was dressed in traditional black attire and had a scowl on her face that would have scared the mightiest beast away. The two simply despised one another. There are no words to describe the animosity that exists between them. Perhaps this is one reason why my cousins, and Tony and I, have always detested Great Aunt Gina. The woman herself had never married, and she lived completely alone without even the companionship of a pet for as long as we had known her. At family gatherings, she was the first to scold and chastise us for nothing more than regular child's play. Her only enjoyment in life seemed to be the food she consumed in amazing proportions. At Christmastime she always was generous enough to bring the four of us gifts. They consisted of a piece of fruit and the current special of the week from a cheap discount store. Sue, Vito, Tony, and I had hence christened her with the name Grinch from the time we were able to talk.

The guests had begun to arrive and the evening began. As each different relative and friend sat down to greet my grandmother, they were bombarded with an emotional outburst. My grandmother seemed determined to unleash her grief upon anyone who would listen. Great Aunt Gina had repositioned herself so that she now occupied the seat next to my grandmother. She actually seemed quite content. The somber atmosphere on this once-festive occasion suited her idea of Christmas quite well.

Sue and I, as well as my cousin Andrea who had just arrived, were engaged in conversation when I noticed something quite out of the ordinary. The men who at this point were usually part of the family gathering had set up the dining room table and begun to play cards amongst themselves. The young children were nowhere in sight. They too on previous occasions were part of the storytelling and family discussions that had followed the arrival of family and friends. The communal sharing and enjoyment, which had been present on previous holidays, was not in evidence this year. Whenever the men would raise their voices above a murmur, Great Aunt Gina would clear her throat so as to hush and remind them that riotous voices and fun were not meant to be part of this Christmas.

By 9:30 that evening, the anxiety, tension, and somber atmosphere were quite thick in my aunt's home. All family members who had recently or not so recently lost loved ones were gathered on the chesterfield with my grandmother. A sequence of five elderly women, all dressed in black, decorated the sofa. Each was wiping her tears and relaying the stories of her beloved departed. Needless to say, I was getting quite frustrated and a bit upset at constantly being reminded that my mother was absent. It was at this point that I summoned Aunt Annette into the kitchen. We both agreed that this was the worst Christmas imaginable. I told her that we should try to get grandmother to bed before she drove herself and everyone else over the brink of hysteria. Aunt Annette readily agreed and said that some of the tension would be dissipated if we could get grandmother to retire.

We entered the living room to accomplish our feat when Erik seemed to appear out of nowhere. He positioned himself in front of my grandmother, in full view of everyone, and exclaimed that he had a joke to tell. Great Aunt Gina looked appalled, but Aunt Annette seemed desperate enough to try anything, so she called for everyone's attention. Andrea and Sue were the only ones to ignore her request and kept on whispering to each other about the arrival of Nicky's new baby. Erik proceeded to clear his throat and inquired, "How does a Newfie pull up his socks?" Aunt Annette began to translate the joke into Italian for the benefit of some of our non-English speaking guests.

I was in total shock; I knew the punch line of the joke and couldn't believe that Erik would actually go through with it. After all, on the couch sat five mourning women, one of whom was my virginal and ghastly Great Aunt Gina. But before I could say anything or try to stop him, I started to laugh, covertly at first and then quite outwardly. At this point Erik proceeded to pull down his pants and pull up his socks. I couldn't believe it. I lost total control as I saw my Great Aunt Gina gasp and cover her eyes. I thought Erik insane to risk the acceptance of new family and friends for a few laughs.

The only thing that could be heard in the entire room was my laughter. Everyone else seemed to be focused on my grandmother. A moment of thick silence hung in the air before I heard my grandmother's familiar chuckle. This signaled her acceptance, which was totally unexpected, and everyone else joined in and began laughing. Sitting at my grandmother's feet and still laughing uncontrollably, I was privy to her comment as she leaned over to Great Aunt Gina and said, "Don't be such a pious witch Gina; after all, that is the closest you've ever come to the real thing." I was the only one to hear this secret exchange and it sent me further into fits of laughter.

It took me close to an hour to bring myself under control, while everyone else had quieted down long before. When I finally gained my composure, I realized that the men who had previously been engaged in a card game had rejoined the group. The younger children, upon hearing the laughter, had also come to sit on their mothers' laps or play at the feet of the adults.

The laughter provided a release for the tension that had built to a phenomenal height during the course of the evening. It reunited the family and helped them embrace Erik as one of their members. My grandmother's unexpected reaction allowed everyone to relax and begin the traditional celebration we had all previously enjoyed. Although the evening was not as rambunctious as other Christmas holidays, it would have turned out to be disastrous if my grandmother had taken offense and wailed out a sob rather than laughing at Erik's antics.

After they presented their stories, I required the students to begin analyzing their experiences, to ferret out what they thought were the necessary conditions for funniness to have occurred. They began with a search for the sources of tension and arousal and the bisociative perceptions that they might have entertained in their minds. In class the students were to share their stories with each other in small groups to begin this analytic process. The more compelling stories were then dealt with by the entire class of some 20 students. The previous story was one of that year's best and it led to considerable back-and-forth, which I will attempt to re-create in the following section. It was in such discussions that we often touched on the very issues that humor researchers raise as they try to understand and interpret humorous events.

AN INTUITIVE APPROACH TO UNDERSTANDING HUMOR

This Christmas dinner story offered much "grist for the discussion mill." It provides evidence of the role of tension in the making of a humorous experience; it provokes our curiosity about the personalities of comics like Erik that allow them to be so audacious and about the personalities of persons like the grandmother, who can respond so positively to the antics of others. These issues—the sources of humor production and humor appreciation, and the role of arousal in humor—are compelling subjects in humor research.

One of the primary factors responsible for the laughter of the participants was, obviously, the clowning behavior of Erik, without which the event would not have occurred. How in the world, we may ask, does someone become so bold? Did he ever consider what the consequences would have been if grandmother had taken offense? What could have possessed him to pull off such a prank under the circumstances? What did he know about the situation and the people involved that allowed him to believe he could get away with it? The making of comics and clowns has been discussed at length by the Fishers (Fisher & Fisher, 1981) in their book *Pretend the World Is Funny and Forever*, an apt title, as we shall see later. Subsequently we will be examining the Fishers' research findings about comedians. Suffice it to say now that people like Erik are not easily found. They represent an extreme on the dimension of humor productivity.

Another salient ingredient in this story is the heightened tension noted repeatedly by the author ("the anxiety, tension, and somber atmosphere were quite thick"). There were good reasons for emotional arousal on this occasion. First, there was a conflict of expectancies among the participants, including the writer. This was a family gathering at which enjoyment, pleasure and fun were the norm. But this year, the writer's mother had died, albeit six months earlier. Since the deceased had customarily been one of the three major contributors to the occasion, her absence was palpable. In addition to the grief-related emotions attendant upon her absence, there was, no doubt, uncertainty about what constituted appropriate behavior under such circumstances. Should the family celebrate the holiday as they had in the past, or should this be an occasion for mourning? In addition, there was evident conflict between the two grieving matriarchs—the revered grandmother and the despised great aunt. While these two women competed in their displays of mourning, the writer and the other relatives at the gathering were held hostage to their demands for somber behavior. The anger, remorse, and uncertainty aroused by the sum of these circumstances could have resulted in a depressing evening for all. The writer herself, may have been feeling considerable anger at the incessant grieving by her relatives and especially Great Aunt Gina, for whom she had little affection. It not only served continuously to remind her of the loss of her mother but may have engendered subtle feelings of guilt as she started to experience any pleasant holiday feelings.

In this story we can see the operation of those characteristics that Koestler deemed necessary for the experience of humor. Tension was everywhere, and it was brought to a peak by Erik's clownish behavior. The potential for bisociation was great given all the uncertainties and ambiguities involved in trying to have a joyous occasion while still feeling mournful. Beyond these general features, different ingredients that contributed to the making of this humorous event can be explored. Here is a more formal sampling of questions that occurred to me and were likely to emerge from class discussions in response to the story:

- First among the issues that must be included in any list of variables responsible for humor is the presence of tension and arousal. As noted, tension is often seen as a necessary precondition for humor, and the tension in this situation was self-evident. If so many sources of emotional arousal were not present at the event, perhaps the writer would not have been so amused by Erik's "performance art." His performance, being so unexpected and so incongruous with the mood of the mourners, no doubt added to the already-high level of tension at the gathering. The "joke" then provided an opportunity for relief which, in turn, provoked further joking.
- How might the "chemistry" of personal interactions become a source of humor and laughter? Here, the known animosity between the grandmother and her sister-in-law provided an extra spark of hilarity for the writer. In essence, her grandmother's quip reflected and confirmed the feelings between the two matriarchs and the allusion to her sister-in-law's lack of knowledge of sexual experience provoked the author into further gales of laughter. Since the young often cannot conceive of the elderly as having any interest in sexuality, this quip could easily have given rise to bisociation. Two mutually exclusive ideas—old ladies in black mourning clothes and a prurient interest in a young man with his pants down—collide. Bisociation along with arousal result in uncontrollable laughter. That the writer is close to her grandmother and distant from her great aunt would also predispose her to enjoy the put-down of the latter by the former. The grandmother's quip could be regarded as a "poison dart" that undermined the mourning performance of the great aunt and signaled the end of the grandmother's solemnity.

  Among the other elements of social "chemistry" that may have contributed to making this experience a humorous one was the laughter of the writer herself when she anticipated what Erik was about to do. Her laughter may have helped to "prep" her grandmother to accept his behavior as funny and not offensive. Erik's novelty in the family made him an unpredictable person for some, which also may have added to the uncertainty and tension as he took the floor. And resentment toward the elderly great aunt who was squelching others' holiday spirits may have made her "humiliation" that much more pleasurable to others when she became the target of a jest.

- What personality characteristics account for the behavior of clowns and humorists who initiate comic experiences, especially in tense situations? As noted, we will review the research pertaining to characteristics of comedians in a subsequent chapter. But from the author's observations of Erik we can at least surmise that risk-taking was not unfamiliar to him. The gamble undertaken to expect laughter was a great one. There was a good possibility that his joke would fail. He was a newcomer to this family, and although he may have been led to believe that grandmother had a good sense of humor, his own experience in the family was minimal. Was he then a particularly gifted reader of behavioral probabilities? Did he have a certain psychological savvy by which he discerned that this was the "right" situation and time for such a comic intrusion? At his disposal, of course, was his recall of the Newfie joke and a willingness to act it out even in circumstances that seemed inappropriate. If we can generalize from Erik's case, comedians often seem to be audacious but knowledgeable, aware of when and where they can "get away with" certain routines. In this story, joking seemed to be a tool with which Erik the clown tried to rescue the evening from declining into a morass of melancholia. A depressing occasion, while unpleasant for some, might be anethema for the would-be comic. Perhaps the comedian is a person for whom depressing events are less tolerable and thus feels compelled to use humor to reverse the slide toward despair.

- Why are some people more responsive than others to potentially funny events, showing their appreciation by laughter and possibly ripostes? Although not necessarily good comics themselves, some people do differ from others in their readiness to respond to funny events. In a later chapter we will examine research into individual differences in responding to humor. Our own scales (Martin & Lefcourt, 1983, 1984) and those of others have been used to examine the correlates of readiness to respond with laughter or humor.

In the story, the writer was ready to laugh when Erik proceeded and her grandmother was quick to follow her lead, whereas Great Aunt Gina was less likely to be responsive. Of course, since some of the laughter was at the great aunt's expense she would not have appreciated the humor. However, from the writer's description, Great Aunt Gina would probably not have been responsive even if she were not the target of a joke. On the other hand, the noted "familiar chuckle" of her grandmother suggests that she was known to be more readily mirthful.

The grandmother's social position was also much closer to the others' than the great aunt's, so she probably felt more secure in expressing mirth, revealing a shift in direction away from her previously mournful demeanor. Great Aunt Gina, on the other hand, was in a precarious position, being a center of attention that others, especially the writer, felt she did not deserve. Consequently, she would have felt less secure about how she would be received had she laughed at Erik's "assault." Such security differences may account for observed differences between persons in their readiness to respond with humor to events like the one described.

- How do we know whether someone is actually responsive to humor? At first this question seems to be silly or at least, academic, in the worst meaning of that word. However, we do know that people laugh for different reasons. Laughter, like smiling, can be a social response that serves to punctuate communications between individuals, encouraging a speaker to continue (Provine, 1991, 1993). Laughter and humor are said to be distinct though often related. The laughter in the story would most certainly have been related to humor, the jokes having produced a major change in the emotional atmosphere of the family gathering. The changes in the observed behavior suggest that the humor heralded a reinterpretation of the night's festivities, reducing the uncertainty about how the participants were supposed to behave.
- Are the characteristics of those people who initiate humor different from those who appreciate humor? Are some of us higher in a general trait of humor than others, better able to cause others to break into laughter and more ready to respond with laughter ourselves? Are the producers of laughter apt also to be highly responsive laughers themselves? In our research we have found some evidence of the independence of humor production and humor appreciation (Lefcourt & Martin, 1986). Rather than being a pervasive trait, laughter seems to be highly contingent on characteristics of the speaker, the listener, and the interaction between them (Provine, 1996). As we explore characteristics of people who differ in humor responsiveness and humor production (comedians), we will observe the relationship between these facets to ascertain whether humor is more accurately described as a pervasive trait or as situation-specific, and we will begin to develop terminology with which individuals can be profiled according to their unique blend of humor components. For example, a person might be

said to be easily provoked to laughter in groups of like-minded peers by sexual jokes but not by jokes that ridicule the opposite sex. The same person might also be said rarely to make an active contribution to elicit laughter from others.

• Do the different forms and purposes of humor have different effects on their intended audiences? The humor in the Christmas story was deliberate and intrusive. There was much pleasure in "getting back" at the elders who were making the evening so unpleasant for everyone else. Here, aggression in the guise of humor played a big role in changing the atmosphere. However, there was also a sharing form of humor. The grandmother became allied with her grandaughter. Perhaps she had felt compelled to mourn along with her sister-in-law, not wanting to seem frivolous in the year that her daughter died. Erik's antics, a really brazen assault on the matriarchs, helped her to shift away from the "folie à deux" and allowed her to collude with her grandaughter in shared laughter instead. There was humor, then, which was divisive, acting like a scalpel to cut out the imposed solemnity, and there was humor that bonded the others together, laughing at the antics of Erik the clown whose behavior, while shocking, was also a corrective. As we will see, different kinds of humor—self versus other-directed, hostile versus perspective-taking—have different portents and possible value for reducing the impact of stressful events (Lefcourt & Shepherd, 1995; Lefcourt, 1997b).

• What circumstances might have quashed the levity in this situation? What emotions would likely have become salient had the joke failed? If the author's mother had died more recently, the mood probably would have been more completely somber. When people feel depressed, humor becomes a less likely response. One must "be in the mood" for humor. If the grandmother had been profoundly despondent, Erik's joke might have fallen flat and people might have felt anger at his impertinence and "insensitivity." It is difficult even to consider the failure of his joke because it would have resulted in such a resounding rejection that the evening might have been brought to a premature close— with the matriarchs leaving the scene in a self-righteous fury. Had the writer herself still been mourning and in a depressed state, she might not have responded to Erik's jest either. But both she and her grandmother were ready to be rescued from solemnity. Finally, if Erik were a true stranger or held in low regard, his joke might have been more likely to be regarded as oafish and contemptible. The mood had to be right, the perpetrator acceptable, and the shift from solemnity something to be welcomed. Otherwise, humor would not have prevailed.

CAN WE TRULY UNDERSTAND THE ROOTS OF HUMOR?

Although humor seems amenable to exploration and explanation it has long been regarded as a difficult phenomenon to study, especially in psychological laboratories. Before we even begin discussing the characteristics of funny experiences it is incumbent upon us to note that many believe humor is an elusive phenomenon, not easily studied without eviscerating its humorous nature. As suggested in this cartoon by Jack Lefcourt, an editorial cartoonist (and my son), humor as an object of study can have little in common with humor as it is experienced.

As one becomes acquainted with the rapidly growing literature on the nature and meaning of humor, it is easy to feel overwhelmed by the sheer number of publications emanating from a variety of disciplines—from linguistics and anthropology to physiology and psychology. At the same time the novice also learns that many of those who study humor feel doubtful about the ability to investigate it in a scholarly manner. Humor is often described as ephemeral, subject to evaporation if closely scrutinized and analyzed. Attributing delicacy to a phenomenon like humor that is so often indicated by such a robust response as laughter seems paradoxical. True, the conditions of a funny event must be "just so." Without the right timing, the right verbal and

FIGURE 2-1: "Studying humor is quite different from experiencing it." Humor can be regarded seriously. Copyright by Jack Lefcourt, 1999.

nonverbal facial expressions and body movements, and the appropriate relationships between the participants in a potentially funny situation there would be no humor at all. However, although the conditions must be right, the assertion that humor is therefore too complex to study confuses the number of contributing factors to it with the complexity of theorizing necessary to make the phenomenon comprehensible. Somehow, despite the features necessary for humor to occur, most humans are capable of recognizing and responding to it with speed and spontaneity. As will be observed in the stories presented throughout this book, funny events may require fancy footwork to be comprehended in some systematic way but not to be observed and responded to. There is often fair consensus in particular cultures about what is regarded as funny, although different tastes and proclivities within those cultures will always result in a range of responses to and judgments about something's funniness.

The problems in studying humor—as opposed to experiencing it—derive partly from the fact that humor has been subjected to investigation by scholars from a great variety of disciplines. Because each discipline has its own traditions and methods, it will draw attention only to certain aspects of humor while ignoring others. Towers of Babel sprout readily in such circumstances. However, we should not confuse our difficulties in understanding the language and focuses of different disciplines with complexity in the phenomenon of humor itself. Any area of interest would come to be seen as overly complex if it were examined by varied disciplines.

No object of study can retain an aura of simplicity when subjected to the close scrutiny of scholars. Whether the subject is aggression, altruism, hope, or humor, close scholarly attention will produce uncertainty as well as knowledge. What seems clear when we stand apart from a phenomenon becomes muddled when we draw in closer. I have often felt that when I am "on top of a subject," having reached that point where I have read all the major papers that there are to be read in a given area, my knowledge seems most fragile, capable of slipping through my fingers like water. If we get too close to a subject, probing for its subtle nuances, we are often left with gnawing uncertainties and the feeling that it can never be understood with any confidence. Yet, if we draw back a little, the clarity of the landscape improves and our vision of it becomes more coherent. Many of the books that have afforded me the greatest feelings of comprehension are those which present a broad sweep across widely diverse phenomena. Interestingly enough, such books often appear weakest to me at those points where I have some degree of sophistication and can see the potential failings of the generalizations being drawn. So much for the illusion that we can ever be fully confident in our knowledge of a phenomenon!

A brilliant discourse on the impossibility of knowing anything or anyone with certainty was recently presented in a fascinating study called *Explaining Hitler*, by Ron Rosenbaum (1998). The author examines the scholarly work undertaken by the many researchers who have tried to understand the personage of Hitler. From the study of their positions, he concludes that they tell us more about their own cultures and the human need to explain and understand than they do about Hitler. Rosenbaum's thesis is that we are incapable of attaining a complete and final understanding of any person or phenomenon, and this fact often leads to "explanatory despair" among those who grasp for certainty. As an interesting complement to this contention, the play *Death and the Maiden* by Ariel Dorfman argues that real knowledge of the world resides in the senses and not in the thoughts that conceptualizers rely upon. Here, a torture victim recognizes a visitor to her home as her former tormentor in an Argentine prison, although she had never actually seen him. Her husband wonders how she can be so certain about it that she is willing to kill the visitor, and as a lawyer he raises all the doubts about truth that he can muster. Yet she, relying on smell, tones, and nuances of vocalizations comes to the correct conclusions. These are the same arguments raised by the poet John Keats, who contrasted the genuineness of the senses with thoughts.

In psychology, one strategy for dealing with uncertainties and the awareness that we can never know anything with finality is called *constructivism*. This is the assumption that what investigators study is not so much the phenomenon itself as constructions of it. That is, in our study of phenomena we are always examining and testing our theoretical constructions about the way things or persons in the world operate, and the information gleaned from such study can be useful, interesting, and stimulating, encouraging us to further investigation. However, our research and study never provide us with "final answers" or truths, because whatever we study can also be examined using other constructs. These may actually improve upon whatever knowledge we have obtained through our own constructs. And what are *constructs*? They are the terms we have *constructed* by which we sort, select, and judge facets of our lives so as to make them predictable and coherent. Funniness, for example, is not simply inherent in certain events. Rather, it is we—the participants and observers—who make judgments about funniness through the use of our constructs, which define the funniness of an event. We may recognize that an event is similar to other events that we have labeled as funny. If we are more analytical, we may observe particular characteristics that the event in question shares with other like events that we have found to be funny. When we laugh during those events our laughter reflects our constructions and judgments about funniness rather than about inherent characteristics of those events. For a full discussion of the construct position, the classic two volumes of George Kelly (1955) are indispensable. In addition, a recent article by Willibald Ruch (1999) describes the plight of investigators debating the meaning of certain forms of humor, each from a different construct system.

To return to our discussion of the complexities in understanding humor, if there is confusion about what humor is, and if people are dubious about whether it can be studied with any rigor, it is because they confuse their constructions of humor with the phenomenon itself. In essence, they are taking their own points of view too seriously, a problem that, perhaps could be undone with a dose of humor. This problem of perceived complexity is not unique to humor nor to situations that we are apt to regard as funny, but rather to the mistaken belief that the humor is in acts, events, and situations rather than in the constructions of the observers of those phenomena.

To end these digressions, suffice it to say that the present study of humor will not and could not be exhaustive. It cannot be all-inclusive because of my own limitations as a person and a scholar in psychology. From my own psychological vantage point I often begin simplistically, with a plain and uncomplicated description. For example: humor occurs when there is a discernible happening or an event; at least one person to perceive it; and possibly, although this is not essential, someone else with whom to share it. This bare-bones kind of definition, of course, does not immediately distinguish humor from other kinds of events, including those we might label as tragic or even horrific. Somewhere in the perception of the humorous event there must also be an element of play, whether physical, or verbal, as in the responses we privately entertain as we observe the event. Because we have evolved into highly verbal creatures, capable of talking about talking, thinking about thinking, and imagining all manner of things as we perceive the world around us, our capacity for play is immense. It is from play occurring inside our heads that I believe humor emerges. As a psychologist, my wish is to discuss this "mind play" that may account for our experience of humor, knowing all the while that my approach is incomplete and no doubt replaceable by other construct systems.

I will discuss humor throughout this book from a functionalist-psychological vantage point. Humor will be regarded as a characteristic that has proven useful to our species, aiding us as we attempt to live in what are often unbearable circumstances. The survival of a species requires continuous adaptation to changing circumstances that occur with time, and the characteristics that enhance adaptability become the surviving attributes of any species. I will argue that some forms of humor have helped our species survive, partly because they help us to draw closer to one another. Certain forms of humor enable us to become more socially connected to others and therefore more ready to give and receive support in trying circumstances.

At this point I will not discuss different kinds of humor and laughter; attention will be given to these matters in a later chapter. I will say only that, certain types of humor can be expressions of different intentions. Some forms of humor are not socially supportive, and may even be divisive and hostile, whereas others serve to bring people closer together, allowing them to laugh at what might otherwise be disruptive experiences. Although I will discuss some of the various forms that humor can take, my primary focus will be on the functions of the forms that have survived as useful techniques for enduring in difficult circumstances. The success with which humor can make travails bearable may explain why it has evolved into a recognizable feature of our species, and one so highly regarded that its most successful purveyors are highly recompensed. On a more trivial level, it may also help us understand why many people wishing to attract others through classified advertisements commonly list "a sense of humor" as one of their personal qualities.

CONCLUSION

In looking back at any humorous event in our lives, we can invoke different constructs to make sense of it. The questions we raise will reflect the backgrounds and disciplines in which we have been trained. As a psychologist, intrapersonal and interpersonal characteristics are most salient for me as I try to sense the sources of humor. The inner play that occurs during funny events is a primary focus for me, and each circumstance that elicits and each personality characteristic that facilitates the onset of inner play make up salient variables in the construct system that I draw on to comprehend humor.

Throughout this book I will discuss a number of funny stories of real events that occurred in the lives of my students, myself, and other writers who have shared their experiences. First, however, let us turn our attention to the ways in which humor has been regarded by our predecessors in philosophy, religion, medicine, and psychology.

EARLY CONCEPTIONS OF HUMOR IN RELIGION, MEDICINE, PHILOSOPHY, AND PSYCHOLOGY

A motion picture that won three Oscars at the 1999 Academy Awards raised serious questions for those who view humor as a gift with positive evolutionary significance for our species. *Life is Beautiful* was so well received that it became the biggest U.S. box office hit of any Italian film ever screened in North America. It is the story of a Jewish-Italian man who tries to protect his young son from the horrors of a Nazi concentration camp by pretending that the camp's routines are actually an elaborate game staged for the boy's entertainment. The father who attempts to create this comic vision is played by Roberto Benigni, who was also the film's co-writer and director.

Among his various honors, Benigni was invited to the Vatican to present the film to the Pope. It was one of the very few films that the Pope has seen in his lifetime. After viewing the film with Benigni the Pope embraced him. The Pope seemed to have been overwhelmed by the ressurective theme of the film wherein the horrors of the Holocaust were diminished by humor. However, not everyone was so enamored. David Denby, movie critic for *The New Yorker* magazine, felt compelled to write two separate reviews of the film (November 16, 1998; March 15, 1999) because he was so disturbed by the premise—that agonies such as concentration camp life could be relieved by clownishness. To Denby, the horrors of the Holocaust and the concentration camps were simply beyond the purview of humor. He felt that Benigni was self-deluding in believing that the enormity of such horror could ever be alleviated by so slight a weapon as humor. It was not that humor or laughter never occurred in concentration camps; there have been enough anecdotes from camp survivors to attest to those occurrences. However, to suggest that the horrific oppression of concentration camp life could be so completely altered by humor and clowning was deemed inappropriate and inconceivable by Denby. Showing that humor could undo such horror was said to trivialize it, diminishing the magnitude of the catastrophic and dehumanizing camp existence to the dimensions proposed by Holocaust deniers.

The conflict between the position that anything is fair game for humor and Denby's position—that some things are so evil that we are even profligate to regard them from a humorous perspective—is echoed in discussions of humor by some of the world's leading contemporary writers. In the third book of Robertson Davies' classic Deptford trilogy, entitled *World of Wonders* (1975), for example, there is a prolonged discussion about whether humor and joking isn't the province of the devil rather than a gift from God. The major characters in *World of Wonders* argue that joking about past events is a way to diminish their importance and "veil" their horror. This position certainly reflects what humor theorists mean when they talk of the positive therapeutic value of humor. However, the novel's protagonists contend that this veiling of horror simply prepares people to accept yet further horrors by stopping them from learning to avoid the circumstances that produce misery. Humor is seen as being essentially evil because it prevents us from thoughtfully trying to predict and imagine the near future and learn what we would need to know for survival. As one of Davies' characters notes, "Only the Devil could devise such a subtle agency and persuade mankind to value it" (p. 92).

A similar point of view is expressed in Umberto Eco's marvelous novel, *The Name of the Rose* (1980), which is portrayed as a rediscovered lost manuscript from the 14th century. Here, a puritanical blind monk, Jorge, the curator and librarian of a large collection of rare books in a remote monastery, is shown to have arranged the deaths of several monks. In one way or another each of them had come in contact with writings about humor in the library, the most significant work being Aristotle's second book of poetics. Significantly, Jorge had hidden that volume away in a remote corner of the library for more than 20 years. Each monk who finds or touches the manuscript, which explains and praises the virtues of humor, ends up a grisly corpse. Near the end of this novel, there is a dramatic encounter in a deep labyrinth inside the library between the intellectual sleuth William, a monk who has been invited to the monastery to help solve the mysterious deaths, and the murderous Jorge. The two intellectually gifted monks engage in a reasoned but tense dialogue about the nature of humor after William accuses and Jorge admits to the murders, contending that the killings were prompted by his God-given duty to prevent others from learning of this tome that extolled the virtues of humor. Jorge reveals his hatred and dread of humor, arguing that it is blasphemous, that it has the potential to destroy faith and the "order of the universe" (p. 474). He argues that if humor is allowed to undo the fear of God, humans would come to revere the profane, "the dark powers of corporal matter" (p. 477). Jorge believes that the consequence of this metamorphosis would be Armageddon. All that is holy would fall, and what is base would ascend. Jorge's case is that humor is an antidote to obedience and a tool for insurrection. This is also a point well made by George Mikes (1954) who stated:

> If it is the philosopher's aim to discover a higher and better inner order where other people see only apparently unconnected phenomena, it may well be the humorist's task to see a higher and inner disorder in things where others see only system and orderliness. (p. 118)

William counters Jorge's arguments, much as humor theorists might, with the assertion that Jorge himself is the devil incarnate; his puritanism is the very hell that threatens to make life an agony in the here and now. The use of fear and terror, while supporting order, reflects the devil's "arrogance of the spirit, faith without smile, truth that is never seized by doubt"(p. 477).

Like Davies, Eco presents along with affirmative evaluations of humor the argument that humor can be construed as "devilish," a force for undoing the seriousness and fear that restrains humans from participating in acts that would destroy the established order. As we will note in later chapters, this view that comedy and humor contribute to rebellion against authority and order is a recurrent theme in writings about humor.

Keith-Spiegel (1972) has described how different thinkers and philosophers vary in their estimations of humor, from those who view it as a "gift handed down from the gods" to those who see it as a "scourge delivered up from the devils" (p. 25).

In a delightful article entitled "A Laugh a Day: Can Mirth Keep Disease at Bay?" Jeffrey Goldstein (1982) presents selected opinions about humor and laughter from early writings in medicine, philosophy, and religion. Among religious writers, Goldstein contends, laughter has usually been held in poor regard. Quoting Robert Barclay in his *Apology for the True Christian Divinity*, Goldstein notes that comedy, along with games, sport, and play, has been said to be inappropriate for Christians because these activities "disagree" with "Christian silence, gravity, and sobriety" (p. 23). Disdain for laughter among the "religiously correct" was likewise manifested in the beliefs of the Pilgrims in America (p. 23). In fact, Goldstein contends, laughter in public has been socially acceptable only for approximately a hundred years.

Before accepting an assumed relationship between religiosity and a lack of humor, however, we should differentiate among religions. As noted by Berger (1997), it is largely the "Abrahamic religions," the monotheistic Judaism, Christianity, and Islam, that "are comparatively underprivileged in the department of mirth" (p. 268). The lack of mirth in Christianity is said to have prompted

Nietzche to have made his renowned quip that he "would find Christianity more believable if only the Christians looked more redeemed."

In contrast to the Abrahamic religions, laughter and humor is common among Zen monks, Taoist sages, and Sufi practitioners, and if one may draw inferences from the multitude of laughing Buddhas on display in the shops of most Chinatowns, laughter would seem to be quite acceptable among Buddhists as well. As noted by Horne (1996), however, "seriousness" is the usual demeanor of Christianity, and Berger (1997) speaks of "Christian theology as a depressingly lachrymose affair" with only occasional exceptions, such as the humor of Martin Luther, which was often used by his critics to discredit him.

Throughout the biblical texts of Judaism and Christianity there are few references to laughter and even fewer to humor. Not until more modern times do we find theological writers like Karl Barth (1928) and Reinhold Niebuhr (1946) speaking favorably about humor. Both perceive it as congruent with religious virtue. Barth notes:

> Like art, humor undoubtedly means that we not take the present with ultimate seriousness, not because it is not serious enough in itself, but because God's future, which breaks into the present, is more serious. Humor means the placing of a big bracket around the seriousness of the present. In no way does it mean—and those who think it does do not know what real humor is—that this seriousness is set aside or dismissed. (p. 511)

In Barth's view, play and humor are necessary to human existence because we are transitory, finite creatures in contrast to the limitlessness of God. For Niebuhr, humor and faith are the human response to the incongruities experienced in life:

> Humor is concerned with the immediate incongruities of life and faith with the ultimate ones. Both humor and faith are expressions of the freedom of the human spirit, of its capacity to stand outside of life, and itself, and to view the whole scene. . . . Laughter is our reaction to immediate incongruities and those which do not affect us essentially. Faith is the only possible response to the ultimate incongruities of existence which threaten the very meaning of our life. (p. 200)

Both Barth and Niebuhr, then, see humor as an expression of human awareness of being fragile, uncertain, and of small consequence. Our knowledge and acceptance of mortality would seem likely to leave us all too aware of incongruities that form the foundations of humor: we make daily choices and pursue goals seriously, knowing all the while that we are mortal and that, in time, whatever our choices and goals, they will have little lasting importance.

It is in these more modern theological viewpoints that we find resonance with what we will discuss as *perspective-taking* or *distancing* in humor, the characteristics that may account for humor's role in moderating the toxic effects of stress. Like theologians, certain modern philosophers have cast humor in a favorable light, whereas for earlier philosophers humor was in poor repute.

Discussions about humor can be found in the writings of Plato (*Philebus*), Aristotle (*Poetics*), Hobbes (*Leviathan*), and Rousseau (*Lettre à M. d'Alembert*). These works most often focused on the derisive qualities of laughter, asserting that it is most often directed at the ugliness and deformities of others and always has a tinge of venom. Consequently, laughter was said to reflect the more undesirable, aggressive qualities of humans that result in the victimization of others. Aristotle suggested that "comedy aims at representing man as worse, tragedy as better than in actual life" and "the ludicrous is merely a subdivision of the ugly" (Piddington, 1963, p. 153). Bergson (1911) argued that humor and laughter represent powerful social correctives that are used to humiliate and correct persons who do not conform to social expectations. Perhaps the most pejorative comments about laughter were offered by Hobbes, who noted that "the passion of laughter is nothing else but some sudden glory arising from some sudden conception of some eminence in ourselves, by comparison with the infirmity of others or with our own formerly" (Piddington, 1963, p. 160). In Hobbes's consideration, humor resulted from a sense of superiority accompanying the disparagement of other persons or our own past ways of acting or thinking. Zillman (1983) pointed out that where Plato and Aristotle suggested that it is the powerful and unblemished who laugh at the infirm and ugly, Hobbes viewed laughter as characterizing the imperfect and blemished, who laugh at others who are even more unfortunate than themselves to enhance their own self-respect. From this point of view, laughter would seem to be a compensatory act.

These philosophical considerations are often clustered into a grouping defined as *the superiority theory of humor*. Other philosophers, however, were more attentive to the mechanics of humor than to its social ramifications. Many of these *conflict* or *incongruity theories of humor* bear similarity to Koestler's concept of bisociation (Koestler, 1964). Among the earliest writings in this vein is an essay by Beattie (1776, cited by Berlyne, 1969, p. 800) who noted, "Laughter arises from the view of two or more inconsistent, unsuitable, or incongruous parts or circumstances, considered as united in one complex object or assemblage." Schopenhauer (1819) expressed this view most clearly when he described laughter as arising from a sudden perception of an incongruity between an object and an abstract concept under which the object has been subsumed. He ascribed wit to the intentional relating of two radically different objects to the same concept. Spencer (1860) likewise spoke of "descending incongruity" as the essential condition resulting in laughter.

Reviews of philosophical deliberations on humor can be found in several sources, including Kimmins (1928), Piddington (1963), Lauter (1964), Monro (1963), and most recently, in *The Philosophy of Laughter and Humor* (Morreall, 1987).

The changeover from a negative to a positive view of humor and laughter is evident in the writings of Freud. His first and larger exploration of humor, *Jokes and Their Relation to the Unconscious* (1905) dealt prominently with aggressive and tendentious humor. Humor and laughter were perceived as veiled expressions of unconscious wishes, often of a sexual or aggressive nature. Freud's later paper (1928), while brief and less noticed for a good length of time, dealt with what he formally called "humor," a definite gift of forgiveness and reassurance internalized from parental responses to childhood misdemeanors. This form of humor was seen as a more intrapersonal occurrence whereby persons lighten their self-judgments, muting their fears and anxieties with the kinds of reassurances that parents might have offered them when they were children experiencing failures and discomforts.

This transition from perceiving humor and laughter as negative attributes to regarding them as having virtue and therapeutic value may reflect changes in the relationships between people in different ages. Right up until the end of the 19th century, for example, it was routine for the fashionable to visit mental institutions to enjoy a good laugh at the expense of pitifully disheveled inmates who were often shackled to their cages. The film *The Elephant Man* offered a good reminder of how people would visit carnivals to view and laugh at deformed and diseased persons.

Among physicians, however, humor—or at least laughter—seems to have been held in positive regard for some time. The first association drawn between health and humor is a biblical maxim attributed to Solomon that states, "The joyous heart is a good remedy, but a crushed spirit dries up the bones" (Proverbs 17:22). Goldstein (1982) noted that the idea that laughter could be therapeutic occurs frequently in medical writings throughout the centuries. Citing the contributions of physicians and philosophers from the 13th through the 19th centuries, Goldstein presented a series of priceless testimonials to humor's value for health. Gottlieb Hufeland, a 19th-century professor, is quoted as follows:

> Laughter is one of the most important helps to digestion with which we are acquainted; the custom in vogue among our ancestors, of exciting it by jesters and buffoons, was founded on true medical principles. Cheerful and joyous companions are invaluable at meals. Obtain such, if possible, for the nourishment received amid mirth and jollity is productive of light and healthy blood. (p. 22)

In the 13th century, Henri de Mondeville, a surgeon, suggested that laughter could be used as an aid in the recovery from surgery: "The surgeon must forbid anger, hatred, and sadness in the patient, and remind him that the body grows fat from joy and thin from sadness" (p. 23).

Another testimonial noted by Goldstein was from Richard Mulcaster, a 16th-century physician who believed that laughter could be thought of as a physical exercise promoting health. He wrote that laughter could help those who have cold hands and cold chests and are troubled by melancholia, "since it moveth much aire in the breast, and sendeth the warmer spirites outward" (p. 22).

In his *Treatise on Laughter*, Laurent Joubert (1579), another physician, discussed how laughter could alter the direction of illnesses, though he also warned how "inordinate laughter" could have untoward effects that might exacerbate some medical conditions. Describing how the presence of pet monkeys caused mirth and recovery from illness, Joubert went on to say:

> In these illnesses the pleasant acts of the monkeys (an animal laughable in itself) excited and raised up the nature that was burdened, broken, and as if suffocated by sickness. The pleasure acquired from laughter can do this very easily. For such joy moves the languishing and crushed heart, spreads the pleasure throughout the body, and makes it come to the aid of Nature, which, seizing upon these means and proper instruments, finds itself once again healthy, and strengthened by such help, combats the sickness with great vigor until it vanquishes the illness. For it is, properly speaking, Nature that cures illness. The doctor, the medicine, and the aid of the assistants are but the helps which encourage Nature. . . . The dignity and excellence of laughter is, therefore, very great inasmuch as it reinforces the spirit so much that it can suddenly change the state of a patient, and from being deathbound render him curable. (p. 128)

Finally, in the spirit of his forbears, J. J. Walsh, a physician and medical professor at Fordham University in the early years of the 20th century, wrote a book entitled *Laughter and Health* (Walsh, 1928), in which the following appears:

> There is nothing that makes us forget so completely about functions of the body that we may have been solicitous over as good hearty laughter. It dissipates the intense concentration of attention on some bodily function which so often proves to be the principal cause of the disturbance in that function. All the varied "cures" that have cured for a while, and then would not cure anything, demonstrate that the state of mind is the most important thing in the world for a great many patients. (p. 143)

He goes on to say:

> The best formula for the health of the individual is contained in the mathematical expression: health varies as the amount of laughter. . . . This favorable effect on the mind influences various functions of the body and makes them healthier than would otherwise be the case. (p. 143)

It would seem then that where many philosophers, theologians, and those concerned with morality and religion in earlier centuries excoriated humor and laughter—which was said to derive from malicious delight at the failings and misfortunes of others—physicians were more observant of the benefits of laughter and humor for restoring health. Joubert wrote about how laughter helped to create healthy-looking complexions and vitality in facial features due to the excessive blood flow that accompanies it. In turn, this was used as evidence that laughter was aligned with recuperative forces that contributed to a patient's wellness.

Given the relatively brief history of psychology as an empirical science separate from philosophy, what we will call early psychological contributions to the literature on humor are really quite recent. Beginning in the 20th century, social psychologists and sociologists concerned with our species' social nature spoke of "instincts" such as "primitive passive sympathy" (McDougall, 1908). This instinct would result in our sharing emotions with others, crying when others cry, feeling angry when others express anger. This tendency was said to make us highly vulnerable to emotional arousal during our social interactions. Along with suggestion and imitation, emotional arousal—derived from primitive passive sympathy—was seen as a source of irrational behavior. Social theorists like Le Bon (1895) regarded these forces as helping to produce a "group mind," which submerged rationality in the rush to group–directed, emotionally charged behavior.

It was McDougall (1903, 1922) who first suggested that laughter could play a role in reducing the impact of these social forces that undermined rational behavior. Laughter was described as a device for avoiding excessive sympathy, saving us not only from depression and grief but from all other forms of vicarious sympathy, a position not unlike that of recent writings about humor serving to alleviate distress (emotional arousal):

> The possession of this peculiar disposition (laughter) shields us from the depressing influence which the many minor mishaps and shortcomings of our fellows would exert upon us if we did not possess it, and which they do exert upon those unfortunate persons in whom the disposition seem to be abnormally weak or altogether lacking. It not only prevents our minds from dwelling upon these depressing objects, but it actually converts these objects into stimulants that promote our well-being, both bodily and mentally, instead of depressing us through sympathetic pain or distress. And now we see how the acquirement of laughter was worthwhile to the human species; laughter is primarily and fundamentally the antidote to sympathetic pain. (p. 299)

Although technically not a psychologist, Sigmund Freud examined the subject matter of concern to psychologists, albeit from limited samples of behavior. His book *Jokes and Their Relationship to the Unconscious* (1905) was a landmark in the literature about humor, later amplified in the writings of others (Koestler, 1964). Working from a "closed energy model," Freud described laughter as a release of defensive tension that had been aroused by circumstances preliminary to the laugh. The tension was said to be created by anything that could provoke primary emotions, anger, and sexuality in situations where their expression would be inappropriate (subject to superego condemnation). When the ego defenses preventing the release of id-derived emotional expressions prove to be unnecessary—as when a joker provides a punch line to his story and relieves listeners of possible emotional responses—the energy exerted to inhibit responses is released in laughter. Though Freud's focus on energy is now regarded as a quaint reminder of the scientific thinking of the 19th century, his writings, like McDougall's, hinted at the beneficial effects of humor as a means of reducing the impact of emotional duress.

These "relief" or "tension-reduction" theories of humor have their roots in the earlier philosophical writings of Descartes (1649), Hartley (1749), Sully (1903), and Kline (1907), each of whom believed laughter resulted from a relief of strain and the induction of a playful mood with pleasurable consequences. Freud, similar to Kline, emphasized the role of "mentation" (mental play) in reducing the tension deriving from controlled thought or rationality.

As already noted, Freud's view of humor as a tension-reducing mechanism is reflected in Koestler's (1964) analysis, whereby bisociation dispels the emotional arousal accompanying some anticipated threat to the superego. Freud's later paper entitled *Humor* (1928) was another pioneering effort that has had a delayed but welcome effect on the literature concerned with humor. Freud suggested that humor represents parental forgiveness that, having been internalized into the superego, enables the individual to gain perspective and absolution from dissappointments and failures. Reinterpreting failures as being of lesser importance than initially believed, "mere child's play" becomes a means of coming to terms with them and therefore of averting anxiety and depression. It is this form of humor that eventually comes to be regarded as among the most mature ego defenses (Vaillant, 1977).

More detailed descriptions of the early history of psychological writings about humor can be found in chapters by Flugel (1954) and Berlyne (1969) in their respective volumes of the *Handbook of Social Psychology*.

CONCLUSION

In the writings of many early philosophers, especially religious philosophers, humor and laughter were thought of in critical terms, in contrast to the way they were evaluated by early physicians and psychologists. The former emphasized the derisive and hostile characteristics of humor and laughter, whereas the latter addressed their virtues as stress reducers. Among the seminal thinkers of the 19th century, Charles Darwin (1872) suggested that laughter was an innate expression of joy and a form of social communication that fostered survival. This positioning of humor within the cluster of survival-enhancing instincts probably influenced Freud, who described humor and laughter as instinctive means of reducing emotional arousal and thus emphasized their positive effects. Conceivably, the different evaluations of humor by early philosophers and later psychologists may reflect their times. Innocuous or nonhostile, self-deprecating forms of humor may actually have become more common in recent years. On the other hand, it is also plausible that writers with greater interest in religious matters may have been more attentive to the "subversive" qualities of humor, as Umberto Eco's novel described. Laughter, with its associated dismissal of seriousness, may have been seen to lead humans astray from the very things they should regard with utmost seriousness. These antithetical viewpoints are mirrored in recent psychological research into the role of mourning. Whereas it has long been thought that humans are helped by fully expressing thier grief in mourning, recent investigations have found that laughter, humor, enjoyment, and amusement exhibited during interviews six months after the loss of a spouse were good predictive indicators of how well persons had been able to come to terms with bereavement (Bonanno & Keltner, 1997; Keltner & Bonanno, 1997). These investigations will be described in greater detail in a later chapter. For now, we see that seriousness and humor have been considered in widely contrasting ways. Those with religious proclivities emphasized the need to remain serious and emotionally engaged in tragic events, whereas others viewed humor as a means of escaping from the persisting agonies of life. The latter would argue that tragedies are all too common and that humor allows us to escape their deleterious consequences.

But if we take a more circumspect view of seriousness and humor, or tragedy and comedy, we may find that they are not mutually exclusive. As Charlie Chaplin once astutely noted: "Life is a tragedy when seen in close-up, but a comedy in long shot." That humor is associated with distance and tragedy with proximity to agonizing circumstances reinforces the idea that humor serves a defensive purpose, allowing an observer a more remote perspective from which emotional arousal may be muted. Although there are times when seriousness is the only appropriate response, as some philosophers and religionists would argue, there are also times when humor is most appropriate and even necessary for our well-being.

If humor is a "hardwired" characteristic of our species that has evolved because of its usefulness as a defense against becoming emotionally overwhelmed, then we would expect it to be universal. In the following chapter we will look at evidence for the pervasiveness of humor and whether it is universal among humans and exclusive to them.

CHAPTER 4

THE PERVASIVENESS OF HUMOR

Astronomers often wonder whether we are alone in the universe, whether life exists on other planets in other solar systems. An analogous question for psychologists, ethologists, and other social scientists is whether we humans are alone among species in being abstract thinkers, users of language, empathizers, and perpetrators of and participants in humor. A common assertion is that we are alone in appreciating humor, that we are the sole jokers on our planet. If our species is alone in appreciating and producing humor, we may wonder whether humor exists in all cultures and enjoyed by all individuals in those cultures. Are there funny stories or jokes that would have universal appeal—that would find receptive audiences despite differences between cultures and individuals—as was suggested in the Monty Python skit, "The Killer Joke?" And finally, are there some human experiences that no human would subject to humorous play?

IS HUMOR UNIVERSAL IN THE HUMAN SPECIES ?

If laughter were the sole criteria for assessing the presence of humor, the answer to the above question would be self-evident. Though the appropriate time and place for laughter may vary from one culture to another, laughter seems to be universal in our species. Investigators of emotional expressions (Ekman, 1973) report finding the same identifiable expressions of emotion from the simplest to the most complex societies. Smiles and laughter occur in all human societies.

However, there can be laughter without humor—as a sign of victory, for example. A famous picture of Hitler shows him doing a jig with a seeming expression of laughter on his face after hearing of the fall of France. But al-

41

though he has been said to have been relatively humorless, even Hitler was known to joke and laugh, as will be noted in a later chapter.

When it comes to humor, however, the phenomenon is more complex. If humor can be seen as a form of social interaction that includes play between the performers that becomes an occasion for laughter, then we can assert that humor too is universal. But, as we will see in reviewing observations of other species closely related to us, this definition makes it clear that we are not alone in our use of humor and laughter.

When considering whether humor and laughter are universal characteristics of our species, it is important to ask if these features have an evolved basis. If humor and laughter are inherent in our species, then it means that these behaviors were selected for in evolution and offer some benefit for our survival. To test for the evolved basis of humor and laughter, methods pioneered by Darwin (1872) are used. These involve assessing for the universal prevalence of humor and laughter within a species, early onset (prior to socialization), specific neurophysiological mediation, presence in related species, and stereotypy. Making use of these methods, Weisfeld (1993) asserts that there is ample evidence for the evolved basis of humor and laughter.

As noted earlier, the universality of humor and laughter has been reported by investigators of emotional expression such as Ekman (1973, 1984). Early onset of laughter has also been established, though with some variability in age reported (McGhee, 1979; Sroufe & Waters, 1976; Young, 1973). Generally, laughter seems to emerge at about four months of age among humans, arguably making it innate.

Specific neural structures or pathways that mediate humor have been found in the literature concerned with the location of lesions and a range of pathological conditions. The hypothalamus and limbic structures of the temporal lobe have been implicated in the expression of humor and laughter along with numerous other emotions that are found throughout the species and are assumed to have an evolved basis. In one remarkable case described by Weisfeld (Martin, 1950), a patient who had a cyst removed from his brain under local anaesthesia laughed, joked, and uttered obscenities whenever the hypothalamic region of his brain was touched but stopped when sensation ceased. Martin concluded that a "humor center" exists in the hypothalamic region. Right-hemisphere lesions have been found to result in inappropriate joking, and the appreciation of humor has been associated with right frontal lobe activity (Brownell & Gardner, 1988).

Most recently, Shammi and Stuss (1999) have found confirming evidence for locating the sense of humor in the right frontal lobe. Among subjects who had suffered strokes, tumors, or damage from surgery, they found that patients with right frontal damage were unable to recognize the correct picture to complete a comic strip in a funny way. These patients could identify funny endings if the comic strip consisted of slapstick humor, and they could identify endings that logically fit with the preceding pictures. However, if the comic strips consisted of more sophisticated jokes, patients with frontal lobe damage were unable to identify the endings that were crucial for understanding the joke. This localization of sense of humor adds to the information in support of humor and laughter having an evolved basis.

With regard to phylogenetic continuity, laughter seems to occur in our nearest related species. Robert Provine (1996) has examined the auditory characteristics of human and chimpanzee laughter, and while different patterns of sounds are evident between the species, the occasions for the occurrence of these sounds make it evident that chimpanzees do laugh. As Provine notes (p. 196), "From at least the time of Darwin . . . it has been known that chimpanzees and other great apes perform a laugh-like vocalization when tickled or during play."

Much like the play of children in a schoolyard at lunchtime, laughter occurs among chimpanzees during physical contact or the threat of same, and during wrestling, tickling, and chasing games, especially among the "chasees." Where we differ most from other species is in the laughter during conversation that characterizes adult human interaction.

Jane Goodall (1968) made similar observations of laughter during bouts of wrestling and tickling among chimpanzees, and Aldis (1975) found laughter-like vocalizations among gorillas, orangutans, baboons, macaques, and entellus langurs. Among chimpanzees and gorillas that have learned to communicate with sign language there is also evidence of joking. McGhee (1979, cited in Weisfeld, 1992, p. 145) reports that these animals sometimes give incorrect linguistic signs accompanied by laughter, and that "chimpanzees have been observed to throw debris at or to urinate on people, and then to sign 'funny,' a sign that is also used in tickling and chasing games."

In this fourth test of humor's evolved basis, evidence again suggests that our species is "prewired" for humor. Finally, with regard to stereotypy, laughter is clearly alike and identifiable in far-ranging and radically different cultures. It would be hard to mistake a laugh for some other emotional expression.

These observations led Weisfeld (1993) to suggest that laughter and presumably humor have an evolved basis in humans. As far as we can ascertain, laughter and probably humor as well can be said to be an inherent characteristic of our species. Therefore, the answer to our first question is yes, humor is universal among humans. Why should such a characteristic have evolved? In a later chapter we will elaborate on Norman Dixon's (1980) hypothesis that humor may be a "mechanism that substitutes for the primitive adrenergic response one [that is] more appropriate to the sorts of stressors with which humans . . . have had to contend" (pp. 281–282). Furthermore, Colin Turnbull's (1972) observations of humor in a devastated society, discussed later in this chapter, lead us to view humor as a means of avoiding emotional trauma, of finding distance from life events that would leave us bereft of a desire to continue living.

ARE HUMANS ALONE IN THE USE OF HUMOR AND JOKING?

The earlier descriptions of chimpanzee laughter would seem to preclude the need to ask whether we are the only laughers on this planet. However, if humor, as opposed to laughter, requires the ability to think abstractly, to be able to consider alternative, contrasting ways of viewing things, to be able to guess at the thought processes of another, then many would contend that it is simply beyond the ken of other species.

The prominent philosopher Noam Chomsky has long argued that we, alone among species, are capable of learning language and thinking abstractly. Consequently, although it may be begrudgingly admitted that nonhumans can laugh, it would seem inconceivable that they could joke or produce humor of whatever kind. This position, however, has been challenged, especially by a little male bonobo (a close relative of the chimpanzee) named Kanzi, who was reared in the labs of Sue Savage-Rumbaugh (Savage-Rumbaugh & Lewin, 1994). Kanzi was the son of a female bonobo who was the subject of language training in Savage-Rumbaugh's labs. When Kanzi was six months old, he began accompanying his mother to these training sessions, to which she was indifferent. After observing these futile lessons with his mother for a two-year period, Kanzi surprised his mentors by showing evidence that he was "catching on" even though he had never been directly trained or reinforced for language learning. By the time he was four years old he had mastered a board of lexigrams (abstract symbols of things that bonobos find interesting), communicating by pointing to specific signs. He used these signs to indicate what he intended to do, like "chase, tickle." In essence, Kanzi knew what he was about to do, or had an image of his own upcoming behavior. This suggests also that Kanzi had an image of himself or was self-conscious, and that in communicating information to another, he revealed a sense of himself, that he was different and separate from the person with whom he was communicating. Although this much is interesting, Kanzi also came to reveal that he understood spoken English. When asked to do something, like "put a rock in a hat," he would do so. Not wanting to be accused of the "clever Hans" phenomenon whereby that famed horse presumably solved arithmetic questions but was really responding to the nonverbal cues of his trainer, Kanzi's handlers demonstrated that he understood requests and commands that were delivered through earphones through which no visual cuing was possible. This research

(Savage-Rumbaugh & Lewin, 1994; Rumbaugh, 1990; Savage-Rumbaugh *et al.*, 1993) has unsettled much of our thinking about the skills that we may share with other species.

Among other cognitive processes that would enable humor to be produced or appreciated is self-consciousness. Because humor and laughter most often occur in social situations during communication between individuals (Provine & Fisher, 1989), joking and laughter probably require the ability to perceive the state of mind of the person or creature with whom one is in communication and with that of the object or target of the joke. Premack and Woodruff (1978) found data that allowed them to conclude that chimpanzees have "a theory of mind." That is, they are aware of their own versus another's "personhood" or mind. Research with chimpanzees has demonstrated that an individual animal who has learned to do a difficult task that must be done in cooperation with another individual (e.g., lifting and moving a table to another location) often knows whether the other animal understands what must be done for them to succeed. In such instances, the knowing chimp will try to take the place of the ignorant chimp in helping the experimenter, or instruct him or her about what it is they should do. In other words, the chimp who understands knows that he is different in what he knows from the other chimp.

How, we might ask, can we discern whether animals such as chimpanzees are truly self-conscious? Without some means of communication, how can we find out if a chimpanzee has a sense of himself, an identity, that differs from that of another chimpanzee? This question was answered wonderfully in the so-called mirror experiments of Gordon Gallup (1977). In most species, the presentation of a mirror either excites indifference, or in some cases, as with certain pugnacious fish, elicits fighting behavior. My dogs have never shown any interest in their own images. They have failed to recognize themselves even when seeing their paws or head being manipulated by me and simultaneously feeling those sensations. If they responded at all it was as if the image were of another dog. Curiosity never seemed to be aroused by images, though one of my Welsh terriers, Eddy, did once run behind our television set as if to follow a group of squealing pigs shown on the screen running off into the distance. My guess is that it was the sound of the high-pitched squealing in that instance that triggered his response. If it were possible to have olfactory stimulation as well, although ghastly for me, he, I'm sure, would have been wildly responsive.

But chimpanzees, orangutans, and even dolphins reveal that they *can* identify the creature in the mirror as themselves. Gallup would put a paint smear on the animals' heads where it could not be seen except when they looked at themselves in the mirror. After a little practice and becoming accustomed to looking in a mirror, these animals would reveal their awareness of themselves by touching their own and not the reflected image of their heads where the paint had been smeared. In other words, these animals knew that the image in the mirror was their own, and that the paint smear on the image in the mirror was a reflection of what was on their own heads. From this behavior, Gallup could argue that chimps, bonobos, orangutans, and dolphins are conscious creatures. In order to recognize itself in the mirror, the creature has to know that it exists separately from others and that it can monitor itself in much the same way as an observer would. For a delightful compendium of the research that reveals greater genetic closeness among species, readers should consult *Shadows of Forgotten Ancestors: A Search for Who We Are* (Sagan & Druyan, 1992). Carl Sagan may not have lived long enough to witness evidence of life on other planets that he so hungered to see, but he did get to relish some of the discoveries that show we are not alone in our self-awareness, that we have conscious partners in life on earth.

Although we are not totally alone on earth in being self-conscious animals, it must be noted that we do not have overly much company. On the other hand, if we examine another contributor to the ability to create humor—playfulness—we find evidence of what we share with a much greater number of species.

Play is frequently discussed as a strong correlate of humor. In the second edition of the *Handbook of Social Psychology,* Daniel Berlyne's chapter is entitled, significantly, "Laughter, Humor, and Play" (1969). Apter's theory of psychological reversals likewise positions humor in the company of play (Apter, 1982). He posits that at any moment an individual will be in one or another of two states—one telic, the other paratelic. The former refers to a state in which a person is goal-directed and serious; the latter is when an individual is involved in some ongoing activity where the ends are less important than the immediate activity and the individual is said to be playful. When people become emotionally aroused during telic activity the result is said to be irritation, because goal-directed action suffers with arousal. However, when people are playful, arousal is said to heighten the pleasure of the ongoing activity. Similar to Freud's focus on a rapid shift from arousal to relief, Apter interprets humor as deriving from a shift between telic and paratelic states. However, unlike Freud, Apter asserts that as we suddenly move from the serious to the playful, laughter signals an increase in arousal (instead of tension reduction), which reflects pleasure. In any case, playfulness, whether seen as relief from seriousness or an opportunity for pleasure, is viewed as being closely related to humor. To put it most succinctly, playfulness may be viewed as a necessary though insufficient cause of humor and laughter. An excellent article linking humor, playfulness, and interest or curiosity is available (Weisfeld, 1993).

Although pet owners may be accused of anthropomorphism when describing their pets' behavior, the fact that play characterizes some of the behavior of animals lower on the phylogenetic scale than chimpanzees is undeniable. Often said to be rehearsals for later predatory or defensive activity, playful activity among the young of many species is easily discerned. As dogs age their playfulness is retained even if such states are interspersed with long periods of indolence and somnolence. With dogs, the difference between seriousness and playfulness is often stark and not at all pleasant as their owners sometimes discover.

My Welsh Terrier Eddy was a friendly but strong animal who loved to wrestle with my son or myself, mock-biting us as he struggled to take a stick from our hands or grab a squeaking rubber toy. He was also obsessed with balloons. I could get him to swim a considerable distance in pursuit of a balloon that I had tied to a string attached to my bathing suit. On one occasion, when he was rapidly catching up to the balloon, my wife called out that I shouldn't let him get it since he had a penchant for swallowing deflated balloons, which could result in intestinal blockage. Grabbing for the balloon at the same moment as Eddy resulted in my losing the tip of one finger. On sensing this assault and witnessing the blood gushing from my finger, I quickly came to know Eddy's capabilities when he was serious. He seemed contrite as he watched me respond with shock, and we both instantly ceased being playful. Suffering this injury made me aware of how much he was "pulling his punches" when he played. In some way, all dog owners know that their dogs can hurt them. When it happens, it reminds us of their power and how much they restrain themselves to remain in our good graces.

That dogs play is also obvious on their faces. Darwin discussed the "canine smile," and investigators of play and humor have discussed the closeness between the "play face" and laughter. "Horseplay" and slapstick (mock-fighting) are easily observable among many primates. Even birds engage in play and "fooling around." The Australian Galah, a pink-and-gray cockatoo (*Cacatua roseicapilla*) is well known as a clown whose playfulness is a source of distress for hydroelectric power linemen. Galahs love to twirl around power lines, spinning like whirling dervishes until the insulation is stripped from the wires. The word *mischievous* is often used to describe the cockatoos' behavior. It is obvious that though verbal humor is largely limited to humans and their nearest relatives, playfulness is widely found among many species.

The answer to our question is, then, that we as a species are not alone in the use of humor and joking if we take account of all those behaviors that are close to humor and laughter. With regard to the verbal play that largely makes up our form of humor we have few companions among other species, though it seems that a few others share the self-awareness, cognitive capacities, and skills of empathy that are prerequisites of humor and laughter.

ARE THERE UNIVERSALS IN THE FORM
AND CONTENT OF HUMOR?

Is there nothing too sacred to be spoofed? It is often surprising and at times dismaying that the most awful circumstances will generate joking responses almost immediately. Jokes about disasters that undermine the confidence of humans are to be expected, and as the Internet allows for communication at lightning speed this phenomenon is likely to increase. On certain chat lines, jokes flash like meteorites the moment a tragedy or disaster strikes. The following cartoon, another by Jack Lefcourt, appeared in newspapers upon the heels of yet another school shooting, this time in Alberta, Canada, which had followed quickly upon the prominent Colorado shooting that riveted public attention.

Perhaps natural calamaties such as tornadoes, earthquakes, and hurricanes, and man-made disasters such as "ethnic cleansing," school shootings, serial killings, and the like are "naturals" for humor. They cause emotional arousal—ranging from anger to sorrow—and yet, if we are far enough from the scene we also are glad not to have been at the epicenter of the event, to be the lucky ones. Bisociation obviously can occur: "That is terrible—those poor people—I feel so bad for them—thank God it's not me and mine who were in

FIGURE 4-1: Horrific school shootings became the subject of humor when they began occurring with some frequency in the 1990s. Copyright © Jack Lefcourt, 1998.

it—I feel good that it didn't happen to us." These are the kinds of thoughts we cannot admit to unless the event is so far from us that we are barely able to sympathize with its victims, or if the victims are people or animals whom we do not particularly revere—saltwater crocodiles, for example. Gary Larson's cartoons often deal with such awful but funny events involving the interactions between humans and other animals.

Although nothing seems to be beyond the pale of humor, the particular targets of jokes often seem to be diagnostic of particular cultural viewpoints. The *fatwa* leveled by the Ayatollah Khomeini against Salman Rushdie for writing *The Satanic Verses* (1988) is a case in point. Either because of his realistic description of the historical as opposed to the mythical prophet Mohammed or because of his humorous treatment of the Ayatollah himself, Rushdie and his publishers and translators were threatened with death, and, in fact, a few of them were murdered. Fundamentalist Muslims in Iran seemed unable to accept the existence of alternative ways of viewing their religious leaders. Although it is not possible from a distance to know how pervasive is this inability to accept diverse viewpoints, the absence of controversy in the Islamic world would lead one to guess that bisociative thought processes would be difficult if not impossible for fundamentalist muslims. Or at least the fear of publicly expressing tolerance for diversity would make the likelihood of humor about religion all but impossible.

Many of us have had the experience of looking at cartoons in magazines from other cultures and wondering what could possibly account for their assumed funniness. Even *Punch*, the humorous English magazine, offers cartoons that are often wholly enigmatic to non-British but English-speaking people. Humor frequently seems nontransferable from one culture to another though if it is explained by a person from that culture it can become comprehensible. Nevertheless, some examples of humor seem to defy comprehension.

Sadistic humor, for example, seems incredible. How can humans find funniness in the horrific? Nazi soldiers, particularly the Gestapo, were known to laugh as Jews panicked during attacks on them. The agony of Jewish victims seemed to arouse mirth and even camaraderie among the ranks of their oppressors. Although benign humor often has this effect, finding humor in others' suffering would seem baffling and rare if it were not for the fact that such observations have been made elsewhere as well.

In a fictionalized work based on the reporting of actual field observations, anthropologist Laura Bohannan, writing under the pen name Bowen (1954), described a reunion in a village in Africa after the rampages of disease had resulted in many deaths and much suffering there and in the surrounding areas. The epidemic had been of such magnitude that villagers had banished their own relatives when they exhibited any sign of disease. Consequently, loved ones were separated and consigned to neglect and death. After the epidemic finally terminated, a young child named Accident mimed the handicaps and disease symptoms at a village gathering. The survivors, observing the caricatured disease symptoms that had so recently terrorized them, giggled and laughed uproariously. Bowen joined in the laughter herself and noted, "In such a situation one must either laugh or go mad, laugh at the reality or be mad in the illusion. . . . In an environment in which tragedy is genuine and frequent, laughter is essential to sanity" (p. 295).

Although this was a fictionalized account of field observations and we do not know how much was fiction and how much fact, laughter nevertheless seemed to be less derisive of the victims and more a release from the fear and misery that had been the villagers' lot. On the surface, though, this form of humor could seem akin to that in which others' hardships are parodied to become a source of laughter—the very kind of humor that early philosophers condemned as revealing feelings of superiority to the victims.

If fear is so intense when life is in jeopardy, how can humor be found in it so readily? A woman whom I knew some years ago had lived in Amsterdam throughout World War II. The Gestapo headquarters, she told me, were located across the street from her parents' home. My vision was of their living in constant fear. I was taken by surprise, then, as she described her family's laughter whenever their small dog would chase the Nazi officers as they marched in and out of neighboring houses. The officers would apparently try to jump out of the way, showing fear of the dimunitive aggressor. That humans can laugh under such daunting conditions is both marvelous, and apparently, not uncommon.

During my first stay as a visiting scholar at the Rockefeller Foundation Institute in Bellagio, Italy, in 1985, I was fortunate to meet two African diplomats who were attending a conference at the Villa Serbelloni where we scholars were housed. After they questioned me about the project I was working on at the time, which involved writing chapters in my first book about humor (Lefcourt & Martin, 1986), they looked at each other, broke into broad grins, and related a story.

Both men had been high-ranking public officials for many years in the government of an African nation and were currently enjoying that status again when I met them. Throughout their respective political careers, however, they had not always been as fortunate as during this period. On one occasion a year or two before our conversation, one of them had been overseas when he received a cable ordering him to return home for important consultations. Upon arrival, he discovered that his country was in the midst of "yet another coup d'état" (the third in his experience). He was led away from the airport in handcuffs and taken to a prison in the center of the capital city. The drama peaked when he was unceremoniously pushed into a cell and an iron door slammed shut behind him. Here was the moment of truth and terror. He described the clang of the slamming door as the signal of impending doom: the end of his career and possibly his life. But, as his eyes accommodated to the cell's darkness, he recognized several fellow ex-officials, including the second diplomat with whom we were talking, all of them wearing the same look of bewilderment, surprise, fear, and shock. After the few seconds required for the reality of the moment to sink in, these deposed officials simultaneously broke into hysterical laughter. Subsequently, whenever the prisoners were brought together in an exercise yard, this hilarity was repeated.

The two men again burst into a round of long and hearty laughter as they told of these experiences. On my probing for the source of their laughter after we had regained our composure, one explained most succinctly: "If we didn't keep laughing, we would've died."

This interpretation of laughter bears similarity to that discussed in Bowen's book. Laughter in the face of desperation prevents a slide into madness or death. As we will see in a later chapter, Brian Keenan, a hostage of Palestinian terrorists in Lebanon, wrote that laughter-provoking zaniness saved another hostage from slipping into a depth of despair that would inevitably have ended in death.

In a field study conducted by the anthropologist Colin Turnbull (1972), we find more evidence of humor and laughter occurring under circumstances in which most "civilized persons" would never anticipate it happening. Turnbull studied a mountain people, the Ik, a nomadic tribe residing in the mountains between Uganda and Kenya. Although normally nomads, they had recently become constrained in their wanderings because of the creation of a national park in Uganda's Kidepo Valley.

These hunter–gatherers were finding it extremely difficult to sustain themselves. Food and water had become scarcities to be hoarded and guarded lest they be stolen. In addition to the threat of starvation, their natural surroundings were often violent and unpredictable. Flash floods, predatory animals, and drought were all features of their new landscape and were making their lives mean and short.

With all of the hardships that these people endured, their ability to laugh did not diminish. But, the content or objects of their humor became grotesque. Given the inevitability of personal misfortune, humor and laughter derived from seeing others undergoing misfortune, and in some cases laughter arose from a person's own misery. For example, in one of many instances when Turnbull heard distant shouts of laughter, he found that a small crowd had gathered at a cliffside to laugh at the spectacle of an elderly blind woman who, in trying to make her way down the mountainside, had tripped and fallen to the bottom of a canyon. She lay there writhing weakly while the little crowd above watched and laughed at the spectacle.

Teasing the elderly such as in moving their food beyond their reach and laughing at their weakness in trying to get it back was common sport. Turnbull himself came close to becoming such an object when his Ik "guides" faded away while they were on a trail where sight was obscured by tall grasses. As Turnbull continued on the path, he drew up short when he discovered that the "path suddenly turned and dipped so violently that I slipped and almost fell." He discovered that before him was the very "edge of the escarpment with 1500 feet between" himself "and Kenya below." When his guides reappeared a half-hour later he was scolded by one of them, who accused him of taking a wrong turn which might have led to his fall over the cliff. Turnbull was actually pleased at what seemed to be concern on the part of his guide. However, he then "heard a muffled snort behind" him and found another guide doubled up with laughter, which in turn set the others off into gales of laughter of such intensity that tears streamed down their faces. Turnbull mused, "It is difficult to tell whether they would have laughed harder if I had fallen, or would have felt deprived of future possibilities for fun" (p. 273).

The story told by Colin Turnbull in *The Mountain People* deals with a topic larger than humor, concerned as it is with human nature itself. His contention is that societies reduced to "individualism" through scarcity and unpredictable misfortune reveal that "caring" for others is not hardwired into our species, that we are not naturally social animals. People can become, if not each other's worst enemies then only convenient means for each other's survival: the lives of others become important only insofar as they enable "me" to survive.

For the purposes of this chapter, the examples of laughter that Turnbull recorded in his remarkable anthropological investigation reveal that people are capable of laughing at anything. Hardships, accidents, death are all potential sources of laughter and humor. In several instances, Turnbull even notes how the Ik people came to laugh at their own accidents and misery as much as others did, and that it was crying and sympathy that were the real omissions in that degraded society. Humor as defined by Freud—somthing that derives from sympathy and forgiveness—were obviously not to be found in the Ik society, though Turnbull notes that "in olden times" the Ik too were said to be caring and supportive. But in the reality of their lives in the 1970s, their humor seemed to derive largely from feelings of superiority toward those upon whom ill-fate had exercised itself.

Humans seem to be quite malleable, responding to the changing circumstances of their lives. One constant seems to be a tendency to find mirth in living even if the objects of that mirth for one culture may be horrific in the eyes of another.

CONCLUSION

Although we can readily summon up images of individuals who seem incapable of laughing or even smiling, humor and laughter are present in most if not all cultures, and there is enough evidence to assert that our capacity for humor is an inherent characteristic of our species (Weisfeld, 1993). The pervasiveness of humor and laughter and the range of events that can provoke them encourage us to acknowledge the importance of humor as a human characteristic for dealing with terrible conditions. At the same time, as Turnbull's observations make abundantly clear, the distancing that humor can provide may also reflect a capitulation to conditions that should never have to be tolerated by anyone.

THE MANY FACES OF HUMOR: VARIATIONS IN THE TYPES AND DEFINITIONS OF HUMOR

As I noted earlier, most phenomena seem to become more complex the closer we get to them. When we speak of humor we often refer to a *sense of humor*, by which we might mean the degree to which persons respond to potentially funny events. Alternatively, we may reserve the term to describe someone who is capable of creating funny jokes or stories that provoke laughter from listeners. However, although laughter may be thought to be a good indicator of a humorous occurrence, not all laughter is related to humor. As Provine (1993; Provine and Fisher, 1989) has noted, many instances of laughter serve to punctuate conversation and may express friendliness or pleasure rather than humor. Even the laughing sounds we make come in great variety, as was so well presented in the scene in the film *Mary Poppins* when Ed Wynn found himself floating near the ceiling because he couldn't stop laughing. In that scene a full range of the varied sounds that could be recognized as laughter was demonstrated. Some manifestations of laughter are easily associated with humor, but some laughter can convey menace rather than humor. Humor itself is not a homogeneous phenomenon but rather a concatenation of expressions—some verbal, some nonverbal—that reveal a great variety of intentions, purposes, and reactions. Obviously, understanding humor, let alone laughter, can become a very complex and convoluted undertaking when humor is examined closely, and this is the very reason why some people feel that studying humor is impossible—that it evaporates when subjected to scrutiny.

Keith-Speigel (1972) has discussed the myriad ways in which humor has been regarded through the ages. Describing a "brier patch of terminology," she riffles through a host of theories, assumptions, value judgments, and assertions about the meanings of humor that can leave one feeling overwhelmed and liable to lose the dedication to make sense of the roles that humor may play. I do believe, however, that humor may be used to describe certain features of human behavior, and that it represents a stable personality characteristic. In addition, I believe that humor has a place in determining the ways in which individuals interact with each other. Given the potential complexity that can obscure these important aspects of humor, I shall try to focus only on what are thought to be functional differences, and among those I will concentrate only on differences that I have come to see as having important psychological ramifications. To this end, I will speak of certain consequences that accompany the exercise of specific forms of humor that lead some to see it as a blessing and others, as a curse.

FREUD'S CONTRIBUTIONS TO THE LITERATURE ON HUMOR

Freud was a remarkable man. In addition to spending long hours in clinical practice he wrote prodigiously about his personal and clinical experiences, constructing theories about the origin of dreams, anxiety, intrafamilial conflict, humor, and so on. His curiosity seemed to be unquenchable. For example, if he laughed at a joke during a dinner party, he would subsequently muse about the event, haunted until he could explain what it was that had provoked his mirth. Nothing seemed to escape his theoretical conceptualizing. Given his penchant for interpreting most human phenomena in terms of intrapersonal conflict and tension, it was almost inevitable that he would apply the same arousal and tension-reduction processes to explain humor that he had previously used to interpret intrapersonal conflict, dreams, and parapraxes or "slips of the tongue."

Freud interpreted laughter as a dispelling of energy that was no longer necessary for inhibiting the arousal of repressed impulses or "forbidden ideas." In essence, jokes were said to toy with repressed impulses, arousing id-related desires that would require repression by the ego if the superego were to be assuaged. To translate this into commonplace terminology, let's imagine a man telling a story that contains erotic details to a woman. If the woman suspected that the purpose of the story was, in fact, a test of her receptivity to his advances, she might begin to feel uncomfortable as the story progressed, especially if she were morally averse to such propositions. The discomfort would reflect an active attempt to subdue her own possible prurient interest in the erotic story and her potential sexual arousal in response to the assumed overture by the storyteller. However, if the story ultimately ended as a joke, this inhibitory action on her part would become superfluous and the energy spent in self-constraint could be discharged as laughter. When the punch line of the joke or story makes it clear that the anticipated inhibition was not really required and that the teller was not really making an advance (it was just a joke), the energy aroused for countercathexes is dispelled with laughter. This process involved in joking and laughter is described in *Jokes and the Unconscious* (Freud, 1905), which gives a fair portrait of the ways in which Freud conceptualized the everyday experiences of his patients, himself, and his friends alike. Today's readers might be less than enamoured of this book because the jokes seem stale and much of Freud's theorizing about energy conservation appears dated or at least out of touch with modern conceptualizations. Nevertheless, some of Freud's contributions in that early work and in a later paper on humor (1928) seem prescient.

To begin with, Freud distinguished between three forms of humor: *jokes, the comic,* and what he referred to as *humor.* Jokes were initially seen as provocative stories that allowed for the expression of normally repressed libidinal impulses. It is from the expression of these impulses, primarily associated with sex and aggression, that the pleasure involved in joking was said to derive. The pleasuresome characteristics of jokes that were associated with libidinal sastisfactions were referred to as a joke's *tendentious nature.* Satisfaction from contemplating aggression toward one's foes or sexual activity with attractive men or women made up the tendentious aspects of jokes. In addition, the "jokework"—the ways in which the listener's inhibitions are aroused and then "let down" by the joker—affords further pleasure. This is referred to as the *nontendentious aspects* of jokes. Koestler (1964), a major advocate of the Freudian perspective on humor, places a greater emphasis on the nontendentious jokework in explaining humor. Bisociation, the sudden convergence of at least two ill-fitting or mutually exclusive cognitions brought together in some context, make up the larger or more salient factor resulting in laughter. However, like Freud, Koestler believed that the jokework is necessary but not sufficient for explaining laughter. The added ingredient of *arousal* is said to be the seasoning without which the process would not create laughter. Bisociation accompanied by a "splash of adrenaline" is the essence of the joke process. Straightforward stories that do not include ambiguity but dwell on sex or aggression are more likely to be seen as obscene or pornographic than humorous. Alternatively, convoluted or incongruous thoughts dealing with nonarousing material—such as the pros and cons of taxation policies— will rarely elicit laughter. Only when the incongruities concern an arousing subject is humor or laughter likely to be found. Figure 5-1 provides an illustration.

The cartoon in Figure 5-1 is funny because of its elicitation of bisociative thinking and emotional arousal. Microsoft executives are not the sort from whom we expect violence. The contrasting *Star Wars* figures remind us, how-

FIGURE 5-1. Pleasure derives from a bisociative process that allows for the expression of anger at an all-too omnipotent force. Copyright © Jack Lefcourt, 1998.

ever, of their power and the arrogance with which they responded to the government probe into unfair business practices. Our envy of their wealth and resentment for making current computer software obsolete not long after we purchase it is easily aroused. The caricature allows us to see them in a way that contrasts with their public demeanor and highlights the features that elicit our ire.

In contrast to jokes, Freud referred to the comic as the conservation of mental or ideational energy when anticipated events do not unfold as expected. Slapstick comedy and the teasing by clowns are usually presented as examples of the comic. In comic humor, people are jarred by violations of their expectancies. The clown is not really hurt when crammed into a car full of 20 other clowns; nor does he really suffer when he is assaulted with brickbats or when he falls from a tightrope. What makes the scene comical is the sense that we have been duped, led to expect something that we come to see as untrue and often impossible. This form of humor is thought to be most appealing to children, whose sense of constancy has formed just well enough to recognize that the scene before them is not real, that the tragedy is a parody, and that the danger is false. Although scholars have paid the least attention to the comic form of humor, it seems to me that the funniest events I can recall in my life have been of the comic form. As Freud suggested, where jokes reflect the active provocation of laughter by another person, the comic scenario of incongruities "finds us" and elicits our response. In essence, the comic is kind of "natural joke," a display of arousal and incongruity that was not necessarily intended to be funny. An example from my early years as a graduate student in clinical psychology may help illuminate the comic form of humor.

Whenever we begin a new stage in our lives, we are bound to experience uncertainty and anxiety. We often do not know exactly what is expected of us, and we are consequently unsure of how to proceed with the new tasks at hand. At these times we are easily provoked into states of arousal, fearing the ill consequences of making mistakes.

In my first clinical placement as a psychology graduate student I reported to a Veteran's Administration hospital where I was to be well paid (relatively speaking) for the summer as I learned how to operate as a clinical psychologist-in-training. My fellow interns and I were led from one staff member to another, who explained their functions; we filled out myriad forms; and we received detailed instructions on our roles and responsibilities.

One day early in the summer session we were led through a maze of halls in different buildings on the hospital grounds to complete a round of prerequisite tasks, including making blood donations to the Red Cross. After many stops and several detours we were led into a small, airless, green-walled office where a short rotund man with the distinct air of a bureaucrat who is rather low in the pecking order, lined us up in front of his desk and instructed us that we would be taking oaths of allegiance to the institution. We understood that our official employment would not begin until we completed these oaths of allegiance. This event occurred in the late 1950s when the influence of Senator Joseph McCarthy was strong, especially in conservative states such as the one we were in—Ohio. We shuffled our feet uncomfortably, wondering what we would be asked to do. The bureaucrat had us raise our right hands and then proceeded to read slowly the oaths that we were to repeat after him. Although scoffing and contemptuous of the activity we nevertheless acceded to his request. After all, our summer salary was to be greater than the sum total of the scholarships and assistantships we had received during the academic year. All was proceeding in an orderly and tedious fashion until the final oath, when we were told to swear that we would not attempt to overthrow the government of Ohio. That did it! Laughter tore through our group of seven or eight graduate students, and we found ourselves unable to contain this outbreak. This nonplussed the oath-giving bureaucrat, whose incredulous expression sent us into further paroxysms of laughter.

What happened here? We were young and inexperienced in the roles that we were undertaking. We were concerned lest we foul up the delicate relationships between the psychology department and the larger medical staff at the hospital. As most novices do, many of us probably felt fraudulent in taking on the mantle of professionalism. We were surrounded by a largely psychotic patient population, some of whom probably frightened us, if not with physical danger then with challenges to our fragile confidence as professionals. With such uncertainty, we were probably at least moderately aroused throughout these early days of initiation rites. The oath-taking, which was anathema to most liberal-minded despisers of Senator McCarthy, was to be tolerated if we were to become salaried, and we fully expected to pledge allegiance to the federal government and deny any loyalty to communist influences of whatever flavor. But to swear that we would protect the government of the state of Ohio—that very state government which financially starved our university and was host to a legislative circus wherein fisticuffs occasionally enlivened sessions in the capitol building—was, in essence, a joke. This sudden juxtaposition of state and federal government, the blending of the serious concern with federal politics and the casual disregard with which we held state politics, the pairing of actual threats to federal and fantasied threats to local governments provided the necessary bisociative elements to complement our states of arousal as we plodded through our day. The jokework was complete. In a sense, we expressed our disdain for the oath-giver, for the process that "blackmailed" us into conforming to absurd political demands, and for having to express allegiance to a hapless state government that worried more about communism than about state-related concerns like education. We enjoyed ourselves in demeaning the process, allowing ourselves the tendentious pleasure of aggression expression. At that moment we did not inhibit our disdain and the surfeit of energy became raucous laughter.

The comic form of humor "happens" to us when we become disabused of the seriousness with which we have regarded some behavior or phenomenon. The clown has not really been maimed, and the victim of slapstick violence has not been killed. In our example, we had not been seriously pushed to compromise ourselves in swearing allegiance to the state of Ohio. We simply went through the motions and discovered that our perceptions of the intiation rites were overblown. The preparatory inhibitions of anxiety, resentment, and irritation were unneccessary as we confronted one bureaucrat after another. As noted earlier, the most memorable occasions of uncontrollable laughter are probably those that consist of comic humor, but it is this form that has received the least study from researchers.

The third form of humor advanced by Freud was actually called "humor" and was described in a brief article of that name (Freud, 1928). Unlike jokes or the comic, humor was thought to derive from a saving of energy that would have been spent in the expression of negative emotions. Freud defined the "essence of humor" as a process by which "one spares oneself the affects to which the situation would naturally give rise and overrides with a jest the possibility of such an emotional display" (p. 216). In this sense, humor can be thought of as an emotion-focused coping behavior or a defense mechanism that allows people to remain in difficult situations without being overwhelmed by the emotions those situations aroused. Humor reflects the way in which people come to terms with their own responses as opposed to the focus on external events that characterizes jokes or the comic.

Freud referred to humor as the highest of the defense mechanisms, a position also taken by Vaillant (1977) and Andrews, Franz, and Stuard (1989). To Freud, humor was distinct from other forms of levity because in addition to a liberating element it has "something fine and elevating, which is lacking in the other" forms of humor. What is fine about it is "the triumph of narcissism, the ego's victorious assertion of its own invulnerability. It refuses to be hurt by the arrows of reality or to be compelled to suffer. It insists that it is impervious to wounds dealt by the outside world" (p. 217).

Humor is clearly reflected in the contribution by author Derek Maitland that is presented in Chapter 9. In this recollection, he describes how his feelings of despair were dispelled by a jest of his father's that gave social support and perspective on an emotionally wrenching occasion.

As noted earlier, my own interest in humor derives in part from observing laughter and humor at my father's funeral. Coming to terms with the death of a loved one is perhaps the ideal occasion for the observation of humor's beneficial effects. If the emotions attendant upon the death of a loved one could not be undone through the use of humor or other means such as religious observance and belief, we would possibly become debilitated by the loss, succumbing to depressive forces that might serve to hasten our own demise.

The dynamics are similar in each of the three forms of humor explicated by Freud. Arousal following some form of incongruity is reduced through the realization that the emotion or thought that was aroused is unnecessary. The release from the inhibition results in amusement. If considerations of energy are downplayed, these do not seem like archaic propositions, although the distinction between the three forms of humor does not always seem obvious.

OTHER DIMENSIONS OF HUMOR

In contrasting jokes, wit, and the comic, one difference discussed by Freud has to do with the activity versus passivity of the persons involved. The wit or joker is obviously active in trying to convey or perpetrate humor on others. However, within this category there are those who simply pass along jokes or stories that they have heard and others who construct their own. The creators of jokes and funny stories can be said to be more "productive" in their humor than the relayers of jokes, who appreciate humor but are less capable of producing it. In a later chapter, I describe a study in which we used a range of humor measures to assess how well humor performs as a moderator of the effects of stressful experiences. In those studies we made use of measures that differed in their degree of humor activity. Humor scales inquired about the subjects' likely responses to comical or stressful situations. In addition to self-descriptive measures of humor responsiveness, we had subjects make up humorous stories or monologues to accompany an anthropological film depicting male genital mutilation during Australian aboriginal rituals that was stressful to watch. It might seem an impossible task to make light of such horrors, but it proved to be a powerful predictor of stress moderation. In brief, although moderator effects were found with all of our humor measures, the effects were most prominent when we used active humor-production measures. At that time we regarded humor productivity as a better stress moderator than humor responsivity simply because it was "more portable." That is, the humor producer has joking and laughter at his or her disposal, whereas the humor responder requires other people or circumstances to provoke it. Consequently, humor responders might not be as able to make use of humor in difficult circumstances as producers of humor.

On the other hand, this distinction between production and responsivity may not be as clear as it seems. Someone who is highly responsive to potentially humorous circumstances may be thought to be as highly perceptive of and aroused by incongruities as the humor producer but less given to sharing their funny responses with others. I note this to indicate that the categories that we use to describe humor suffer the same failings as most classifications when phenomena are closely examined. It is for this reason that we must consider most dimensions used in the study of phenomena such as humor to be arbitrary, though some may prove to be more useful than others.

This contrast between responsiveness and production is analogous to Freud's distinction between wit and the comic. Wit was said to be humor that one "makes," whereas the comic was something funny that one "finds." More will be said about the contrast between responsiveness and production in the following chapter on individual differences.

Although jokes can be thought of as a singular category of productive humor, they differ substantially in their targets and impact. Some jokes can be said to be cruel, some clever, and others genuinely funny. If we were to analyze the nature of what is thought to be cruel we would probably find that jokes that rely on denigrating individuals or groups of individuals earn this sobriquet most often. Referred to in the psychological literature as examples of *hostile humor*, these jokes play up the inferiority of others. Clever jokes, on the other hand, would probably be judged to be so because of the "jokework" that went into them. The complexity and convolutions through which our minds are made to leap in order to grasp the jokes meaning help define its cleverness. For Freud, these complexities consisted of condensation, displacement, unification, and indirect representation—the same cognitive leaps that characterize dreams, that fool the superego into allowing some expression of libidinal desires. In contrast, puns, which rely only on phonetic features, are usually regarded as nonclever jokes and usually elicit groans rather than laughter.

Those jokes or stories that people deem genuinely funny are less likely to depend completely on disparagement. Although they may cast some aspersions, funny stories more often center on frustrations suffered by the narrators or someone close to them. The jokes are genuinely funny because they don't necessarily require compliance with unshared prejudices. The experiences described are most often comprehensible to the listeners who can sympathize, if not empathize, with the storyteller. Jokes or funny stories that capitalize on the misfortunes of the narrator or offer sympathetic renditions of others' misfortunes are those that are usually described as genuinely funny. Raconteurs and writers like the late Jean Shepherd, Garrison Keillor, Bill Cosby, and Stuart McLean are all examples of the genuinely funny humorist who is capable of rendering sympathetic accounts of life's tribulations. It is interesting to note that each of these performers has a devoted following and the spontaneous and warm laughter of their audiences attests to the affection and enjoyment with which their stories are greeted.

The kinds of jokes that are regarded as genuinely funny might also be closer to what Freud referred to as humor rather than jokes or the comic. In essence, the person or target of the story being told often accounts for whether the story will be interpreted as an instance of cruel joking or genuinely funny humor. If the target is another person or group, the joke will likely be seen as cruel unless it is done sympathetically, as when the teller suggests that the events could have happened to him or the listener—that there but for the grace of God go I. In contrast, wit and joking, usually do target others and most often without sympathy. Thus, the joke relies more on its tendentious elements and possibly less on the jokework involved. Humor is mostly self-directed because it concerns the ways in which persons manage their emotional responses by adopting humorous attitudes.

Avner Ziv (1984) has discussed the differences between what he refers to as the *aggressive* and *defensive* functions of humor. Aggressive humor relies on the disparagement of others, whereas defensive humor undoes fear or reduces the emotional responses to threatening experiences. Similarly, a German psychologist, Reinhard Lempp (cited in Berger, 1997), distinguishes between what he calls *sociopositive* and *socionegative* laughter. The former is said to enhance solidarity in a group, whereas the latter is malicious humor derived from the exclusion of someone from a group. Lempp asserts that the more "innocent" form of humor "can be a great help in meeting the exigencies of life" (Berger, 1997, p. 51). These forms or functions of humor parallel the contrast between hostile jokes and the genuinely funny stories that are more often self-directed.

This differentiation between jokes that are cruel or genuinely funny will be seen to have important consequences for the way in which we view humor and assess its value as a means of dealing with life's vicissitudes.

CRUEL AND HOSTILE HUMOR

Although hostility and aggression have been major topics of interest in psychology, aggressive or hostile humor has not been investigated extensively. Humor would seem to have been a peripheral subject or maybe even an oxymoron when coupled with hostility for those concerned with understanding the sources and consequences of hostility. Nevertheless, there has been some research into hostile humor as a reflection of attitudes toward select others and the ways in which it has been used to "even the score" with persons who have given offence.

Disparagement humor has been said to be enjoyable because it allows for the ridiculing of persons who are disliked. Much like Freud's assertions about the tendentious nature of jokes, Zillman and Cantor (1976) contended that people enjoy disparaging jokes when they have negative attitudes toward the victims of those jokes and positive attitudes toward the jokers themselves. Supportive evidence for their "dispositional theory of disparagement humor" comes from their own work (Cantor & Zillman, 1973) and that of others (LaFave, Haddad, & Marshall, 1974; Wicker, Baron, & Willis, 1980). Additional support for the dispositional theory of disparagement humor derives from earlier research, which indicated that persons who are characteristically aggressive or easily angered have been found to prefer hostile humor to more benign forms of humor (Grziwok & Scodel, 1956; Murray, 1934).

A few studies have examined how humor can play a role in vindictive behavior. For example, in a study by Dworkin and Efran (1967), subjects were demeaned by an experimenter for the way in which they had completed autobiographical sketches that they had been asked to write. Following this deliberate provocation of anger, subjects completed a mood adjective checklist on which they readily acknowleged their anger. Subjects in an experimental condition were then asked to listen to and rate for funniness one of two humor tapes—one containing decidedly hostile and the other nonhostile humorous skits which subjects were to rate for funniness. The control group, in contrast, listened to nonhumorous tapes, which were to be rated for interest level. A second measure of mood states was then obtained.

The resulting data revealed that there were significant decreases in hostility scores among subjects listening to either set of humor tapes, whereas no changes were found among those who listened to the control tapes. Contrary to the investigators' hypotheses, hostile humor did not differ from nonhostile humor in serving to lessen the hostility scores. Similar effects were found for anxiety scores obtained from the mood adjective checklist. That is, the humorous tapes served to lessen the anxiety reported by subjects after they had been berated by the experimenter. These findings led the authors to conclude that humor mitigates feelings of hostility and anxiety.

Another study by Berkowitz (1970), a psychologist well known in research into aggression, dealt with the role of humor in lessening anger. In his study, female university students believed they were listening to a job applicant who spoke disdainfully about college women. The experimenter then said he had to leave the room to get the "correct forms" to continue the study and asked the subjects as a favor to listen either to a tape of skits by a hostile (Don Rickles) or nonhostile (George Carlin) comedian and then rate it for humor. These tapes were presumably going to be used in another study. After the rating was done, the experimenter reappeared and gave subjects the forms on which they were to record their judgments about the job applicant and their affect states on a mood scale.

The findings revealed that the subjects who had listened to the hostile humor thought more unfavorably about the irritating job applicant. Descriptions and ratings were decidedly more negative. Most importantly, on the mood measure, those who had listened to the hostile humor tape characterized themselves as forgiving–kindly and refreshed–pleased in contrast to those who had listened to the nonhostile humor tape. The latter rated their moods in a way similar to control subjects who had been exposed to a nonirritating job applicant. The hostile comedy skit thus was seen as relatively tension-reducing for the young women who had been angered.

In a study that was conducted during a period of intense racial strife in the United States, Singer (1968) found a marked decrease in tension and aggressive impulses among black adults following the presentation of a tape in which white segregationists were the targets of hostile humorous monologues. This effect was most prominent among subjects who were tested late in the summer of that year, when racial violence in the southern United States had exploded. Arousal levels were much higher than they had been at the beginning of the summer, and the "cathartic" effect of hostile humor proved to be greater at that time. In these studies, therefore, humor seemed capable of altering prevailing negative mood states, and in two of them hostile humor, in particular that which derogated persons who had offended the subjects' demographic groups, helped lessen feelings of anger or tension.

More recently, Jim Olson and his colleagues have attempted to observe the effects of being witness to hostile put-down humor. In one publication describing the results of two experiments, Janes and Olson (2000) found that people who watched videotapes of a comedian humorously ridiculing someone else subsequently behaved in ways that indicated increased conformity and fear of failure. This contrasted with behaviors of subjects in response to nonhumorous presentations and to humorous presentations with the identical content as noted but with the same comedian directing the jokes at himself rather than at others. Similar findings were obtained in a second experiment where the videotape included the target of the humor along with a laughing bystander. In addition to the conformity and fear-of-failure effects resulting from ridiculing humor, Janes and Olson found a heightened responsiveness to rejection-related words on a lexical decision test among those who had viewed the humorous ridiculing of others. This contrasted with the responsiveness of subjects in the self-directed humor and nonhumor conditions.

Janes and Olson concluded that observing the comic derision of others, even when the manipulation is only a proxy for the actual experience, inhibits the actions of observers. Subjects become more conforming and fearful of being "singled out" as the "next victim."

In another study, Olson, Maio, and Hobden (1999) found no effects on stereotypes and attitudes among those who were exposed to disparaging humor about certain groups. Although it is heartening to learn that comedic put-downs may have little impact on observers' attitudes toward the disparaged, the authors demurred from taking pleasure in such a conclusion. Their "targets" of jest were higher-status persons (men and lawyers), who were deliberately chosen in lieu of more vulnerable persons because the investigators feared that there could be repercussions from humor that ridiculed the latter. They had previously obtained partial support for that conjecture from evidence showing that stereotypes are reinforced when ridiculing humor makes elements of the stereotype more salient. They had found this to be the case when the target group had been Newfoundlanders (Maio, Olson, & Bush, 1997). In Canada, Newfoundland is often the target of jesting; it has a rural character and education and literacy were traditionally at lower levels than in the other provinces. In cultural jokes, "Newfies" are often bumpkins, friendly but naive. Even when the targets are not from vulnerable groups, such as lawyers, attitude effects were found under certain conditions that followed upon disparagement humor (Hobden & Olson, 1994).

In these studies, even with seemingly weak manipulations and many possible constraints on expression of attitudes, there has been some evidence that hostile disparaging humor can have damaging effects. Negative stereotypes are sometimes strengthened and people become more fearful of rejection themselves when observing others being ridiculed. In consequence, they seek to avoid drawing attention to themselves after being subjected to the comic derision of others by a hostile "joker."

Mark Twain, cited by Janes and Olson, stated that "there is no character, however good and fine, but it can be destroyed by ridicule, howsoever poor and witless" (p. 474). Also cited by these authors, Thomas Hobbes (1651) noted,

"It is no wonder . . . that men take hainously to be laughed at or derided, that is, triumphed over" (p. 203). In essence, to be laughed at is to be defeated, and that arouses all manner of anxiety and desires for revenge, as will be noted subsequently.

At this point, I will share a story written by another of my students that depicts how she was manipulated by an aggressive "comedian." It is of particular interest because the writer conveys the inner processes that can be set in motion when one becomes the target of a hostile jester.

Three first-year co-op students were the subjects involved in the following incident. We all had just completed the first four months of the first year of our university's engineering program. This was the beginning of the co-op aspect of our program and we ended up working in the same building for our first term at IBM.

We were all a little anxious about beginning a job after only four months of an education that we basically felt confused us and made us even less self-confident. This anxiety was compounded by the fact that we were employed by "the great and wondrous" IBM. I was even more apprehensive than most because I was studying chemical engineering but was doing a computer engineering job at IBM; the other two students were at least in electrical engineering and supposedly understood what they were doing at IBM.

I had previously become acquainted with one of the other students during our freshman orientation but had not been more than acquaintances when we got to IBM. The other two individuals were good friends because they were in the same classes at the university. Through my acquaintance, I had met the third person at the IBM general orientation meeting on the first day of the work term. As it turned out, we three were assigned to the same IBM building; my newest acquaintance and I were even appointed to the same development group and ended up sharing an office; we quickly became very good friends. The third individual worked in the library department two floors down.

Because we were all students from the same university together in this intimidating work environment, we soon became a group. In this environment it was only natural that the co-op students would associate with one another instead of the "regulars" because we felt more comfortable with each other than with the full-time group. Eventually, we ate lunch together everyday and started to go out together in the evenings. During the workday we generally kept in touch through computer messages. Soon, we knew each other's business and began to trust each other. We also discovered that we all had "a sense of humor"; we shared sarcastic jokes and pranks all the time and began to become comfortable with and dependent on one another—we became friends.

There was a corporate and fairly professional atmosphere at IBM, or so we thought at the beginning of our first work term. This was our first time in a professional atmosphere—the first time we had to be responsible for understanding and completing tasks that were important in the development of communications software. People were relying on us and expecting us not to make mistakes. I was even more intimidated because I felt like I was pretending not only to be "professional" but also to be capable of a computer engineering job. Even though we were proud of ourselves for having been hired by IBM, the circumstances were frightening and tense to say the least.

We also came to realize that IBM had many convenient and beneficial pluses. For instance, we could obtain free office supplies and disks. IBM also had tie-lines, or direct telephone lines, set up with many cities across Canada and the United States, so; we could talk to long-distance friends for free. IBM's great computer communication system also allowed us to send messages to anyone working at any IBM location who was identified on the system. We could even do conference computer calls and talk to up to eight other students at once! Needless to say, as the "poor university students" we were, we took advantage of all these "extra benefits" that IBM had to offer. We were aware that we were taking advantage of the system, but it was free and we could get away with it. Since it was so easy to get away with, we did not give our actions much serious thought. We initially joked about what would happen if IBM knew that they were supplying disks for every IBM-employed co-op student who owned a computer. But, eventually it seemed to us that IBM was not blind at all and had planned for and accepted such violations. With this belief we continued to make free phone calls and collect office supplies for our school term.

The incident took place in the office I shared with one of the other co-op students. We were in the process of writing the third person of our group midmorning computer messages; this was one of several messages in our habitual and daily correspondence. Next to ours was a second office also shared by two co-op students whom we were just getting to know. This was a typical day; it followed the routine of hard brain-teasing work with frequent breaks in between—or should I say frequent breaks with work in between.

My friend from the library downstairs and my officemate and I were sending each other messages for about 10 minutes when a strange message popped up on my screen. The sender was AUTOTASK and the message suggested that we had been corresponding with each other long enough and should perhaps consider getting back to work. I was totally shocked; in all the time we had worked there and been sending messages, I never seriously considered that someone might be monitoring our discussions. I immediately turned to my officemate and asked him if he had received a strange message. There on his screen sat a similar message from the same user ID. I typed as quickly as I could and asked our third correspondent what was happening on her machine. She responded by saying that she had to get back to work and was turning off her messages. I got really worried now; usually, she was not so abrupt. Something was going on there too.

I went to the office next door and brought in another co-op student to show him the message and asked if he had ever seen it. By the time I returned, there was another message on my machine asking me why I was not getting back to work like the other two people I had been communicating with. The person I brought in said he had never seen that type of message or user ID before; I really started to panic now. My officemate had a message telling him that they had been keeping tabs on his long-distance phone calls and that his monthly bill was unusually high for a co-op student. I turned to my own screen and saw a horrible message. Basically, I was told that they were monitoring all my computer messages and phone calls for an unspecified length of time until they were sure I dealt with only business matters during these occasions. At this point, I was nervous, frightened, and paranoid. I was sure my manager was keeping a close personal eye on me and that he was not impressed.

I was really scared; the fear is almost indescribable. Horrid images whirled in my head. Essentially, I saw the deterioration of my whole future. Obviously, IBM was not impressed by my actions and would get in touch with the university about the ethics of their co-op students. Certainly, I would not only lose my job but would also be dismissed from the co-op program, probably from engineering, and who knew if even the university would want me any more. There was no way I could hide this from my parents, either. I was afraid that my whole future was lost; I envisioned it collapsing completely. What's more, I could not even begin to imagine what I could possibly do to prevent this sure catastrophe. I was panicking. It did not take long to realize the consequences of my previous actions; all the imaginable repercussions were disastrous. The guilt was also incredible. I was truly ashamed at the thought that I had taken advantage of IBM. I felt even more of a fraud now. Considering that they were offering me a great opportunity and salary, I realized that my misconduct seemed unforgivable. I had never perceived how dishonest my activities were and what consequences they could generate. Now I felt terrible about what I had done, but there was no excuse—I had done it and IBM knew. I was ruined and bound to be a "loser" in life. Obviously, as the old saying goes, crime really does not pay.

Without delay, the co-op student from the library rushed into the office. The look on her face reflected that she felt exactly what I felt; we were both on the verge of tears. Someone was watching us. She explained that someone was sending her messages and that they knew about the long-distance phone calls she had made recently and about the package of disks she had signed out of the office supply room. Apparently, this person was wondering if these occurrences were work-related. She said that she had panicked and logged off when she was told to end her correspondence with me and get back to work. At this point, all four co-op students in the office were confused, worried, and scared.

My officemate was still at his computer and received a message asking was there a staff meeting going on in office 3011 or was it a social gathering? We all flipped; the tension and fear in the room was incredible. Terrified, everyone rushed back to their own office; I decided to log off for a few minutes. I logged back on in 10 minutes and there sat a message thanking me for finally starting to work for the day. I was just about in tears. I tried to send AUTOTASK an apologetic message, but the computer indicated that there was no such user ID. Now completely persuaded that someone was watching me or at least monitoring my computer, I silently got up from my desk to whisper my anxiety to my officemate. He was furiously typing away at his keyboard and did not see or hear my approach. On his computer screen he was typing out the message:

"Please get back to work; all your co-workers are doing so. "_____ I yelled, "You ass! It was you all along!" He started to laugh. We had all failed to notice that throughout this whole ordeal he kept "working" at his computer. He had been frantically typing and sending individual messages to all of us, including himself, from some weird program that automatically generated messages without specifying the person's real ID. The relief was instantaneous; my life and future were restored in a flash. I had been so gullible, paranoid, and irrational that I did not think about the fact that all the messages completely followed our actions. I had easily let myself be fooled. But, of course, no matter how relieved I was, I still wanted to kill my officemate for getting me so frightened.

I had screamed at him so loudly that the students from the neighboring office came rushing in. I just pointed to my officemate and said, "He's that 'AUTOTASK' ass." We all looked at one another and started to laugh uncontrollably. Tears were running down our faces and we could not stop laughing; my stomach hurt from the laughter as we stared at one another in disbelief. When the laughter died down, we all started to bombard our friend in the library with AUTOTASK messages. Soon enough, after many abusive messages, she once again came rushing upstairs to our office; she looked anxious and scared and did not understand the laughter she generated as she rushed in. All it took for her to understand was me pointing a finger at my officemate. She whispered, "Oh my. You are terrible," and joined in the laughter.

Although the perpetrator of this "practical joke" was obviously enjoying the distress that he provoked, the joking relationships that he had with the targets of his jest make his joke seem less hostile than it might have. Friends can sometimes be excused for taking advantage of each other in such joke-making. In fact, this practical joke probably enhanced the positive feelings among these students. Nevertheless, the writer's distress before discovering that it was a joke reveals how hostile humor can affect its targets. For the victims of the joke this was not funny until the ruse was revealed. Prior to the revelation it was a humiliating and threatening situation. To be the target of such a joke is to be made miserable. Only with the discovery that this was a joke did relief from misery translate into humor and laughter.

When the writer alluded to being ready to kill the joker, though she probably said it in jest, her feelings were quite clear. Had he not been a friend, her hatred would have been palpable. He had made her distraught, and inflicting revenge on him would have been sweet. If they had not been friends and shared the pleasure of joking with each other previously, it is possible that she would not have been so magnanimous when discovering that she had "been had." Anger might have predominated and any hint of a relationship put in jeopardy.

Being belittled by hostile humor can obviously arouse feelings of outrage and a desire for vengeance. When people are the target of hostile humor they do not ordinarily think of it as funny but more likely consider it humiliating.

To be laughed at is to feel that you can be dismissed as of little worth, which is in itself a good instigator of hatred.

In a stunning book by Ron Rosenbaum (1998), varied attempts by scholars to explain why Hitler unleashed the Holocaust are subjected to close scrutiny. Rosenbaum queried prominent Holocaust scholars about when and how the idea and plans for the Holocaust could have been conceived. In comparing and contrasting their viewpoints Rosenbaum clarified the assumptions that each theorist seemed to have made about human nature and man's place in the larger universe.

After reviewing the diverse writings on Hitler's role in perpetrating the mass murder, Rosenbaum turned to Lucy Dawidowicz (1975) in *The War Against the Jews* as providing the most convincing portrait. Dawidowicz, who had been a graduate student of English literature at Columbia University, seemed to be more ready to find meaning in subtextual material in Hitler's communications than many other Holocaust analyzers have. Instead of taking his commentaries literally, she sought to analyze his pronouncements and show his likely deceptions and attempts to disguise his purposes by indirection. The portrait of evil that Dawidowicz unveiled led Rosenbaum to feel that the picture of a "laughing Hitler" who hungrily anticipated the Holocaust has greater coherence and plausibility than other, more charitable portraits of him.

Whether there were actual incidents in which Hitler felt that he was being laughed at, or whether he was using metaphors to express his feelings of rejection and humiliation, Hitler often referred with venom to the Jews whom he believed had laughed at him. Hitler had been extremely patriotic in World War I, volunteering repeatedly for dangerous assignments on the battlefield. In fact, his military experience was a high point in an otherwise feckless youth. Consequently, he was likely to have taken umbrage at the public statements of Jewish celebrities like Albert Einstein who were critical of patriotism and Germany's involvement in the war. Consequently, he might have felt that his heroism was denigrated and "laughed at" by such "notable Jews." This is not unimaginable since it was commonly rumored that Jews and communists were responsible for Germany's surrender at the front.

Hitler's pronouncements and discussions with his inner circle, recorded by stenographers, provide some fuel for the proposition that his antisemitism derived from feelings of being laughed at. Here are some quotes from Rosenbaum (1998, p. 387).

> They [Jews] may still laugh today at that, exactly as they laughed at my [other] prophecies. The coming months and years will prove that I also saw correctly here.

> The Jews laughed once also in Germany at my prophecies. I do not know if they are still laughing today, or if their laughter has not already subsided. But I can also now only assert: Their laughter everywhere will subside.

If Jewry perchance imagines that it can bring about an international world war for the annihilation of the European races, then the consequence will be not the annihilation of the European races, but on the contrary it will be the annihilation of Jewry in Europe. I was always laughed at as a prophet. Of those who laughed then, countless ones no longer laugh today, and those who still laugh now will perhaps in a while also no longer do so.

Rosenbaum's thesis, echoing that of Davidowicz, is chilling: the Holocaust may have been perpetrated as revenge for an assumed humiliation, the Jews' laughter at Hitler's prophesies and at Aryan greatness, with which Hitler identified. Rosenbaum notes that in recorded discussions between Hitler and his inner circle, there was sometimes laughter about the vengeful killing of the Jews and the deceptions used to deny the horrors that were being committed.

The thought of such horrors is so mind-numbing that it is possible to forget the purpose of this digression, which is to assert that hostile put-down humor, even if largely imagined, can have terrible consequences. That Hitler's hostile "joke," whether it was in response to perceptions of being laughed at or to projections of his own hatreds, may have been a cause of the destruction of Europe and its peoples, underlines this point further. Whether it is in conforming behavior, fear of failure, or the desire to reap revenge, the result of hostile humor is not likely to be as positive as one would expect from humor. The distinctions that Lempp and Ziv drew between positive humor that encourages group solidarity and affords defense against emotional upset, and negative or aggressive humor that separates, divides, and excludes, is perhaps the weightiest dimension on which humor may be evaluated.

HUMOR

Genuinely funny humor, as opposed to hostile humor, is largely self-directed and defensive. That is, it reflects a retreat from seriousness and the assumption of a perspective that affords relief from negative emotions. As noted earlier in this chapter, Freud (1928) defined humor as being among the best of the defensive processes, a means by which we can dispel the impact of emotional experiences that would otherwise leave us depleted. In a similar vein, Allport (1950) stated that "the neurotic who learns to laugh at himself may be on the way to self-management, perhaps to a cure" (p. 280). Others have spoken of humor as a sign of perspective-taking. Rollo May (1953), for example, suggested that humor has the function of "preserving the sense of self . . . It is the healthy way of feeling a 'distance' between one's self and the problem, a way of standing off and looking at one's problem with perspective" (p. 54). Similarly, Viktor Frankl (1969) asserted that "to detach oneself from even the worst conditions is a uniquely human capability" and that this distancing of oneself from aversive situations comes "not only through heroism . . . but also through humor" (pp. 16-17). Raymond Moody (1978) also suggests that the ability to detach oneself is intrinsic to humor: "A person with a 'good sense of humor' is one who can see himself and others in the world in a somewhat distant and detached way. He views life from an altered perspective in which he can laugh at, yet remain in contact with and emotionally involved with, people and events in a postitive way" (p. 4).

This kind of humor, as we shall see in subsequent chapters, does not separate us from others. If anything, self-directed humor seems to encourage group solidarity. Of course, there may be exceptions to this rule, especially in interaction's between the sexes. Morreall (1999) helps us comprehend the power of humor when he describes the contrast between comic and tragic visions of life. The former is said to be associated with mental flexibility—as characterized by complex conceptual schemes, tolerance for disorder and ambiguity, acceptance of the unfamiliar, critical thinking, emotional disengagement, playfulness, and the like. Tragic vision, on the other hand, is linked with mental rigidity—characterized by simple conceptual schemes, intolerance for disorder and ambiguity, preference for the familiar, uncritical thinking, emotionality, seriousness, and so on. It would be hard to think of Othello as flexible and playful, having second thoughts about his own obsessions and finding humor in them. It would likewise be strange to find Bill Cosby becoming a venemous, vengeful person even after his son was murdered by a wanton drifter.

Humor that encompasses perspective-taking and playfulness, I will contend, provides protection from the effects of stressful experiences. As opposed to hostile humor, self-directed perspective-taking humor helps us remain embedded in our social groups, encouraging others to approach and remain with us. Where hostile humor may weld fellowship in an in-group that shares its animosity to other groups, its ultimate end is divisive so that the even in-group members themselves become suspicious of each other, fearing that they will become the next targets of ridicule.

More will be said about this contrast between hostile and perspective-taking humor in later chapters. For now, I wish to emphasize that this difference in the form and nature of humor is one of the more important dimensions on which we can assess the role of humor. It is this contrast that allows us to understand the conflicting views that philosophers have offered when considering whether humor is a blessing or a curse.

In Figure 5-2, the cartoon elicits laughter about our tendency to treat figures with increasing reverence the more they recede from our memories. This self-directed humor would be an example of perspective-taking humor. It invites us to laugh at ourselves and to take ourselves less seriously.

FIGURE 5-2. "Elvis Worship" provides an example of perspective-taking humor directed at typical human proclivities. Since it is a pejorative commentary on human behavior, it also contains some tendentious characteristics. Copyright © Jack Lefcourt, 1997.

CHAPTER 6

THE DEVELOPMENT OF HUMOR: ACCOUNTING FOR INDIVIDUAL DIFFERENCES

When we think about the people whom we have come to know well throughout our lives, it is not difficult to draw comparisons among them with regard
to humor. A few of our acquaintances are apt to be funny, quite capable of
telling stories and acting in ways that make us laugh aloud. More of our friends
may not be terribly funny themselves but seem ready to respond to funny
stories with laughter or to appreciate humorous circumstances as they occur
in their social interactions. Others, on the other hand, may seem to be opaque
about potentially humorous events, oblivious to the funniness of stories told
or jokes relayed.

At the Christmas gathering described in Chapter 2 we encountered Erik,
a young man who seemed audacious, an exhibitionist who stepped into the
breach when tension had mounted to uncomfortable levels. The author's grandmother proved to be highly responsive to Erik's antics. Why are some persons
so ready to find humorous events funny, laughing with glee at their occurrence? Why are others so capable of entering into the roles of comedian and
clown, shucking off constraints and inhibitions? We can also ask equally relevant questions about humorlessness. Some persons just do not seem to perceive funniness when it is apparent to others, and some can be counted on
never to make a funny remark.

What do we know about personality characteristics that are associated
with humor responsivity and humor production, and how do they develop?

Perhaps what we think of as "everyday" examples of humor are not at all equivalent to the "extreme" humor displays that we associate with clowns and comedians. As we will note in this chapter, people like Erik, who can be thought of as amateur comedians, are not necessarily to be understood in the same terms as people who are humorous in more ordinary ways. Might humor mean something different to clowns from what it means to the rest of us?

RESEARCH WITH NORMATIVE SAMPLES

One of the more consistent findings concerned with individual differences in humor is that children who are known by others to have a good sense of humor or who describe themselves as funny are more likely to be assertive in their interactions with peers and in their social and academic activities. In some studies, however, this humor-related assertiveness has been defined in terms of verbal and physical aggression, dominance, and talkativeness (McGhee, 1980; Bell, McGhee, & Duffey, 1986). In other words, it has been associated with what could seem to be objectionable characteristics. In other studies, assertiveness has been related to engagement in the school milieu, popularity, sociability, leadership (Masten, 1986; Pelligrini, Masten, Garmezy, & Ferrarese, 1987; Sherman, 1988) and communicative competence (Carson, Skarpness, Schultz, & McGhee, 1986), all highly commendable characteristics.

Still, the association between humor, assertiveness, and activity level seems to be reliable and mirrors earlier studies in which my colleagues and I found significant relationships between humor and locus of control (Lefcourt, Sordoni, & Sordoni, 1974a; Lefcourt et al., 1974b; Lefcourt, 1982). Humor was more likely to be found in quasi-tense situations among persons who perceived themselves to be active and assertive in their life experiences (internals) than it was among more fatalistic (external) and passive persons.

We found that when subjects discovered that we had deceived them about the purposes of our investigations (essentially having perpetrated a joke on them), those who revealed amusement and sometimes responded with humorous repartee were almost always the more confident subjects who described themselves as capable of effective behavior in their daily lives. Externals, on the other hand, who characteristically are more passive, were slower to discover our deceptions, and when they finally succeeded in doing so, were less apt to be amused and almost never could respond with humor. Because internals are more likely to actively pursue their purposes than externals, these results with locus of control and humor would seem to cohere with the more recent studies focusing on children's assertiveness and humor.

These observations indicate that individuals with a good sense of humor are more likely to take an active stance toward their own experiences than are those with a lesser sense of humor. Therefore, it is reasonable to surmise that people who have a good sense of humor would also be more active in attempting to alter their unpleasant mood states rather than endure them passively. This contention is supported by the above-mentioned studies on children: those with a lesser sense of humor were found to be shier, less engaged, and more socially distant from their peers, characteristics that would suggest passive endurance of emotional experiences during social interactions. Also interesting is a common finding about the lives of comedians: their childhoods were often replete with unsettling events to which they responded by becoming funny and in this way succeeded in changing their parents' behaviors.

Further indications that humor is associated with more activity or "approach" rather than "avoidance" coping styles are found in two studies that linked humor with self-monitoring. Turner (1980) found that high self-monitoring college students—who are presumed to be more socially astute and have greater mastery of interpersonal skills than low self-monitors—were better able to produce humor on demand. In one study, they created funny stories that drew upon their making connections between assorted objects on a table in front of them. In a second study, in which they engaged in group interactions, high self-monitoring subjects were most likely to make humorous remarks and to be adjudged funny by their peers. Similarly, Bell, McGhee, and Duffey (1986) found that college students who commonly engage in self-monitoring of their expressive behavior were more likely to describe themselves as frequent initiators of humor. In a regression analysis of their data, these investigators found self-monitoring to be their strongest predictor of humor.

From other studies directly concerned with coping styles associated with humor and/or positive affect, further evidence accrues for the relationship between activity level and humor. Positive mood states were related to humor: Mannell and McMahon (1982), for example, found evidence that the number of humorous incidents and the frequency of overt laughter recorded in a "humor diary" were positively correlated with elation and surgency and negatively correlated with anxiety, fatigue, and hostility on the Nowlis Mood Adjective Checklist (Nowlis, 1965). Similarly, in our work with humor and moods (Lefcourt & Martin, 1986) we have repeatedly found our humor scales positively related to the Vigor subscale of the Profile of Mood States (McNair, Lorr, & Droppleman, 1971). Therefore, humor may often be an instigator or at least a correlate of positive affect, though positive affect states can obviously occur under different circumstances in the absence of humor.

In laboratory experimentation where positive affects have been induced by humor or the receipt of small gifts, Isen, Daubman, and Nowicki (1987) found that subjects exhibit improved performance on tasks that require creative ingenuity for their solution: Duncker's (1945) candle task and the remote associates test (Mednick, Mednick, & Mednick, 1964). In contrast, the arousal of negative affect, or periods of exercise in which there is physical arousal but no accompanying emotion, failed to have a similar impact. Positive affect, then, especially that which is aroused by humor, would seem to be associated with more flexibility and/or ingenuity in problem solving.

In another study of coping styles associated with humor, Rim (1988) examined the relationships between an extensive measure of coping and both the Situational Humor Response Questionnaire (SHRQ; Martin & Lefcourt, 1984) and the Coping Humor Scale (CHS; Martin & Lefcourt, 1983) measures. More than 100 students completed a measure of coping styles as well as the two humor measures. Among the coping styles evaluated were *minimization*, whereby people minimize the magnitude of their problems; *suppression*, which denotes the avoidance of even thinking about displeasing things; and *replacement*, which indicates flexibility when people feel thwarted in the pursuit of their usual activities. Five other coping styles were also described. But it was on these three coping strategies that the results for both sexes and both humor scales were the most uniform. The humor scales were positively associated with minimization and replacement and negatively with suppression.

These findings complement those described earlier. Minimization and replacement reflect a "carrying on" despite adversity whereas suppression reflects an avoidance or failure to contend with the details of one's stressful experiences. Rim's findings, then, mirror the approach-versus-avoidance and activity-versus-passivity dimensions that characterized persons differing in their sense of humor in other investigations.

What may we conclude from these studies with regard to the ways in which people deal with the affective consequences of stress? It would seem that people with a good sense of humor are less likely to passively accept the negative effects that accompany stressful experiences. Humor seems to signify an active and assertive orientation that augurs a readiness to change feelings and perhaps an impatience with negative affects such as anxiety and depression. The tendency to minimize and to replace one pursuit with another suggests that persons with a good sense of humor do not as easily accept the experiencing of negative emotions for a lengthy time as do their less mirthful peers.

It is still somewhat mysterious and perhaps beyond the purview of psychological methods, given ethical constraints, to know what occurs at the exact moment when people begin to suffer from an aversive situation. Most often psychological data consist of descriptions of events and experiences that have already transpired. To examine the moment in which a person shifts from one affective state to another or closely observe the process of recovery from mourning, for example, might more clearly reveal to us how certain persons draw on humor to reverse their slide into negative emotional experiences.

SOURCES OF INDIVIDUAL DIFFERENCES IN HUMOR

If differences in assertiveness, activity levels, approach versus avoidance tendencies, and the like are associated with humor, our next question might be to ask how those differences arise? Although there is no definitive answer in the psychological literature, we do have some suggestive leads.

Fortunately, a few programs involving longitudinal research still retain data collected in years past, which continue to be mined for the myriad purposes that researchers can bring to them. One such project focusing on the effects of child-rearing practices throughout a period of the life span was conducted in the Institute of Human Development at the University of California at Berkeley. Under the aegis of Jack and Jeanne Block much data have been made available for investigators concerned with antecedents of adult behavior.

In a book chapter exploring the antecedents of field dependence–independence (Witkin, Dyk, Faterson, Goodenough, & Karp, 1962), Nat Kogan and Jack Block (1991) described the relationships between parental and child behavior beginning when the children were age 3 and ending when they were 18. The assessments had been made at ages 3, 4, 5, 7, 11, 14, and 18, and were later subjected to Q-sort ratings. *Field independence,* which is assessed through the subjects' capabilities at disembedding figures from within patterns (Embedded Figures Test) and at resisting the influences of distorting contextual backgrounds in judging verticality (Rod-and-Frame Test), has often been found to be positively associated with characteristics such as autonomy and personal identity. *Field dependence,* on the other hand, which is typified by yielding to contextual influences and inability to disembed figure from ground has more often been found to be correlated with dependence and emotional immaturity.

The findings reported by Kogan and Block (1991) are interesting and relevant to the linkages found between humor, assertiveness, and activity. The data with particular reference to humor have not been published earlier but were collected by Nat Kogan (personal communication, 1991) who graciously shared them with me.

The study made use of a sample of 120 children whose involvement began when they were enrolled in preschools at age 3. The number of participants at the end of the investigation, when the subjects reached 18, was 105, indicating a high subject retention rate. In addition, 91 mothers and 81 fathers had completed the Child Rearing Practices Report (CRPR), a 91-item Q-set of ratings, when the children were 3 years old.

As is the case with most field-dependence research, the findings seemed most germane to the male children. Relationships with measures of field dependence–independence were close to negligible for girls. Among boys, both responsiveness to and initiation of humor at age 18 were at least moderately related to field independence in 6 out of the 10 assessments that were made over six age periods (3, 4, 7, 11, 14, and 18 years). Correlations ranged between .27 and .52, the latter relationships having been obtained with embedded figures testing when the child was 3 years old. That is, the ability of male children to extract figures from within complex designs at age 3 was positively related to their observed responsiveness to and initiation of humor at age 18.

Of greater relevance to understanding the sources and antecedents of humor were data linking parental child-rearing practices with field dependence–independence scores. In 7 out of 10 assessments of field dependence–independence, the degree to which mothers joked and played with their 3-year-old sons was significantly related to the boys' field independence scores. Beginning at age 7 and lasting through the final sessions when the boys were 18, all measures of field dependence–independence were significantly associated with the mothers' behavior with them when they had been three years old. These relationships ranged between .32 and .62, with mothers' playfulness with their 3-year-olds always positively associated with their development of field independence. Again, these results were negligible for girls. Futhermore, the same findings were not replicated when the descriptions of mothers' child-rearing practices derived from when their children were 12 years old.

When the fathers' child-rearing practices were examined, the results were highly similar to those obtained with their spouses. In 6 out of the 10 measurements of field dependence–independence, the fathers' joking and playing with their 3-year-old boys was positively associated with the boys' subsequent field independence scores, obtained from the ages of 7 to 18. Correlations between fathers' joking and playfulness and their sons' field independence scores ranged from .32 to .76.

What do these data convey? If either of the parents are playful and joking with their 3-year-old male children, and assumedly, the years leading up to that age, the children seem to obtain a headstart in becoming field independent. The data did not indicate the outcomes that might have resulted if both parents were joking and playful. However, one would guess that children with two such parents might have proven even more likely to become field independent than those with one playful parent. What makes these parental behaviors most relevant to our concerns is that field independence, in turn, becomes positively associated with responsiveness to and initiation of humor among the children, which became most evident when they reached age 18.

From this longitudinal study we may conclude that the active and assertive style of behavior found to be associated with humor among children may begin with the parents creating a playful and joking atmosphere when the children are young and most vulnerable to the parents' behaviors. That parents' behaviors when a child is 12 prove irrelevant to the field dependence–independence test scores may reflect what parents often find most disconcerting: their power to affect their children's development wanes as children enter adolescence and become more vulnerable to peer influence. We must remember, however, that these findings were found largely among males. It is beyond the purview of this writer and the purposes of this book to inquire into the meaning of the sex differences in the linkage between humor and field dependence–independence. However, as we will see in later chapters, sex differences are relevant to the ways in which humor is expressed and humor may play different roles in the lives of men and women.

In a second longitudinal investigation into the development of humor, Paul McGhee (1979) made use of the data files available from the Fel's Research Institute, which was then associated with Antioch College in Yellow Springs, Ohio. Although the data in this investigation often made use of singular impressions from professional home visitors, and consequently could not be tested for reliability, a considerable number of observations were made by multiple observers while the children attended a semiannual Fel's nursery school (for ages 3 to 5) and an annual Fel's day camp (for ages 6 to 11).

McGhee used a cognitive framework deriving from the work of Jean Piaget (1952, 1962) to explain the emergence of humor among children. Given the necessity of a child's ability to apprehend the incongruous among otherwise familiar objects, McGhee describes the development of humor as beginning after a child has come to recognize and become familiar with the objects that surround him. Smiling and laughter exhibited during infancy are not regarded as indications of humor. Rather, they are said to originate with spontaneous central nervous system activity and eventually reflect recognition of stimuli such as human faces. This process involves the child's development of a schema for faces, allowing him or her to recognize that a given set of lines and figures make up a human face. This recognition, then, becomes a trigger for smiles and occasional laughter.

When children begin to engage in playful fantasy, at around age 2, they are said to be in the process of becoming capable of humor. McGhee posits four stages of humor development beginning at this age that reflect an increasingly greater ability to perceive incongruities from the normative. These stages are characterized as follows:

- Stage 1 involves taking incongruous actions toward objects. The child laughs while engaging in fantasy play with objects that is at odds with "reality." A stone, for example, is treated as a food object, or more likely, a food object is treated as some kind of toy.
- Stage 2 is similar to Stage 1 except that the play is more verbal. That is, the child is still involved in playing with objects but comes to do so

verbally. Playing with the names of objects or persons is typical at this stage, reflecting the child's increasing skill with language. This is thought to typify the end of the child's second year. When children rename objects or deliberately use a "wrong name" they are exhibiting an early form of play and humor through the use of symbols.

- Stage 3, characteristic of 3- and 4-year-olds, consists of the development of *conceptual incongruities*. At this time, the child does not merely play with the names or labels of objects but plays with more abstract classifications, such as boy, girl, dog, and so on. For example, I managed to encourage one of my grandsons to eat breadcrusts by shaping them into "crust men" who cried as he chewed them. His joy and laughter at inflicting such pain on his crust men gave me mixed feelings even while enjoying my power to alter his behavior. In this case, however, an incongruous admixture of food and people with voices (falsetto soprano) were mixed together to create pleasure in the violation of conceptual categories.

- Stage 4 involves the developing awareness of multiple meanings that is common around age 7. This allows for the expression of bisociation and approaches what is meant by adult humor. Double entendres, puns, and the like become possible because the child has developed language skills well enough to know that there are errors to be made even when, phonetically, the responses seem accurate. Illogical but superficially accurate, the child can joke about waking up the sleeping pills and the like.

Given these "natural" stages, McGhee questions how different children navigate their way through them, and it is here that he makes use of the Fel's longitudinal data. He sought to draw links with children's behaviors studied during home visits, semiannual sessions in nursery school and annual day camp after the child was 6 years of age, and maternal behavior observed every 6 months during the child's first 6 years in the home. He looked for connections between maternal behavior, early childhood behaviors, and laughter and "behavioral and verbal" humor initiatives after the children attained their 11th birthday.

The first findings of note were similar to those of Kogan and Bloch. During the first 3 years mothers' interactions with their children had decided impacts on the preschoolers' developing sense of humor. Aside from the mothers' encouragement, modeling of laughter, attention, and affection McGhee (1979) noted that "boys and girls with a heightened sense of humor had a history of very positive relations with their mothers." Mothers of such children were described as "warm and approving," and the children were described as being "raised in an environment free of conflict, danger, and difficult-to-solve problems" (p. 191).

However, after this young age, the impact of parental behavior seemed to change. Children who had a more developed sense of humor assessed after age 3 seemed to have less affectionate mothers and to have had to cope with more problems and conflicts than their peers. As McGhee describes it, humor development comes to be associated with "toughness." If anything, joking, clowning, laughing, and other forms of humor initiation come to be associated with physical and verbal aggressiveness. However, where physical forms of aggression may meet with criticism and punishment, humor that allows for social domination may be not only socially acceptable but appreciated by others and rewarded.

These observations from the Fel's longitudinal data have a somewhat different complexion than those in the Berkeley studies. Where the two agree is in the association of humor with activity, assertiveness, and even perhaps cognitive development, without which the perception of incongruities would be impossible. The portrait of family life for the young child before age 3 is similar to that of the Berkeley study. In both studies, the parents of children with a good sense of humor seem warm and nurturing while also being more playful and humorous in their interactions with their young children.

Although parental behavior effects were not replicated when the children were older in the Berkeley studies, there was no suggestion that a "reversal" in correlates with parental behavior could have occurred. Possibly, the humorousness of children from less conflicted backgrounds "goes underground," becoming unrecognized for what it is when the child emerges "into the world" and plays against a background of noisy aggressive humor. The portrait deriving from the Fel's studies emphasizes the role of humor as a coping device that the child learns to use to resolve difficult familial conditions. The development and use of humor to undo and reshape the problems of family life is exactly what becomes apparent when we examine the lives of an "extreme group"—persons who become professional comedians.

HUMOR AS A COPING TOOL
AMONG PROFESSIONAL COMEDIANS

A recent article about the comedian Richard Pryor (Als, 1999) makes evident that Pryor's childhood was fraught with potential danger and horror. From Pryor's description, his mother was a prostitute who was "scarier than God." When his father hit his mother across the face, she turned "blue with anger." After cursing him in menacing tones and words, she then "ripped his nutsack off" with her "finger claws." His grandmother, likewise, was described as mean. Her job, he said, was to "scare the shit out of people."

In the face of his frightening family life, Pryor found his comic role when he discovered that falling off a "railing of bricks" on purpose seemed to make these dangerous people break into laughter. When he subsequently ran to his grandmother and skidded through some dog poop he elicited more laughter. Consequently, he repeated the act and achieved a more intense response from his family. They called him "crazy" while laughing at him, and he referred to it as his "first joke." As he stated it, he "was really on to something then."

What was Pryor on to? He could transform the potentially angry faces of his mother and grandmother into laughing faces, converting a dangerous situation into one that was far less menacing. McGhee (1979) describes how Norman Lear, likewise, responded to the albeit less extreme but nevertheless persistent discord in his family. His only way to deal with it was to find something funny to do, such as scoring points during parental fights, ascribing scores to each verbal assault, thereupon monitoring who was winning and who was losing. Carol Burnett has described how she clowned around in an effort to reduce the strife between her alcoholic parents. Her perceived choice was to rise to the challenge of stopping their battles or succumb to the agony of accepting them.

The lives of such comedians have been chronicled in articles and books (Janus, 1975; Fry & Allen, 1975; Fisher & Fisher, 1981). The Fishers' study was based on of a set of interviews with and test performances of comedians. In addition, the Fishers obtained interviews with some of the comedians' parents, and for comparison, interviewed and tested entertainers other than comedians as well as children on their way becoming comics or "amateur comedians." Common to all studies of comedians is one implicit question: Are they qualitatively different from the rest of us?

The life of Charlie Chaplin would seem to indicate that comedians' lives are different. Chaplin's parents were both stage performers who died so early in his life that he was left to be a real "little tramp," begging on the streets while still a small child. He had no formal schooling other than what he learned on the stage. Self-educated, having read his way through dictionaries and the like, Chaplin became a sophisticated comic who could interact with such intellects as Albert Einstein. Was he a fluke, a deviate, a one-of-a-kind who happened to end up as one of the 20th century's great comedians?

When I spoke with the Fishers about how they managed to enlist the cooperation of the participants in their study I was surprised that they felt they had been able to secure their subjects easily. While traveling through strange cities on their way from one "gig" to another, stage performers apparently welcomed the invitation to share their lives with the Fishers, especially talking about their childhood. Interestingly, the Fishers did not find them willing to speak about their current families; rather they seemed protective of or secretive about their spouses and intimate lives. Though this may have been a meaningful characteristic of comedians it may also have reflected an adult sense of privacy and the belief that such intimate information was not relevant to understanding their professional lives.

After examining the data they obtained, the Fishers' conclusions seemed congruent with the stories about Richard Pryor and other comedians' lives. The comedians' mothers seemed to have been less nurturing than the mothers of noncomedians, while their fathers often seemed to have provided the care and nurturing that their mothers had denied them. The Fishers contended that professional comedians often seem to have suffered from not having had a real childhood, a time of prolonged dependency in a secure and loving home. If anything, as children they often felt they had to assume responsibility for the welfare of their families, sometimes in a financial sense and often in the sense of maintaining the family's morale. Their role seemed to be one of protecting their insecure parents. In essence, the children who later became comics had to entertain their parents, or more precisely, appease their mothers while protecting their fathers, making up to the latter for what he seemed to have sacrificed for the child. The Fishers described the child as having a headstart in seeing what children should not see at an early age: that the facades of adult life are not what they might seem to be. The comedian seems intent on revealing the man behind the curtain, as in the *Wizard of Oz*. The comedian reveals what is dimunitive behind what looks big or important. As the Fishers put it, comedians, unlike clowns, often feel like anthropologists watching people from afar and searching to uncover the absurdities of their daily lives.

Though the Fishers found some similarities between comedians and other stage performers, the differences seemed to lie in the comedians' mission to reveal inanities, to subvert pomposities and pretense, and to make clear what is preposterous in daily life. All this, while at the same time feeling small like the orphaned or nonnurtured child.

Certainly, this portrait of the comedian seems to differ from that of a "normal" individual with a good sense of humor. As we will see in subsequent chapters, and as has been intimated in earlier chapters, humor seems to be a tool for alleviating the effects of stress and therefore saving us from the adverse effects of emotional arousal. Insofar as humor can reverse the stress—emotional arousal—illness pathway, one would imagine that humor would be associated with *greater* health and well-being. This, I will contend, is the case for those who find humor in their daily lives, who take themselves and their experiences less seriously than they might, and consequently become somewhat impervious to the potential threats around them.

In contrast, comedians, beginning with the "child schlemiel" discussed by the Fishers, seem in a sense to be at war with the world of pretense around them, even if that world includes themselves. For them, humor may be more a weapon with which to protect themselves against the absurdity of others than a reflection of reduced self-importance. A more apt metaphor for the comedian maybe that humor is like a life preserver necessary to avoid drowning. Were it not for humor, perhaps, the child in the rejecting home would become withdrawn and manifest psychopathology or delinquency rather than comedy.

The longitudinal studies that were discussed earlier provide us with some contrasting and at certain points convergent pictures. Nurturance during the child's earliest years along with parents who can joke and be playful seem to produce children who, at late adolescence and early adulthood, have a good sense of humor. In the Berkeley study we do not sense that the investigators are speaking about comedians or extreme cases of humor producers. Their meaning of a *good sense of humor* would seem to be of the sort that is associated with assertiveness, activity, involvement in school, leadership, and the like. The Fel's sample, likewise, showed that a sense of humor is affected by mothering during the youngest years, before the child is 4 years old. But after that age the data seem to be reversed. The less nurturing mother and the more strife-filled home was associated with humor. Subsequent findings about the behavior of funny children in school seem to be more comprehensible when we consider their home life to be fractious. For children from such homes the linkage between humor, aggressiveness, and dominance does not seem untoward. For these children, humor is a tool they can use to control others, something they have learned in their dealings with the warfare in their own homes.

My contention is that warmly nurtured children come to see humor as something that characterizes their relationships with their parents. Their humorous efforts are appreciated by their parents and their use of humor is not seen as a tool for reducing hostility. For example, my 3½-year-old grandson sent our family into paroxysms of laughter after a moment of stunned silence that followed his spilling a glass of water on the dining room table. His exclamation, "That's life!" immediately earned him congratulatory plaudits and the reduction of tension all in one. I do not think he will become a comedian, though he has shown that he is capable of humor at his young age, rising to the occasion in a few other irritating circumstances and altering the moods of the adults around him.

The comedian seems to have to face a more uncertain world. Parents need to be appeased because they can denigrate and inflict pain on their offspring. Consequently, humor becomes a weapon necessary for psychological survival rather than something that can be enjoyed and reveled in by parents of more typical children. For the latter, humor may simply add to an already secure and loving relationship.

Findings from two other studies offer more food for thought on this subject. In another longitudinal study, also from California, we see a sobering note. Friedman *et al.* (1993) searched for predictors of longevity throughout the seven-decade-long study initiated by Lewis Terman in 1921 (Terman & Oden, 1947). Because it was conducted with gifted children it is not very representative of the general population. Nevertheless, the findings are compelling: cheerfulness, including optimism and a sense of humor, was found to be *negatively* related to longevity among the 1,178 girls and boys who participated in this investigation. Survival into old age (70 and over) was negatively related to an assessment of cheerfulness at the time when the child first began participating in this investigation, at the age of 11. Children who were seen to be funny and optimistic at this age eventually died at younger ages than their less funny and optimistic peers.

Another recently reported investigation into longevity by Rotton (1992) presented evidence that comedians were likely to die at younger ages than other kinds of stage performers. Why should this be the case? If humor is associated with less emotional arousal and therefore less incidence of illness, why should comedians and funny 11-year-olds eventually die at younger ages than their less comic peers?

Without going into lengthy deliberation at this time, I will assert that it is in the nature of the humorous behavior that we may find the clues. Comedians' humor may be more of a weapon, a tool with which they lacerate opponents, "puncture their balloons," and control their behavior. Comedians may be seen to be at war, using humor to counteract and control emotional encounters both in their families and later in their confrontations with audiences. The humor of comedians, then, may reflect emotional arousal rather than its reduction and to be more tendentious, offering pleasure from the effective controlling of others.

Noncomedians too may use humor as a tool for ameliorating difficult situations. However, there may be less urgency in their behavior because the circumstances in which they function may seem less dangerous. Their humor, therefore, may appear to be less habitual, less manic, and less controlling of others than that of comedians.

This less driven and less urgent kind of jesting will be referred to as *perspective-taking humor* in subsequent chapters. This is a benign form of humor for which anger and aggression are less important than is the distancing function of humor whereby individuals come to accept absurdity as a normal part of life. In contrast, more tendentious and hostile humor may characterize the jesting of comedians and will be seen as possibly having health effects for them that differ significantly from the health effects for those ordinary folks who practice perspective-taking humor.

THE EFFECTS OF STRESS ON EMOTION AND HEALTH

It is commonplace today for people to associate stress with emotional upset and illness, and to think of stress as anything that demands that we change and cope with challenges. This has not always been the case, however, especially with regard to mental illness. Until recently, when people were admitted to clinical settings after showing inordinate responses to daily demands, the approach most often involved examining the character or personality structure of the victim in a search for habitual neurotic or psychotic tendencies. Less regard was given to contemporary events as determinants of personal problems. Few psychologists and fewer psychiatrists would have thought to take into account the immediate circumstances in their clients' lives. Contemporary circumstances, if they were considered at all, would be thought of as remote triggers precipitating some latent abnormal behavior, making visible what would have been already apparent if the client had previously been subjected to closer scrutiny. Rarely were "circumstances" taken to be salient in their own right. To be fair, certain theorists and clinicians did consider situational variables to be, if not preeminent, at least strongly influential in determining the onset of emotional distress and mental illnesses. Psychiatrist Harry Stack Sullivan, for example, placed great emphasis on contemporary events in trying to explain the emergence of psychopathology (Sullivan, 1953), and in clinical psychology Julian Rotter (1954) incorporated situational variables into his predictive formulae so that they were as primary in social learning theory as were habitual personality characteristics for predicting deviant behavior. This emphasis on the impact of the situation in social learning theory became most salient in the writings of Walter Mischel (1968), a former student of Rotter's. Mischel argued that situational variables had greater impact on human behavior than did supposedly reliable personality traits. Of course, the work of Skinner and his followers is notable for attributing behavior totally to situations and circumstances—*reinforcement schedules*, in Skinner's lexicon.

Situational variables did not seriously enter into discussions about the origins of illness until the appearance of a brief article by Thomas Holmes and Richard Rahe (1967). Here, a major link was made between the occurrence of life experiences characterized as distressing and the onset of illnesses varying from viral infections to morbid conditions. In this article, the authors introduced a Life Events Survey, which subsequently was popularized in mass-market magazines. This survey presented a number of situations varying in stress potential, ranging downward from the maximal "death of a spouse" to the relatively innocuous "minor violations of the law." The investigators had judges weigh the comparative demand for readjustment of each event, so that if the death of a spouse was weighted 100 some lesser event such as committing a minor violation of the law was rated 11 in comparison. Subjects would simply endorse whether or not they had undergone the particular events in question during a given time period; the resulting scores consisted of the sum total of the weighted items that they acknowledged had occurred. This score was then used to predict the onset of illnesses and did so reliably and with statistical significance though the relationships never attained high magnitudes. Holmes and Rahe acknowledged their debt to Adolph Meyer, the American psychiatrist who created a "life chart" to be used as an aid in diagnosing medical problems. Meyer had stated that "changes of habitat, of school entrance, graduations, or failures . . . jobs . . . births, and deaths in the family" were important environmental influences in the natural history of many diseases (Lief, 1948). As a point of interest, Meyer had been one of Harry Stack Sullivan's mentors when Sullivan was training to become a psychiatrist, one probable source for his sensitivity to the effects of current situations on mental illness. Since the introduction of Holmes and Rahe's Life Events Survey, a considerable literature has developed concerned with the impact of life events. These life events can be conceptualized as shifts in an individual's relationships with valued others because of illness, death, incapacity, separations, and so on. What Holmes and Rahe and many other investigators found was that people who experienced a great number of life changes in a relatively short span of time became more susceptible to a variety of emotional and physical afflictions.

These findings became common knowledge thanks to the widespread publication of the survey in magazines and newspapers, allowing readers to predict their own likelihood of becoming ill. The popularization of the stress construct has resulted in scores of books about the effects of stress so that it has now become one of the most commonly blamed causes for illness and emotional distress. Investigators such as Hans Selye (1956) would be amazed at the sheer volume of literature about a construct that was not actually named until Selye began his studies on the general adaptation syndrome.

In the 30-some years that have transpired since Holmes and Rahe's seminal publication, numerous scientific books, articles, and monographs have attested to the importance of the impact of life events on moods, illness, and psychopathology. Investigators have explored the responses of people to a great variety of life experiences: the death of loved ones (Stroebe & Stroebe, 1987), the migration or mobility from one community to another (Coelho & Ahmed, 1980), the urban conditions that result in unpredictability and a lack of control (Glass & Singer, 1972), the strains involved in fulfilling difficult roles (Pearlin, 1983), loss of work (Kasl & Cobb, 1980), and even small daily hassles (Lazarus & Folkman, 1984). No longer are current lifestyles and circumstances ignored when thoughtful clinicians and investigators try to understand the onset of a malady, from stroke and coronary attack to flu and depression. However, at the same time that we have come to recognize the role of life circumstances, most researchers also are aware that there is considerable variability in the responses manifested by persons undergoing similar events. As Johnson and Sarason (1979) observed, although the effects are reliable, life events rarely account for more than 10% of the variance in the prediction of stress responses. These researchers came to suggest, as did Rabkin and Struening (1976) and Cohen and Edwards (1988), that predictive accuracy of illness onset is enhanced by the knowledge of the individual differences that can moderate the deleterious effects of stressful events. In other words, the pendulum has swung back toward a midposition. Personality predispositions are now less likely to be ignored in the scientific discussion of stress. However, they do not stand alone. Rather, they are seen as characteristics that serve to minimize or maximize the impact that stress exerts on the organism and are sometimes conceptualized as having assumed associations with different coping styles. Moderator variables such as beliefs about control (Lefcourt, 1982), efficacy (Bandura, 1977), social support (Sarason & Sarason, 1985), intimacy (Miller & Lefcourt, 1983; Brown & Harris, 1978), optimism (Carver & Gaines, 1987), and humor (Lefcourt & Martin, 1986), along with certain coping strategies, have been found to have protective value in helping people withstand the impacts of many stressing experiences. An example of the moderator effect, with locus of control as the moderator variable, is presented in Figure 7-1.

What can we say we have learned from the great volumes of literature that have accumulated since the introduction of Holmes and Rahe's survey in 1967? We know that stress is pervasive, that almost any life event—even those offering positive challenges—can make demands on us and have serious conse-

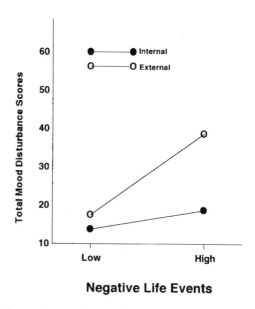

Negative Life Events

FIGURE 7-1. Locus of control as a moderator of the emotional effects of stressful experiences. Adapted from Lefcourt, Miller, Ware, & Sherk (1981).

quences for our emotional well-being. We know that as people encounter increasing demands for change and active coping they become at greater risk of becoming ill. We also know that those who feel least capable of dealing with demands, who feel helpless and ineffectual, who feel most socially isolated, having neither friends nor an intimate other in whom they can confide their problems, who do not have effective ways of coping with the emotions aroused by their experiences, may be particularly vulnerable to the effects of stress, and often succumb to emotional distress and illness when demands are made on them. We also know something of how psychological conditions associated with stress become translated into physiological states that can give rise to illness.

ILLNESS AND STRESS: THE PHYSIOLOGICAL CONNECTIONS

We are indebted to two physiologists who paved the way toward our understanding of how psychological stress can lead to the physiological changes and complications that become manifest in illness. Walter Cannon (1932) was among the first to emphasize the impact of stressors on the organism. When encountering a dangerous situation the adrenal glands were said to secrete epinephrine and norepinephrine, which create a disequilibrium or imbalance in the physiological system. During this imbalance, the organism becomes energized so that it can engage in fighting or fleeing from a threatening individual or situation. This was called the "fight or flight" syndrome, which requires the mobilization of energies released with the secretion of adrenal hormones. Confident that the organism would then return to its original state of quietude through homeostatic mechanisms, Cannon did not view this arousal process as having lasting aversive consequences. Later, Hans Selye (1956), on finding certain stereotypic patterns associated with illnesses among humans and other animals, came to see the arousal process described by Cannon as being in some way associated with the onset of a great variety of diseases. Selye noted commonalities among people at the earliest stages of infectious diseases and also among laboratory animals that had been handled in ways that were distressing to them. The stereotypic set of responses, or syndrome, consisting of an enlargement of the adrenal cortex, gastrointestinal ulcers, and the shrinking of the thymus and lymph nodes, seemed to follow a variety of stressful experiences. Selye initially described this stereotypic pattern of symptoms in a brief article (1936). General adaptation syndrome or GAS as it was later named, appeared regardless of whether animals were exposed to cold, heat, X -rays, noise, pain, bleeding, or muscular work. In essence, these stereotypic physiological responses occurred in response to any of a wide range of circumstances that could be labeled as distressing or stressful. For example, if following a divorce a couple were to struggle for a prolonged period of time over the custody of their children, they would be in a continual state of alarm that could result in the symptoms of GAS Employees anticipating layoffs or downsizing over an extended period of time would likewise be in a continual state of alarm, being persistently vigilant for clues of the crisis that might soon overtake them, and would eventually exhibit signs of GAS.

When people are in this state, glucose and simple forms of proteins and fats are released from fat cells, liver, and muscles to feed those muscles necessary for fight or flight. Glucose is then distributed to the critical muscles accompanied by increases in heart rate, blood pressure, and respiration. Due to the chronicity of the state of alarm, Selye felt, the organism would suffer from a depletion of its homeostatic reserves. Adrenal secretions would become exhausted and the resulting lack of glucose for fueling the embattled stressee would then leave the organism bereft of defenses against possible illnesses.

Selye's explanation for the emergence of illnesses following the onset of stressful experiences rested on this very assumption: that there would be an eventual depletion of the hormones necessary for energizing the organism in its struggle against threats if the stressors continued beyond some unspecified time period. The ensuing state of exhaustion, was thus somehow responsible for the development of disease.

Subsequent research by endocrinologists has provided confirmation for parts of the sequence described by Selye. The physiological events involved in the manifestation of alarm, when an organism takes note of a threat, and then in the organism's adaptation to that alarm, have been confirmed. However, it is the third stage—the exhaustion of adrenal capacity that supposedly gives rise to stress-related diseases—that is regarded as questionable. Current understanding is that it is the stress response itself—the adrenal activity that serves to mobilize the threatened individual, and not its depletion—that can become damaging when it persists beyond a short time span. The adrenal response that is useful or even necessary for short-term encounters with stressors may be highly destructive if it occurs too frequently or for too prolonged a period. This position and the data that support it are well presented in *Why Zebras Don't Get Ulcers* by Robert Sapolsky (1994), a must-read for those wishing to understand the physiological and physical ramifications of stress.

Among the examples that Sapolsky offers to describe the physiological changes occurring with stress, one makes the point most dramatically. In a section labeled "Why You Seldom See Really Old Salmon," Sapolsky addresses the question about why salmon die after heroically leaping over dams and waterfalls to return to the freshwater streams of their birth. After spawning in those locations, most salmon die within a few weeks. Such die-offs are often attributed to exhaustion or to natural cycles in the service of evolution. But Sapolsky notes that salmon at this stage "have huge adrenal glands, peptic ulcers, and kidney lesions; their immune systems have collapsed, and they are teeming with parasites and infections." Furthermore, salmon in this state are found to have very high concentrations of glucocorticoids (a steroid hormone that controls the metabolism of carbohydrates, proteins, and fats) in their bloodstreams. It seems that during the salmons' massive exertions in leaping upstream against the natural flows of rivers and then spawning, the regulation of glucocorticoid secretion breaks down and the brain, through the hypothalamic-pituitary circulatory system, loses its ability to operate the feedback mechanisms that would moderate these circulating hormones. In essence, the salmon's brain continues to call for more and more secretions from the adrenal glands, resulting in the overabundance of sugar glucose that provides energy during stress. When this emergency process becomes chronic and excessive it can bring about all the diseases that beleaguer the salmon at the time of spawning. If, however—and this is the crucial point—the adrenal glands were to be removed right after spawning, the salmon would go on to live for at least another year (Sapolsky, 1994). The same result from extirpation of the adrenal gland has been found with mice. If the secretion of glucocorticoids from the adrenal glands is arrested through removal of the adrenal glands, the rapid and obvious degeneration of the organism can be halted. Sapolsky goes on to point out that it is the hippocampus that provides the regulating feedback that limits the secretion of adrenal hormones. However, the hippocampus degenerates with age due to lifelong bombardment by the very same glucocorticoid secretions that it endeavors to inhibit. Consequently, as organisms age, the hippocampus in many species ceases to act as an effective inhibitor of adrenal secretions, which through the activation of the sympathetic nervous system may result in the increasing blood pressure and heart rates commonly found among older humans. Given a decreasing capability to inhibit adrenal secretions and the diminished immune system that accompanies it, the elderly become more subect to the ravages of disease. Without going into further detail, suffice it to say that many of the illnesses that seem to follow the experience of stress are probably the result of excessive adrenergic stimulation and the associated diminution of immune system activity. Cancerous tumors, for example, grow more vigorously when the host organism is faced with stressors that it is helpless to avert (Visintainer et al., 1982) and ulcerous lesions grow most markedly when organisms suffer uncontrollable stressors (Weiss, 1977).

A more technical and up-to-date discussion about the ramifications of stress on various endocrine functions is available in a chapter by Tsigos and Chrousos (1996) entitled "Stress, Endocrine Manifestations, and Diseases." The current position expounded in that chapter and in the writings of Sapolsky (1994) is that physiological processes that are less crucial during stress or that encumber responses necessary for the organism's survival in a stressful encounter become inhibited. Among the processes that are deactivated during stressful experiences are those associated with digestion, sexual arousal and reproduction, growth, and immune system activity, and it is the prolonged inhibition of these processes that may account for the development and progress of certain illnesses. Following are brief descriptions of these processes that often occur during stressful experiences.

STRESS EFFECTS ON APPETITE AND DIGESTION

Changes in appetite and digestion are obvious to most of us when we are stressed. When we say that we have "lost our appetite" during and after an emotional upset our statement is most often accepted at face value and elicits nurturance and concern from our loved ones. Gastric upsets are also routinely attributed to stressful experiences. When we are not undergoing stressful experiences, food that is eaten is broken down into amino acids, which are the components of protein; into simple sugars like glucose from more complex sugars and carbohydrates; and into free fatty acids. This reduction of more complex molecules into their simple components occurs by the actions of enzymes in the gastrointestinal tract. The simpler forms are then absorbed into the bloodstream to be delivered when and where they are needed. Cells may then use the simpler forms to construct those proteins, fats, and carbohydrates that are usable by the human body. It is the hormone insulin, released from the pancreas into the bloodstream, that stimulates the transport of fatty acids and glycerol to fat cells where they are stored as triglycerides. Insulin also is responsible for starches, sugars, and carbohydrates being transformed into glucose (stored as glycogen) and converts ingested proteins into amino acids that are synthesized and stored as proteins compatible with human cells. The processes whereby food is turned into useful forms and is stored, then, depend on the secretion of insulin. In turn, insulin secretions require the activation of the parasympathetic part of our autonomic nervous system. Feeling relaxed and comfortable promotes parasympathetic activity, enhancing the likelihood of insulin secretion and the successful digestive processes from which we derive our energies. This is probably why physicians in the past have recommended laughter and fun while eating meals to those having digestive problems (Goldstein, 1982).

When we become threatened by stressors, however, the sympathetic, rather than the parasympathetic, nervous system is activated and insulin secretion diminishes. Initially, the hypothalamus secretes corticotropin releasing factor (CRF). This activates the sympathetic nervous system, leaving the organism more vigilant and aroused, and suppresses appetite. In addition, CRF triggers the pituitary gland to release the hormone corticotropin (adrenocorticotropichormone, ACTH). Once released into the bloodstream, ACTH eventually provokes the adrenal gland to release steroid homones like glucocorticoids. When glucocorticoids have circulated throughout the bloodstream following an acute onset of stress, they work toward restoring the appetite that was diminished at the stressor's onset. However, glucocorticoids also block the transport of nutrients to fat cells. In essence, with a state of arousal accompanying some stressful experience, there is both a decline of appetite and an inhibition of digestive processes. Furthermore, while the hypothalamic–pituitary–adrenal system releases glucocorticoids, parallel sympathetic nervous system stimulation results in the secretion of epinephrine and norepinephrine. Both of these processes serve to block the storage of food and make glucose available for rapid use during emergencies, enhancing the organism's ability to fight or flee. In addition to the decreasing output of insulin, during periods of stress and arousal, glucocorticoids "act on fat cells throughout the body to make them less sensitive to insulin" (Sapolsky, 1994, p. 67). With continued stress, the stress hormones cause more glucose and fatty acids to be released into the bloodstream while the glucocorticoids make the cells more refractory to insulin. This process can in time exacerbate the effects of diabetes when elevated blood glucose levels (hyperglycemia) are not reducible by insulin.

Physiological activation during the encounter with stress, then, can be seen to have an inhibiting effect on the digestive processes, beginning with the reduction of appetite and ending with the prevention of nutrient storage.

STRESS EFFECTS ON SEXUAL ACTIVITY

Sexual arousal and reproduction are also inhibited by the physiological concomitants of stress. Male impotence was commonly observed during the Great Depression, when people worried incessantly about their inability to find work; more recently impotence has been found to be linked to falling income and loss of jobs in a fairly large sample of men (Laumann, Paik, & Rosen, 1999).

The physiological mediators responsible for the diminution of sexual arousal differ somewhat between males and females. For males, stress deriving from injury, illnesss, starvation, surgery, or loss of dominance rank (Sapolsky, 1994) is associated with a decline in circulating testosterone levels. With the onset of stress, the endorphins and enkephalins act to block the release of hormones from the hypothalamus. This blockage, in turn, precludes the release of testosterone. In addition, while stress activates the sympathetic nervous system, its opposite, the parasympathetic nervous system, is what allows for the development and maintainence of penile erection. The parasympathic part of the autonomic nervous system causes hemodynamic erections among humans, which is not apt to occur when the sympathetic nervous system is activated. In consequence, given an arousing stressor that activates the sympathetic nervous system, ability for penile erection is lost. Parasympathetic activity is difficult to maintain in an anxious male.

Among females, stress reduces body weight through the depletion of stored fat. This reduces the concentrations of estrogen and allows for the buildup of androgens, which inhibit the eventual activity of the reproductive system, though androgens do play a part in facilitating sexual excitement. Ovulation also decreases with stress because endorphins that are secreted with the onset of stress similarly inhibit the release of female hormones. As Sapolsky notes, there is a great array of mechanisms through which reproduction is disrupted in stressed females.

Most simply stated, physiological responses to stress interfere with different phases of sexual activity and reproduction, making attraction, arousal, conception, and birth more complicated and unlikely occurrences.

THE INHIBITION OF GROWTH

Given the inhibition of digestive processes, an easy leap can be made to growth problems among children subject to severe and chronic stress. With excessive levels of epinephrine and norepinephrine produced through the actions of the sympathetic nervous system, the release of various digestive enzymes halts and nutrient absorption is interfered with. In addition to this obvious obstruction to growth because of nutritional deficits, glucocorticoids also block the secretion of growth hormone, reduce the sensitivity of growth hormone receptor cells, and interfere with the synthesis of new proteins and of new DNA in dividing cells. More importantly for adults for whom growth is less important than maintenance of body structure, stress hormones disrupt the processes by which the body reconstructs itself through the use of calcium. Stress is responsible for the disintegration of bone.

Glucocorticoids inhibit the growth of new bone tissue by interfering with the division of bone-precursor cells situated at the ends of bones and reduce the supply of calcium to the bone. The glucocorticoids impede the absorption of dietary calcium in the intestines, increase excretion of calcium by the kidneys, and accelerate the resorption of bone. This resulting loss of bone mass can become osteoporosis. With decreased levels of estrogen following menopause women are more likely to suffer bone resorption and if stress were to be experienced at this time of life circulating glucocorticoids preventing calcium replacement could increase the likelihood of osteoporosis or bone degeneration.

Again, simply put, the experience of stress interferes with body growth and restoration by impeding or blocking the incorporation of calcium into bone, interfering with the function of growth hormones and the digestive processes necessary for growth.

THE INHIBITION OF IMMUNE SYSTEM ACTIVITY

Although there is much complexity and uncertainty in our understanding of the relationship between stress, immune system functioning, and illness, there is evidence that immune system activity is suppressed by the physiological processes associated with stress. When glucocorticoids are released by the adrenal gland in response to stressful experiences, they prevent the formation of new lymphocytes in the thymus, which results in the shrinking of the thymus gland. Since the thymus is the source of T-cells, which bring about cell-mediated immunity, their numbers become diminished as the thymus shrinks, and since glucocorticoids also inhibit the release of interleukins and interferons, which "inform" T-cells about infectious agents, those circulating lymphocytes become less responsive to alarms about the arrival of infectious agents. As if this were not enough, glucocorticoids also remove lymphocytes from circulation and can actually kill them.

Without going into the detail on this complex subject that is available elsewhere (Sapolsky, 1994; Tsigos & Chrousos, 1996), I state simply that the activation of the sympathetic nervous system with the onset of stress interferes with some of the processes by which the immune system protects us from invasive infections, inhibiting both the functioning of signal systems and the production of cells that can hinder the progress of infectious diseases.

IS THERE A WAY OUT OF THE VICIOUS CIRCLE OF AROUSAL AND DETERIORATION?

Whenever we take note of the range of destructive forces arrayed against our survival we can become vividly aware of our fragility and begin to feel imperiled. However, though the vulnerability of living creatures to the effects of stress is becoming common knowledge, as was noted earlier many people do not succumb as easily as others to the onslaught of stressors and somehow remain buoyant throughout crises. What might characterize these less vulnerable individuals?

After reviewing many of the deleterious effects of stress upon different organisms, Sapolsky (1994) turned to this issue, questioning whether one could account for examples of resilience among certain individuals. For more than 15 years, Sapolsky has been engaged in longitudinal research with a troop of olive baboons that live in the Serengetti National Park in Kenya and Tanzania. Sapolsky has described this setting as an ideal one for baboons—there is a good food supply and a minimum number of predators. He likens this to the affluent settings in which humans live in developed societies, where the major problems and stresses result more from social interactions, like social comparison and status seeking, than from extreme physical deprivation. The stressors for the baboons similarly involve competition and the struggle for status, which facilitate access to sex, comfort, and food. Not quite a passive observer, Sapolsky would sometimes take blood from tranquilized male baboons, rushing the blood extraction process to obtain his samples before the tranquilizer descended fully throughout the baboon's bloodstream. The physiological indicators of stress among these male baboons and their behavior and social status in their troop has been under study.

Ideally, baboons, like humans, have low basal levels of glucocorticoids in their blood system that may rise significantly when they are distressed but quickly subside when the stress diminishes after three minutes or so. However, if basal levels of glucocorticoids are already high, increases with the advent of stressors will be less evident and therefore less efficient and helpful in the encounter with threats. This latter condition is regarded as pathogenic—likely to result in the kinds of illnesses that were noted earlier.

Similar to research with humans, Sapolsky found that baboons who were at the bottom of the power hierarchy were the most likely to have heightened levels of glucocorticoids circulating throughout their bloodstreams. This makes sense, because those with the least status in their group are the least able to protect themselves from the aggressions of the more powerful members. Consequently, these low-ranking individuals lead the most unpredictable lives, never knowing when they are going to have to move aside and surrender whatever assets they were enjoying. High-ranking baboons, on the other hand, were more likely to exhibit the ideal physiological patterns, with low basal levels of glucocortocoids. The physiological profiles of subordinate animals were likely to make them more vulnerable to stress-related diseases such as atherosclerosis. These findings confirmed those that have been found with humans.

Being a good observer, however, Sapolsky also took note of a number of social characteristics that seemed to lessen the likelihood of finding physiological stress effects in this troop of baboons. First of all, he found that physiological patterns changed when the society within which the baboons lived became unstable, usually through the presence of a new aggressive male in their midst. When a stranger appeared and began to challenge the existing power hierarchy, certain changes became apparent, most notably for those who were threatened with downward mobility. At such a time, those higher in status began to show signs of pathogenic high basal levels of stress hormones. In addition to these social status correlates of physiological stress, Sapolsky noted that there were individual differences among troop members with regard to their responses to threats and stressors. His later observations then were directed at trying to understand these differences in "personality characteristics" that could account for why some baboons succumbed easily to the pathogenic physiological patterns associated with stress whereas others seemed to be less affected by the social circumstances around them. These latter baboons were likened to resilient humans.

Among the features that were prominent among resilient baboons were accurate perceptions of lurking danger, readiness to take an active role in conflicts when they were unavoidable, a range of available behavioral responses for positive and negative outcomes in conflict situations, and displacement of aggression following losses in competition. Finally, baboons who seemed the most "laid back" and affiliative with others, who were more apt to play with the young, who were more likely to groom others even if sex was not in the offing, were likely to have lower basal levels of glucorticoids than were those who were less sociable and more competitive.

These characteristics of baboons that are associated with resilience during stressful experiences have immediate parallels with features found in research with humans, which are discussed in other chapters of this book. Most important for the present discussion is the last mentioned observations of affiliation and "laid-back" behavior.

The more relaxed baboons that Sapolsky describes, who are more likely to play with youngsters and to affiliate with their fellows are also probably less competitive and bellicose. Among humans, people who are more apt to crawl around the floor with their youngsters and enjoy "shmoozing" with peers without perpetually defending their positions and status may also be said to be "laid back." We usually describe such persons as "easygoing" and also assume that they have a good sense of humor, or at least that they are not overly serious. Here is our link with our primary concern: humor. Is it possible that a sense of humor is a gift that enhances our resistance to the destructive potential of stress and therefore increases the probability that we will live longer and with greater comfort than we would otherwise?

In our early research into the feasibility of this idea, we constructed measures in the hope of assessing this ephemeral characteristic, humor. We developed two paper-and-pencil scales. In one, we asked people to describe their most likely responses to situations that could be amusing for some and irritating for others. The responses ranged from not being amused at all to laughing out loud. The other measure questioned whether the subject used humor as a means of coping with difficult situations. Subjects responded with their degree of agreement and disagreement with each of seven items. After completing a number of studies in which we examined the reliability and validity of our instruments, we launched into a set of studies focusing on the role of humor as a moderator of stress. In the appendixes, readers can find copies of these scales, norms, and an up-to-date bibliography of research studies in which the scales have been used.

HUMOR AS A MODERATOR OF STRESS

To test our hypotheses about the power of humor as a stress moderator we began by studying the way in which stressful circumstances affect self-reported emotions. Our hypothesis was that the emotional states of people with a good sense of humor would be less likely to be predictable from the occurrence of stressful circumstances. In other words, persons characterized as being low in humor would be expected to show a predictable rise in dysphoria given increases in the occurrence of stressful events. On the other hand, those characterized as being high in humor would be less predictable with regard to the ways in which they reacted to stressful experiences. Some might become more distressed, some less so, while the largest number might possibly seem to be unmoved or impervious to those stressful events. We began with three studies in which we used a variety of measures to assess humor, stress, and the reports of emotional distress.

Study 1

The first study was conducted with students who completed a series of measures pertaining to stress, humor, and moods that were administered during weekly testing sessions. The questionnaires were introduced as typical scales used in psychology research. The measures of interest in this study were:

Life Events of College Students (Sandler & Lakey, 1982)

This checklist is composed of 112 experiences that are considered germane to college students. Subjects checked off events they experienced during the preceding year and rated the effect that each event had on their lives (very negative, slightly negative, slightly positive, or very positive). A weighted negative life events score was obtained for each subject by adding events that were rated as having had a negative impact, weighting them 1, if slightly negative, or 2, if very negative.

Profile of Mood States (POMS, McNair et al., 1971)

To assess predominant current mood levels rather than transient moods, we instructed the subjects to fill out this scale in terms of general feelings throughout the preceding month. This measure yields scores on five negative moods (Tension, Depression, Anger, Fatigue, and Confusion) and one positive mood (Vigor). In order to avoid redundancy, because these six subscales are quite highly intercorrelated, we conducted our analyses using a Total Mood Disturbance (TMD) score, which is computed by summing the five negative mood scores and subtracting the Vigor score.

Situational Humor Response Questionnaire (SHRQ; Martin & Lefcourt, 1984)

This measure, included in the appendixes, was designed to assess subjects' sense of humor in terms of the frequency with which they display mirth in a wide variety of life situations. It is a 21-item scale consisting of 18 specific situations. For each one subjects estimate the likelihood that they would smile and laugh, rating from "I would not have been particularly amused" (1) to "I would have laughed heartily" (5). The other three items pertain to self-descriptions about humor.

Sense of Humor Questionnaire (SHQ; Svebak, 1974)

This 21-item scale provides scores on three subscales. The first, Metamessage Sensitivity, measures the degree to which subjects report being capable of noticing humorous stimuli in their environment. A typical item on this scale is: "I can usually find something comical, witty, or humorous in most situations." The second subscale, Personal Liking of Humor, assesses the degree to which subjects report valuing humor in their lives. A typical item on this subscale is, "It is my impression that those who try to be funny really do it to hide their lack of self-confidence." Disagreement with this item yields a higher score on the scale. A third subscale, Emotional Expressiveness, was eliminated due to low reliabillity.

Coping Humor Scale (CHS; Martin & Lefcourt, 1983)

In contrast to the above two humor scales, this short 7-item scale, also included in the appendixes, was designed specifically to assess the degree to which subjects report using humor as a means of coping with stressful experiences. A typical item is "I have often found that problems have been greatly reduced when I tried to find something funny in them," with subjects rating items from "strongly disagree" (1) to "strongly agree" (4).

THE RESULTS

The scores obtained with these scales were subjected to a hierarchical multiple regression analysis, the results of which are presented in Figure 7-2. Using the SHRQ as the measure of humor in the regression equation, we obtained a significant increment in the variance that we could account for with the product of Negative Life Events and SHRQ scores. This product is the equivalent of an interaction between these two variables and demonstrated that the humor measure had a moderating effect on the relationship between Negative Life Events and Total Mood Disturbance. In other words, the magnitude of the correlation between these latter two measures changed systematically as scores on the humor measure increased. For subjects who had higher scores on the SHRQ, there was a lesser magnitude relationship between stressful events and emotional distress than there was for subjects with lower SHRQ scores, as we had predicted.

In regard to the two subscales of the SHQ, Metamessage Sensitivity did not produce a moderating effect. However, a significant increase in the variance we could explain was obtained using the Liking of Humor subscale as a moderator variable. This is also presented in Figure 7-2. As with the SHRQ, subjects who had scored low on the Liking of Humor subscale (that is, those who reported a lesser appreciation for humor) revealed a higher correlation between Negative Life Events and Total Mood Disturbance than did those who scored higher on this measure. Again, it was as we had hypothesized.

Finally, a significant moderating effect was also found using the CHS in the equation. This measure also yielded a significant increment in the percentage of variance that we could account for, deriving again from the stronger relationship between Negative Life Events and Total Mood Disturbance for subjects who scored lower on the CHS than for those who scored higher on this measure. This again provided confirmation of our hypothesis.

The results of this first study lend support to the hypothesis that humor reduces the impact of negative life experiences on self-reported moods. A significant moderating effect was found for three of the four measures of sense of humor. As scores on the humor measures increased there was a systematic decrease in the magnitude of the correlations between the number of negative life experiences occurring during the preceding year and current levels of reported mood disturbance.

In this first study, sense of humor had been assessed entirely by self-report measures. In order to avoid the possible biases that are often found with such instruments, a second study was conducted that used a more behavioral assessment of subjects' ability to produce humor. As in the first study, scores from this measure of humor were then entered into a multiple regression equation to assess its moderating effect on the relationship between negative life events and mood disturbance, similar to what we had done in the first study.

Study 2

With a second sample of subjects who were recruited to come to our psychology laboratory, we administered the Life Experiences Survey (LES; Sarason, Johnson, & Siegel, 1978), a more general measure of stress not directly concerned with student life, and the POMS. The life events measure required subjects to check off the events that had occurred during the preceding year and to rate whether those events had had a negative or positive impact on them. The Negative Life Events score was composed of the total number of events checked and rated as having had a negative impact. The Total Mood Disturbance score on the POMS was again used as the dependent variable.

Rather than rely on the self-report measures of humor as we had in the first study, we set out this time to assess the subjects' ability to produce humor. To this end we made use of Turner's (1980) tabletop technique, which had been used to assess humor in a study concerned with self-monitoring. After completing the questionnaires the subjects were individually seated at a table on which about a dozen miscellaneous objects had been placed, including an old tennis shoe, a drinking glass, a beer bottle, an aspirin bottle, and so on. The subjects were instructed to make up a three-minute comedy routine by describing the objects on the table in as humorous a manner as they could. If unable to think of any witty comments, they were simply to describe the objects. A tape recorder was turned on and the experimenter left the room for three-minutes. The tape-recorded monologues were subsequently scored, following Turner's method, for (a) number of witty remarks, and (b) overall wittiness, as rated on the following 0 to 3 scale: 0 = no humorous comments, attempts monologue but simply describes objects; 1 = attempts to be witty but

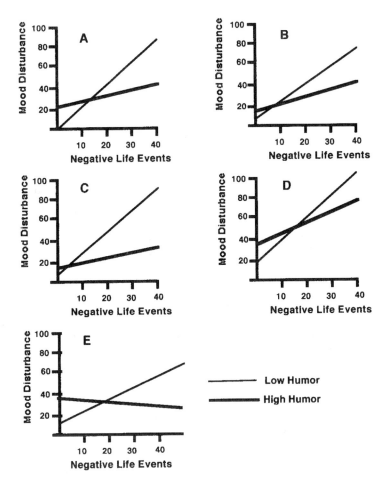

FIGURE 7-2. Five different measures of humor moderate the impact of stressful events on emotions. A = SHRO; B = CHS; C = SHO, liking of humor; D = humor production; E = rating of humorous monologue to subincision film. From Lefcourt & Martin (1986).

with limited success and tries to do more than simply describe objects; 2 = makes a few clearly humorous remarks but routine without a smooth flow of humor; and 3 = a good comedic patter with the total monologue directed toward humorous remarks.

Because the two measures, the number of witty remarks, and overall wittiness were highly related to one another, a composite Humor Production measure was created from these two scores for each subject and this composite score was then entered into a multiple regression equation between life events and mood as in the previous study.

The Results

In this investigation, the interaction between humor as measured by the Humor Production score and the LES measure of Negative Life Events (Sarason *et al.*, 1978) was again found to be significant. As can be seen in Figure 7-2, subjects with low scores on this measure of humor manifested a higher relationship between Negative Life Events and Total Mood Disturbance than did those who had high humor scores, replicating the findings from the first study.

These results provided further evidence for the stress-moderating role of humor. Individuals who demonstrated an ability to produce "humor on demand" in this admittedly difficult task showed a lower relationship between life stressors and disturbed moods than did those who were less able to produce humor in this situation, again confirming the hypothesized moderating effect of humor.

Study 3

In the third investigation of the stress-moderating effects of humor, we again assessed each subject's ability to produce humor but this time in a quasi-stressful situation. In order to create an experimental analogue of stress, the film entitled *Subincision* was shown to each subject as he or she sat alone in a laboratory. This is an anthropological film focusing on ritualized genital mutilation among the Arunta aboriginal tribe in Australia and contains close-ups of incisions being made with sharpened stones into a youth's penis with much display of blood, flies, and so on. It is a difficult film to watch, producing shock in some, nausea in others, and commonly resulting in physiological responses indicative of sympathetic autonomic arousal (Lazarus, 1966). In Lazarus's early lab studies of stress and coping, this film was often used as the "stress stimulus." To assess the potential of humor use during stressful stiuations, we asked our subjects to create a humorous monologue to accompany this film and assumed that the subjects who would be best able to do so would be those who are capable of creating humor in real-life stressful situations. We hypothesized that the ratings of subjects' humor, when entered into a multiple regression equation as in the preceding studies, would demonstrate a strong moderating effect on the relationship between negative life events and current mood disturbance. The subjects had previously completed the Life Events of College Students questionnaire (Sandler & Lakey, 1982) and the POMS, as well as several humor scales in classroom sessions.

The tape-recorded narratives obtained from subjects as they watched this film were subsequently rated for overall humorousness on a scale from 0 to 3 with 0 indicating no humorous comments to 3 being a regular comedy routine with a monologue full of humorous remarks. This was similar to the scoring system used by Turner (1980) for his humor-production task described earlier.

The Results

Again, humor was found to operate as a moderator variable. The ascribed ratings for the humorousness of the narratives created while watching the *Subincision* film were entered as humor scores into the regression equation predicting mood disturbance from life stress. These scores added significantly to the power with which mood disturbance could be predicted from a life stress measure. This interaction, observable in Figure 7-2, revealed that those who could produce a humorous monologue while watching the film showed much less of a relationship between stress and emotional distress than those who were unable to produce as funny a response in this trying situation. In fact, if we examine the regression line for those who scored high on this humor production measure, the line appears to be parallel to the base, showing no increase in mood disturbance as a function of increasing negative life events; that is, the correlation between stress and mood disturbance would approximate zero for those scoring high on this measure of humor. In contrast, those who were less able to construct a humorous monologue while watching the stress film exhibited the more common regression line, indicating increased mood disturbance with an increasing frequency of negative events.

For the third time, evidence of the stress-buffering effect of humor was obtained. As we had anticipated, this measure of humor production which is most germane to the use of humor in stressful situations, produced an interaction term that was substantially larger than those we had found with other less stress-relevant measures of humor in the preceding studies.

The results of these three studies, which were among our first investigations into the relationship between stress and humor, provided considerable support for the hypothesis that humor reduces the impact of stress. Five out of the six measures of humor demonstrated a significant moderating effect on the relationship between recently experienced negative life events and current levels of mood disturbance. In each case, subjects with high scores on humor measures exhibited weaker relationships between negative life events and moods than did those who seemed to have a less well-developed sense of humor.

WHAT MAY WE CONCLUDE FROM THESE DATA?

After acknowledging the negative consequences of arousal for health status, we asked whether there were not some mitigating circumstances that could reduce the impact that stress can have on our systems. As we noted in our discussion of Sapolsky's observations, laid-back male baboons demonstrated less evidence of basal physiological arousal than did their more serious and competitive peers. These fortunate animals, who were more playful and affiliative than the latter, had lesser amounts of glucocorticoids circulating in their bloodstreams and consequently may not have been suffering from the inhibition of those systems, which are so important for health and survival.

In our initial work with humor as a stress moderator, we examined in humans what could be thought of as a parallel to the laid-back and playful characteristics of baboons. In regarding humor as a reflection of an orientation or an attitude toward their experiences, humans said to have a good sense of humor may be those who take themselves and their experiences less seriously than those with a lesser sense of humor. It is possible that, had we been allowed to subject our humans to venipuncture as they engaged in their daily activity, we would also find less evidence of basal physiological arousal among those with this "lighter" point of view. Without giving too much of the story away in advance, I will say that the next chapter will look at some evidence to support this conjecture. Some persons with a good sense of humor do indeed seem be more physiologically serene and therefore less troubled by the inhibition of life-sustaining physiological functions.

HUMOR AS A COPING STRATEGY

If humor among humans does in fact does serve a function that approximates what the laid-back social approach does for baboons, then we should be able to observe a relationship between humor and how humans deal with stress in their everyday lives. In turn, we should find that humor has effects on our health and well-being.

The psychological literature concerned with how humans cope with stress is voluminous; it has been at the forefront of psychological writings since the early 1960s. From the extensive collections published in that decade with the word "stress" in their titles, a model emerged that is most clearly explained in a volume by Richard Lazarus and Susan Folkman (1984) entitled *Stress, Appraisal, and Coping*. This model has become widely known and has been seminal for subsequent researchers. In brief, it describes a process that begins with an event and ends with illness after following the complicated pathway presented in Figure 8-1.

Stress is usually depicted as pressure coming from an occurrence external to us. It might be a demand to achieve, to engage in social contact of some kind, to avoid becoming lost, or any experience that would make us feel anxious if we were not able to rise to the challenge. However, this "external" event is not stressful in and of itself. Rather, it requires an interpretation and response on our part to be considered stressful. It is thus in our responses to potential threats that the psychological description of stress originates.

In Lazarus's model of stress, stress includes both the event and our responses to it, the process beginning when an individual attends to the event and appraises it for its threat potential This, in Lazarus's terminology, is *primary appraisal*. Persons whom we diagnose as neurotic seem ready to believe that the worst is always about to occur; their primary appraisals find threat in many situations that would seem benign to others. In consequence, neurotic

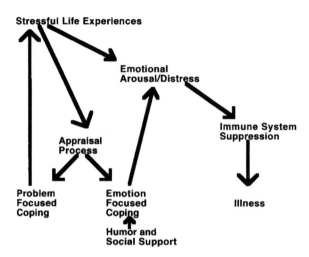

FIGURE 8-1. Humor as an emotion-focused coping response can interrupt emotional distress and reduce the drift toward illness. Where problem-focused coping may subvert the stressfulness of an experience, emotion-focused coping may diminish the emotional responses to it.

persons are often in a state of arousal, suffering the symptoms associated with sympathetic nervous system activation. For such persons challenging situations, which might activate instrumental activity on the part of less frightened individuals, could result in unmitigated emotional upset with ramifications for illness as described in the previous chapter.

However, if a potentially threatening event looks manageable to an individual he or she is likely to engage in what Lazarus terms *problem-focused coping.* This form of coping behavior would follow what is referred to as *secondary appraisal.* In this second appraisal process, people are said to evaluate whether or not they feel capable of dealing with the stressors at hand. If they feel able to deal with what they are confronting, problem-focused coping ensues. For example, if an individual were to receive threatening information from a physician with the advise that it was essential to alter his or her lifestyle, secondary appraisal would occur. Those who believed themselves capable of altering their lifestyles would be less likely to suffer the burden of emotion than those who were less sanguine about their ability to make such a change. A more active stance would result in action taken to make changes so that the medical threat would diminish. But those who doubted their ability would have to deal with their emotional responses, engaging in what is referred to as *emotion-focused coping.* This is not to say that people will always engage in only one or the other kind of coping when encountering stressful events. At some point, regardless of one's capabilities, the uncontrollable will be encountered and emotion-focused coping will occur regardless of one's customary stress-response style.

Excellent examples of how people cope with uncontrollable stressful events abound in biographical writings. Most pertinent to humor as an emotion-focused coping response is Brian Keenan's powerful description of how he and other hostages in Lebanon survived their incredible ordeals during five years of captivity. In the following excerpt from *An Evil Cradling* (1992), we see the process by which morbid depression was alleviated through the use of zany humor when a reprieve seemed remote and unlikely.

I have watched a man lie still for days, his body a living corpse. His face stares back, a pallid mask of the man he was. Nothing will arouse him from his torpor. We are wordless and angry at the constant sight of his silent corpse. We push down our anger, looking to one another to see which of us might have the energy to go in and find this man and bring him home to us. Our empty faces and our shrugging shoulders display our own fearful anxiety.

I speak to him as if nothing strange is happening and the day is like all the others. "Tell me about bees," I suddenly say without knowing where the thought came from, only that I am now at this instant interested in bees. There is no reply. I speak again to him but know that I am talking to myself, and start pulling from the air of my imagination some facts that I know about bees. I talk about them and ask odd questions that occur to me. Nothing, no response. It's time to find another key. I begin talking about cheese-making. I have always wanted to know how to make cheese, but the subject is boring and my knowledge limited.

I jump from one thing to another, desperately tying together disparate ends to find a way in. "You know what I am going to do when I get out of here? . . . There is an island just off the North Antrim coast called Rathlin Island. It's a place where in the 14th century Robert the Bruce went to hide out from the English armies. It's the place where he saw the spider. Rathlin Island is sometimes called the disputed island because the Scots claim it and the Irish claim it and the Brits claim it because they claim a part of Ireland. But as far as I know, and it's only a small island, nobody has ever found the fucking cave where the spider went swinging back and forward, back and forward, back and forward. I think if I get out of here I am going to hunt all over it till I find the cave and if I don't find one big enough I am going to see somebody with a lot of explosives and blow a bloody great big hole in the side of a hill somewhere and call it the Robert the Bruce Cave, and then what I am going to do is I am going to fill the fucking island full of goats and then I'm going to. . . . No, I'm not going to fill the island full of goats, that's ridiculous, 'cause everybody knows about goat's milk cheese and everybody knows about sheep's milk cheese. . . . What I think I'll do is, I'll get a load of pigs, they're cheap, and I'll milk the pigs. . . . When I've made all the milk into cheese I'll put the cheese in this cave and I'll call it Robert the Bruce Cheese and make a killing because with everybody disputing who owns this island how can anybody tax me when

I start selling the stuff, and nobody will ever have eaten cheese like it before because there is nobody who eats pig's milk cheese."

My own lunacy is beginning to intoxicate me. I am sitting close to the dreaming man. I look quickly at him and see what I haven't seen for days. His eye brightening. Pretending not to notice I carry on ad libbing. "I'll have to make this cheese look different. . . . You know, all cheeses look the same but this being a special Robert the Bruce cheese made on this island, which has never been known before and stored in these caves. . . . I think the French store their cheese in caves but how did it get that funny color in it? . . . You know, you get this smelly-sock cheese and it's all marbled with blue, well my Robert the Bruce cheese is going to be mottled green 'cause its obviously going to be Irish cheese. . . . Now how the hell do you get all that green mottling in it? . . . Do you inject some sort of bacteria, or maybe I could get a lot of shamrocks and stick them in it and maybe the bacteria from them would turn it green or something, but then nobody will eat green cheese so I just have to get it mottled the way Danish Blue is. Look at the Danes, they just spread a whole lot of blue ink over their cheese and everybody is buying it."

Laughter beginning to ripple up. Again I continue, "What are you all laughing at? . . . I'm deadly serious, this thing could work, think of it . . . you could make a fortune. . . . Pig's milk cheese, stick Robert the Bruce on it, go to this island, blow a big hole in the wall, who is going to know? Who is going to know if that is Robert the Bruce cheese or not, you get a lot of spiders from somewhere and hang them all over the place; that's your evidence and then how do you get this green stuff into it?" In the middle of the laughter, even the "dead man" begins to come to life. Suddenly his voice says nonchalantly "You need to bury some copper wires in it, Brian, and after a time pull the wires out; it leaves a green mark throughout the cheese." "Fuck me, how did you know that?"

A man emerges back into life, not because of anything I have said, but the lunacy and the laughter that is at the heart of our life beckon him back and he cannot resist it. There are many things a man can resist—pain, torture, loss of loved ones—but laughter ultimately he cannot resist." (pp. 267–269)

In this dramatic recollection Keenan reveals how humor can be summoned forth to help relieve despair. Absurd circumstances seem to call for the most absurd humor. To engage in such zany humor about a future that seems remote and unlikely is an act of defiance or denial or both. That Keenan could rhapsodize in such a fashion was in such contrast to the seeming reality of the moment that the incongruity alone drew attention even from someone in such despair as his fellow hostage. That he could then entertain the future, and in such a zany fashion, would be at least distracting and at most an antithesis to the affect that had created such a pall in their cell. During this interminable incarceration emotional duress, anxiety, fear, or despair would be inevitable. Humor would be a useful strategy for undoing the ravages of emotional distress. In his book, Keenan relates many other instances where humor was a tool for overcoming emotional turmoil. In *Someone Who'll Watch Over Me*, a play by Frank McGuinness based loosely on the experiences of hostages like Keenan, hostages make a point of displaying humor when at their most abject in order to defy their captors, turning their emotion-focused coping into an instrumental act and depriving their captors of the pleasure of seeing them grovel.

To ascertain the role that humor can play as an emotion-focused coping response, we will begin with a review of the literature that followed upon our early demonstration that humor can operate as a moderator of stressful experience, lessening the likelihood that emotional distress will occur after the appraisal of a threatening event. We will then examine the literature concerned with physiological processes and medical conditions that seem alterable through the use of humor as an emotion-focused coping strategy.

HUMOR AS A MODERATOR OF STRESSFUL EXPERIENCES: AN UPDATE

Two investigations were reported shortly after the initial presentations of our research demonstrating that a sense of humor moderated the relationship between stressful events and mood disturbance (Martin & Lefcourt, 1983, 1984). Since one of these subsequent investigations replicated our work and the other did not, researchers might conclude that the role of humor as a stress moderator is uncertain. The disconfirming study by Porterfield (1987) made use of both the CHS and SHRQ and the Life Events of College Students (Sandler & Lakey, 1982) that we had employed. The one exception in method was that instead of the measure of mood disturbance that assesses a range of negative moods (tension, anger, depression, and so on), Porterfield used a singular measure of depression from the Center for Epidemiological Studies Scales (CES-D; Radloff, 1977) as his criterion.

Humor was found to be negatively related to depression, a main effect that we had not found with our measure of mood disturbance. This means that people with a good sense of humor would usually be "in a good mood" or that being "in a good mood" included feeling responsive to humor. Other than this finding, there were no interactions between stress and humor in the prediction of depression. In other words, humor seemed to be more of a correlate of mood than a means of countering the depressing effects of stressful events. Porterfield's investigation had an advantage that make his findings compelling, a rather large sample (N = 220). As Porterfield himself noted, however, there was something substantially different about his subjects. For some reason, this large sample of Oberlin undergraduates registered significantly higher depression scores than had Radloff's normative sample (M = 9.25, SD = 8.58). Mean depression scores in Porterfield's sample were 19.42

(*SD* = 10.12), more than one standard deviation higher than the normative mean. Although Porterfield offered no ready interpretation for the elevated depression scores, he did note that subsequent samples of first-year students at Oberlin manifested similar elevations when tested upon arrival at the campus. In another publication (Lefcourt & Davidson, 1991) we asserted that humor may simply not be an effective stress moderator for those who have already become depressed. Another possible explanation for the failure of humor to operate as a stress moderator in this study may derive from the fact that the depression and humor scores were assessed very early in the students' first year on campus. The elevated depression scores could have reflected the new students' sense of dislocation and loneliness at the beginning of their college years. If many of these students had come from far away, as Oberlin's reputation would lead one to expect, and had not yet established friendships or a sense of belonging on campus, then reports of depressive affect should not be surprising. In addition, since humor requires a social context it may not have been as viable a tool at that time as in later years. Being among strangers during those first weeks on campus, few students would likely feel secure enough to express humor, especially the self-deprecating kind that, as we'll see later, may be the most effective in alleviating distress. Consequently, though humor may be characteristic of an individual in more normal circumstances and prove useful for lessening the effects of stress, it may not be an effective stress moderator when the sympathetic responses of others cannot yet be taken for granted.

In the following year, a major confirmatory study was reported (Nezu, Nezu, & Blissett, 1988). In this investigation both the CHS and SHRQ were evaluated for their moderator effects on the relationships between life stress, measured by the LES (Sarason *et al.*, 1978); depression, measured by the Beck Depression Inventory (BDI; Beck, Ward, Mendelson, Mock, & Erbaugh, 1961); and anxiety, measured by the trait scale of the State-Trait Anxiety Inventory (STAI; Spielberger, Gorsuch, & Lushene, 1970). The assessments of depression and anxiety were made at the start of the study along with the other predictors, and again two months later. During the second test, subjects also completed the LES describing the events that had occurred since the first test. This investigation, then, consisted of two parallel data sets, one cross-sectional, allowing for an examination of the immediate effects of stress, and the other prospective, allowing for the study of delayed effects of stress on dysphoria.

Unlike Porterfield (1987), Nezu et al. found significant main effects and interactions between stress and humor in the prediction of depression at both times of testing. In the prospective analysis, where earlier measures of depression and anxiety were entered as covariates in predicting the later measures (a means of controlling for baseline levels of depression from which subsequent changes are ascertained), the analyses were even stronger than at the first test session in predicting depression. On the other hand, anxiety seemed to be unrelated to humor. In both the cross-sectional and prospective data sets, depression scores were found to have increased with stress primarily among subjects with low scores on either measure of humor. Those who scored high on humor varied little with changing levels of stress and were always less depressed than their low-scoring counterparts.

This replication of our results by Nezu *et al.* offered evidence that our differences with Porterfield probably did not derive from our choice of measuring mood disturbance as opposed to his of depression. However, Nezu's failure to obtain parallel results with anxiety serves to remind us that the particular criterion selected can make a great difference. Anxiety, which is more often anticipatory than retrospective, may be less relevant to humor, which may be better used as a tool for coming to terms with prior events (emotion-focused coping). That the measure of anxiety used was the "trait" form as opposed to "state" form of anxiety may also have limited its predictability from humor measures. Anxiety as a trait may indicate a continued readiness to experience arousal and distress. Be that as it may, the findings with depression offered strong replication for our earlier findings of moderator effects for humor.

Close on the heels of these two early follow-up investigations, three other studies contributed to the interest in and uncertainty about the stress moderator role of humor. In one of these (Anderson & Arnoult, 1989), humor (measured by the CHS) failed to moderate the effects of negative life experiences (a variant of the LES) on health (wellness), illness, depression, and insomnia. However, the health–illness variables were composed of single items only, and depression was measured by an abbreviated form (13 items) of the BDI along with the Multiple Affect Adjective Checklist (MAACL; Zuckerman, 1960). The CHS produced significant main effects at least on the MAACL; the results with the BDI were not reported since the authors ignored any results short of the .01 level of significance.

The failure to find interactions between stress and humor in this study did not lead to clear conclusions. For one, the stress measure had been altered substantially, with subjects being asked to rate each life event twice, once for degree of impact as a positive event and then again as a negative event. Second, the health-related measures were not standardized, known, reliable medical scales. And finally, one of the affect measures was abridged. The CHS was used to assess humor, and though there were ample numbers of males (89) and females (70), sex was not included as a factor. As will be noted later in the book, this may have obscured potentially significant results. In addition to all these points, the authors adopted very conservative tests of significance because there were numerous tests of stress moderation with several variables other than humor. They may therefore have failed to observe meaningful trends, some of which might have become significant had sex of subject been included in the analyses.

In a brief report that was compelling for its ecological validity—the study having been conducted in undeniably arousing circumstances—Trice and Price-Greathouse (1986) found that dental patients who had scored "high" on the CHS, and who had joked and laughed prior to treatment became less distressed during dental surgery than less humorous patients. Given the brevity of the description of the study, however, it was impossible to assess the veridicality of the findings. There was also uncertainty about whether scale scores and observed mirth were both used for subject classification, whether observers of mirth before surgery were different than those of postsurgical behavior, and about how distress was measured. Although interesting, these results were obviously not altogether unambiguous.

In another study, Labott and Martin (1987) examined the joint moderator effects of humor and proclivity for weeping during stressful circumstances as predictors of mood disturbance. These investigators found that the penchant for weeping did interact with stress (CSLES; Sandler & Lakey, 1982) in predicting total mood disturbance measured by the POMS. Those who were more apt to weep showed higher relationships between stress and mood disturbance than those less likely to weep. In a second study, these investigators included the CHS among their measures and found a main effect for humor (the higher the humor score the lower the mood disturbance), and a borderline four-way interaction between stress, humor, sex, and tendency to weep. Although tendency to weep again interacted with stress in the prediction of mood disturbance, humor was found to have moderated that tendency in all groups except males who were "high weepers." Among all less-likely-to-weep subjects, those who were low in humor manifested higher relationships between stress and mood disturbance than did high-humor subjects. Among high weepers, the differences between those scoring low and those scoring high on the CHS were less marked, and among males were opposite to the general findings: high-humor males manifested a greater relationship between stress and mood disturbance. However, these findings are suspect because the number of stressful experiences they reported was markedly lower than that of the other groups.

In this study then, there were some interesting results that, like most data resulting from four-way interactions, are not completely clear. The authors thought of weeping as a cathartic experience and were expecting it to reduce the effects of stress. Their findings, however, were the opposite: weepers were more dysphoric than nonweepers in stressful circumstances. Since the propensity to weep, then, might be thought of as an indication of an enhanced reponse to stress, it would seem that humor is less effective as a stress reducer among those who are most likely to become distraught in stressful events, especially if they are male. Given that weeping is generally less frequent among males, as was indicated in the means of the scale scores, high humor–high weeper male subjects may be more emotionally labile or at least more emotionally expressive than others.

In summarizing the findings from these early investigations, the conclusions we could draw are not dissimilar from those to be drawn from close scrutiny of most research areas. That is, there are tempting suggestions but no certainties to be derived. In certain circumstances humor has been found to alter the emotional consequences of stressful events. In others, humor has been found to be a negative correlate of dysphoria regardless of the levels of stress experienced and in essence similar to traits such as well-being, optimism, or cheerfulness.

It should not be surprising that more recent studies have not completely dispelled the uncertainties about humor as a stress moderator. For example, Overholser (1992) used the LES measure of stress with humor as a moderator variable as predictors of depression (BDI), loneliness (Russell, Peplau, & Cutrona, 1980), and self esteem (Rosenberg, 1965). He found evidence that humor did play an important role in the regression formulae. However, the results were not always as expected.

Among males (N = 46), the CHS measure of humor was unrelated to depression. However, among the 52 female subjects, CHS produced a strong main effect and an even stronger interaction with stress in the prediction of depression. CHS was negatively related to depression, but when the humor scores were used to form a low and a high group divided at the median, the relationship between stress and depression was seen only in the high-humor group, and that relationship was positive. That is, among female subjects scoring in the upper half of the CHS distribution, the relationship between stress and depression was significant (r = .55, p < .01). Among those in the lower half of the distribution, the relationship between stress and depression was negligible (r = .03). With the other dependent variables, CHS produced main effects, being negatively related to loneliness among males and positively related to self-esteem among both males and females. No other interactions were found between stress and CHS scores in predicting these latter variables.

Unless the data were inadvertently reversed in their presentation, these findings are perplexing. On the other hand, because these findings occurred only in the female sample, which had been dichotomized via a median split, the interaction derived from comparisons between the rather small samples may have been overly biased by a few outliers. One way or the other, these results served to increase rather than dispel uncertainties.

In an interesting series of three studies by a research group at Allegheny College in Pennsylvania, the effects of humor on dysphoria have been studied experimentally with mixed results. In one study by Yovetich, Dale, and Hudak (1990), humor, as measured by the SHRQ, was used to predict self-reported anxiety, facial expressions, and heart rate as subjects awaited electric shocks. During this period subjects listened either to a humorous tape, an engaging tape about geology, or no tape at all. Subjects who scored low on the SHRQ reported more anxiety and manifested faster pulse rates than those who scored high on humor. However, the increased pulse rates were found only during the "no tape" condition. In other words, when there were no distractions offered, low-humor subjects evinced greater increases in heart rate than high-humor subjects and than all the subjects who were provided distracting tape recordings to listen to. Other interesting findings involved more smiling among high- than low-humor subjects while listening to the humor tapes, and less reports of anxiety among subjects who listened to the humor tape. Although self-reported anxiety was more obvious among low-humor subjects, especially as the time for electric shock approached, the comparisons of pulse rates at each time period varied extensively. The only reliable finding with regard to pulse rate was the gradual acceleration of pulse rate among all subjects, but this was most notable among the low-humor subjects who did not listen to either of the tape recordings. We could conclude that the distraction of listening to the tapes helped minimize the effects of anticipated shocks and that when there were no distractions available, persons with a lesser sense of humor were more apt to become emotionally aroused. However, in the last time period, just before the expected shock, high-humor subjects who were listening to the humor tape exhibited pulse rates that approached the high levels shown by the low-humor no-tape subjects. Consequently, as noted earlier, there were no clear conclusions but much interesting data.

In a second experimental study from this group of researchers depression was induced by the "Velten procedure" (Velten, 1968), whereby subjects read aloud a series of progressively more depressing statements and are asked to think about and feel them. Danzer, Dale, and Klions (1990) examined the effect of a humorous intervention designed to undo the depressive effects on several variables pertinent to depression. Their all-female sample completed the MAACL before and after undergoing the Velten procedure, and again after the humor or control treatments that followed on the mood induction. The humor treatment consisted of listening to 11 minutes of humorous routines by Bill Cosby and Robin Williams. The control conditions consisted of a recorded geology lecture and an equivalent no-tape time period. The results with the MAACL indicated that depression, anxiety, and hostility all increased substantially following the depression induction. After the subsequent "therapeutic" treatments, most subjects exhibited decreases in their registry of negative affects. However, the greatest changes were found among subjects who listened to the humor tape. These subjects' MAACL scores returned to baseline levels. Similar magnitude decreases were not found among control subjects for depression, anxiety, and hostility. Other data with heart rate and zygomatic muscle tension (smiles) did not produce unambiguous results except to attest to the success of depression induction.

In a third study, Hudak, Dale, Hudak, and DeGood (1991) examined the effect of humor on responses to induced pain, replicating an earlier investigation by Cogan, Cogan, Waltz, and McCue (1987). Where the latter investigators found that tolerance for pain produced by a pressure cuff increased after subjects listened to a humorous audiotape, Hudak et al. found that responses to pain created by transcutaneous end nerve stimulation (TENS) were affected by a humorous video in interaction with trait humor measured by the SHRQ. The humorous video (*Bill Cosby Himself*) or a control video (*Annuals and Hanging Baskets*) was shown to subjects immediately after they signalled that the electrical stimulation was becoming uncomfortable in the baseline condition. Five minutes into the video presentations, pain threshold was again measured in response to the TENS. Those subjects whose scores were in the upper half of the SHRQ distribution exhibited an increased tolerance of pain from the TENS compared to their baselines in both the humor and control conditions. Those in the lower half of the SHRQ distribution showed some increase in threshold for pain from their baseline levels in the humor condition. But most marked was a large decrease in threshold for pain when the low SHRQ subjects viewed the nonhumor tape. In addition, zygomatic muscle tension was highest among high SHRQ subjects viewing the humor tape before the TENS was administered.

Together, these three studies offer some support for the role of humor as a stress reducer. In some circumstances, humor seemed to be more traitlike than a characteristic with specific application to stress. In others, its effects were more notable during stressful or painful moments, suggesting a moderator role. Self-reports, facial expressions, and heart rate indicating distress in aversive situations have all been found to be influenced by humor. However, interactions among variables in these studies have often made the results seem conditional with no certainty about what might be responsible for the variability observed.

To make matters even more unclear, Nevo, Keinan, and Teshimovsky-Arditi (1993) found only weak effects for a measure of trait humor and humor induced by a film on subjects in a cold pressor task. Only one subscale (humor productivity) of Ziv's sense of humor scales (Ziv, 1984), was even mildly related to pain tolerance ($r = .26$, $p < .05$) and the SHRQ was unrelated altogether. One finding of some note was that the funnier subjects thought the humorous film to be, the longer they were able to tolerate the immersion in freezing water ($r = .38$, $p < .05$). In contrast to the humorous film, some subjects viewed a documentary and others saw no film at all. Ironically, when subjects had been classified as low or high in humor on the basis of the Ziv measure, it was the low-humor subjects who exhibited the greatest differentiation in their ratings of funniness between the humorous and documentary film. High-humor subjects seemed to find the documentary almost as amusing as the film that was intended to be funny.

Whether variations in the perceived funniness of the films was responsible for the failure of trait humor to be a major factor in this study, or whether the procedures used in the cold pressor task may not have been controlled (no mention was made about whether there was a "circulating bath") this study failed to replicate the findings from other investigations concerned with pain.

In a study with a somewhat different aim, Kuiper, Martin, and Dance (1992) examined the role of humor in helping individuals maintain positive affect during encounters with negative events. First, these investigators found that positive affect increased most substantially for subjects who scored high on the SHQ (Svebak, 1974). Two subscales, metamessage sensitivity (SHQ-MS), and the liking of humor (SHQ-LH) interacted with the Positive Life Event subscale of the LES (Sarason *et al.*, 1978) in predicting the positive affect subscale of the Positive and Negative Affect Schedule (PANAS; Watson, Clark, & Tellegen, 1988). It would seem that only persons who appreciated humor seemed likely to derive positive affect from their positive experiences. It is of interest, however, that neither the CHS nor the SHRQ produced similar results, pointing to the specifity of certain kinds of humor for producing particular effects in different circumstances. Nevertheless, when all the humor variables were used as moderators of the relationship between negative life events and positive affect, the CHS and SHRQ along with the SHQ-MS did produce significant interactions. These interactions derived from the sharp decline in positive affect that occurred with increasing negative life events among those who had scored low on those humor measures. In other words, positive affect was maintained despite negative experiences by persons who seem to have a good sense of humor. These findings add a new dimension to the work on moderator effects of humor. Consequently, the authors described their focus as being not so much on the reduction of negative affect as upon "enhanced quality of life."

Carver et al. (1993) have reported on the ways in which a sample of women coped with surgery at an early stage of breast cancer. These investigators were most interested in the effects of optimism as a moderator of the illness–distress relationship. At the same time, they examined the relationships between several coping mechanisms and optimism on the one hand and experienced distress on the other. Included among the coping mechanisms was "use of humor." The authors do not describe the measure used to assess this characteristic other than to say that it is composed of three items, as are each of the other measures of coping mechanisms within the COPE Scale, and that it has good internal consistency (Scheier & Carver, 1985).

Among the various coping mechanisms, use of humor correlated significantly only with "positive reframing." But in each of five assessments at presurgery, postsurgery, and then at 3, 6, and 12-month follow-ups, use of humor was positively correlated with optimism which, in turn, was associated with less distress as measured by subscales of the POMS at each point in time. Furthermore, when coping mechanisms were examined for their direct effects on distress at the different time periods, use of humor was found to be negatively associated with distress at all five time periods, though statistically significant at only two of them.

Although use of humor was reliably related to optimism, its relative independence from other coping mechanisms was notable, the only other significant correlation being with "positive reframing." Although brief, the questions in the humor measure may have attained their predictive power from the specificity with which they addressed the stressor under study ("I've been making jokes about it"—"it" being breast cancer). Humor, then, seemed to be distinctive and contributed as a relatively independent moderator of stress. Given the nature of the very real stressful circumstances explored in this study, the results are compelling.

In another study examining responses of patients who had undergone orthopedic surgery, Rotton and Shats (1996) found humor to have some limited use in reducing pain. These investigators provided either serious or humorous films for patients to observe in the two days following surgery. Half the patients in each group (humorous versus serious) were allowed to choose which of 20 films they could see. The other half were shown films of the experimenter's choice. Self-reports of distress and pain showed a marked decline from the first to the second day after surgery among all patients who had been provided films. In contrast, a control group that had not been given the option of watching movies showed little change from day one to day two. No differences were found between those who had viewed comedies and those who had viewed serious films. However, requests for "minor analgesics" (aspirins, tranquilizers) was significantly less for patients who had viewed comedies than for those who had viewed serious films, and choice of films and condition (humor versus serious) interacted in predicting the dosage levels of major analgesics (Demerol, Dilaudid, and Percodan). If the patients could choose the films they were to watch, then humorous film-watching was associated with lower dosages of major analgesics. However, if there was no choice in the films to be watched, then humorous films resulted in greater use of such analgesics compared both to the serious-film and the no-film control conditions. Given the idiosyncratic preferences people have for certain forms of humor, these findings suggest that watching "humorous" films that a person does not find funny may prove irritating enough to exacerbate feelings of pain.

Finally, a few recent publications have focused on the affective responses of subjects to the contemplation of death. In one set of studies, subjects were led to think about their own mortality. The assumption underlying this research is that many of the questions in life event measures of stress contain intimations about the deaths of loved ones and of the subjects themselves. In one study from our labs at the University of Waterloo (Lefcourt *et al.*, 1995), subjects were led to think about their own deaths during a series of tasks: they filled out a death certificate for themselves in which they guessed what would be their cause and time of death; they composed a eulogy for themselves to be delivered at their funerals; they constructed a will disposing of the worldly goods they anticipated having at the time of their deaths, and so on). Mood disturbance measured by the POMS was assessed before and after these "death exercises." As had been predicted, most subjects exhibited an increase in mood disturbance, reporting more depression, tension, anger, and so on. The only exceptions to this trend were subjects who had scored high on a measure of perspective-taking humor. These subjects showed little or no change in their moods after completing of the death exercises. The perspective-taking humor measure consisted of an index reflecting appreciation and comprehension of a set of Gary Larson's "Far Side" cartoons (Larson, 1988) which had been selected for their "perspective-taking" character. Each of the cartoons required a distancing from our own species to be appreciated. That is, people had to be able to see the nonsense in everyday human activity to find humor in the cartoons. In addition to the perspective-taking humor measure, the SHRQ was administered and was found to be negatively related to mood disturbance both before and after the death exercises. Where the SHRQ measure of humor produced main effects on POMS scores, indicating that this measure of a self-reported tendency to laugh in potentially awkward situations opposes the tendency to feel dysphoric in general—the perspective-taking humor measure produced an interaction, indicating that when people think specifically about death, their ability to assume a humorously distant orientation from one's own species and probably, therefore, from one's own self, provides some protection from becoming dysphoric.

In the second study involving the contemplation of mortality as a stressor, humor was used to predict the willingness to be an organ donor, represented by signing the form that is attached to the Ontario driver's license (Lefcourt & Shepherd, 1995). First, form signing was found to be related to a number of other behaviors indicating fear or acceptance of death, such as the willingness to visit a mortally ill friend, to discuss death with parents, and so on. Persons who had signed their organ donation forms seemed less phobic about death-related thoughts and behaviors. In turn, when organ donation signing was examined for its relationship with humor, it was found to be positively associated with humor assessed by the SHRQ and the cartoon measure of perspective-taking humor that we used in the previous study. The interpretation of these data was that humor, especially perspective-taking humor, indicated a tendency to not regard oneself too seriously, and in not being overly serious about oneself, it then became possible to think about and acknowledge mortality and the end of self without succumbing to morbid affect. Because contemplation of mortality is regarded as a stressor in these studies, humor can be said to have moderated the relationship between stressor and mood disturbance.

In another set of studies, Dacher Keltner and George Bonanno have used observations of laughter, humor, enjoyment, and amusement exhibited during interviews six months after the loss of a spouse as predictive indicators of how well people come to terms with bereavement (Bonanno & Keltner, 1997; Keltner & Bonanno, 1997). Although one might question whether humor could cause bereavement outcomes, the readiness to laugh even about difficult subjects such as a deceased spouse would assumedly be associated with a predisposition to respond to stress with humor. Consequently, it is reasonable to assume that showing humor during bereavement might have a similar relationship to acceptance of mortality as we found in our research.

In interviews with spouses whose mates had died approximately six months earlier, these investigators found differences in adjustment favoring survivors who manifest Duchenne laughter while speaking about their former partners. Duchenne laughter involves both zygomatic major muscle action that pulls the lip corners up obliquely and orbicularis oculi muscle action, which pulls the skin from the cheeks and forehead toward the eyeball (Keltner & Ekman, 1994). In common parlance, Duchenne laughter could be described as laughter involving both mouth and eyes, whereas non-Duchenne laughter involves only the mouth. The former is what many regard as a full laugh as the latter appears less wholehearted or possibly overcontrolled.

Those who exhibited Duchenne laughter during their interviews reported that they felt less anger and were experiencing increased enjoyment in contrast to the period of time immediately following their spouse's death. Most importantly these "full-laughers" manifested dissociation from distress assessed by the contrast between their verbal reports of distress and autonomic indications of same. Duchenne laughter was negatively correlated with "verbal-autonomic discrepancy" ($r = -.37$, $p < .05$), indicating that those who engaged in full-laughter displays were less apt to mention emotional responses that were suggested by changes in their heart rates. This indicates that the full-laughter display, like humor as we have described it, reflects a distancing from grief or dysphoria that allows the person to recover and enjoy life more fully. Indeed, Keltner and Bonanno did find that Duchenne laughers were less ambivalent about their current social involvements than those who did not show such humor. As an interesting contrast, non-Duchenne laughter was positively correlated with verbal-autonomic discrepancy indicating that there were greater verbal claims to emotional responses than were indicated by heart rate changes among persons who manifested "less genuine" laughter. This was intepreted as an indication of greater sensitization to as opposed to dissociation from distress.

Also interesting, Keltner and Bonanno found little relationship between non-Duchenne laughter or smiling with self-reported emotions, whereas Duchenne smiles and laughs were both positively associated with positive emotions. However, Duchenne laughter was more strongly related to self-reports of reduced anger ($r = -.49$, $p < .01$, compared to $r = -.28$, $p < .10$ for smiles) and Duchenne smiling was slightly more related to self-reports of reduced fear ($r = -.31$, $p < .05$ compared to $r = -.24$, ns for laughter) and distress ($r = -.49$, $p<.01$ compared to $r = -.36$, $p < .05$ for laughter). Keltner and Bonanno (1997) note that these findings resemble Sylvan Tomkins's (Tomkins & Demos, 1995) observation that laughter accompanies the sudden reduction of anger, whereas the smile of joy accompanies the sudden reduction of fear and distress. Humor as an alternative to the expression of anger was also central to Dixon's contentions about the evolution of humor (Dixon, 1980).

Another finding with relevance for the next chapter in this book concerned humor's role in facilitating social support. Those who manifested Duchenne laughter were judged by observers as being better adjusted and happier, though nonlaughers were more likely to elicit compassion and help. The display of laughter may then have aroused less nurturance from observers while increasing their attractiveness. Laughers were described as more amusing and potentially less frustrating to interact with.

The relationship between emotional display and the attainment of social support was emphasized more strongly in the study by Bonanno and Keltner (1997). Here, facial displays of enjoyment and amusement were found to be negatively related to grief-specific symptoms at 14 and 25 months following the loss, whereas negative emotional displays of anger and contempt were positively associated with those symptoms. Also, the negative emotions displayed facially were negatively correlated with perceived health outcomes at both later time periods, and these results were most marked for the expression of anger ($rs = -.37$ and $-.40$, $p < .05$ for 14 and 25 months postloss, respectively). The authors interpreted their results in terms of the emotional displays that express the desire to participate with others and obtain their social support. As noted, this will be discussed more fully in the following chapter.

Overall then, the empirical literature suggests that humor does play some role in the development and maintenance of mood states. However, that role is rarely straightforward. Nevertheless, the larger percentage of findings do suggest that humor can serve to reduce the effects of stressors that would otherwise result in dysphoric emotions. When humorous material is provided in experimental conditions, a lessening of distress can sometimes be observed, though the effects may vary with the particular humorous presentations. On the other hand, as in the original group of studies examining the moderator effects of humor, some findings have proven to be the opposite of hypothesized effects. Such results do little to reduce our uncertainties about the robustness and reliability of stress moderator effects.

In following the pathways indicated in Figure 8-1, humor's impact can be evaluated through its effects on the incidence of physiological changes that are related to illness. As described in the previous chapter, prolonged arousal with accompanying adrenal stimulation has decided effects on the organism, from loss of appetite and growth to inhibition of immune system activity. In a subsequent chapter we will review research in which humor is found to reverse certain stress-related physiological processes that may be associated with illness. Before turning to that literature, we will focus on the relationship between humor and social support suggested by the bereavement work of Bonanno and Keltner (1997) and Sapolsky's observations about (1994) more affectionate and affiliative baboons.

HUMOR AS A MEANS OF RETAINING SOCIAL COHESION AND SUPPORT

In his captivating book *Guns, Germs, and Steel*, Jared Diamond (1997) contrasts the behavior of humans reared in small bands of hunter–gatherers with those who live in larger food-producing societies. Where the latter are said to be more likely to die of diseases and in war, the former are more often the victims of murder. With particular reference to the inhabitants of New Guinea, where he regularly conducts field studies, and to isolated bands and tribal societies in the Amazon, Diamond asserts that murder among members of different tribes or extended families is a common occurrence. Women report having "serial" husbands due to the murder of one man after another. Central authorities, often chiefdoms, evolve and become accepted because they provide public order, curbing the violence that is so common among members of those relatively isolated hunter–gatherer groups. That humans are capable of violence is self-evident. A quick perusal of most daily newspapers confirms our worst fears. Humans are capable of abuse, murder, torture, and the like, and they commit such travesties frequently with the blessings of their own societies as they wage wars, commit "ethnic cleansing," and so on. In crowded food-producing societies, the possibility of escape into the anonymous crowds of larger urbanized areas probably has served to increase the incidence of murder and violence.

If humans are capable of perpetrating violence on their neighbors even when they live in small groups where they are familiar with each other, secure lives in larger societies where strangers interfere with each other would seem to be impossible. As evidence of the frustration and violence that regularly occurs in urban settings, I have collected newspaper articles for many years that describe vicious altercations between landlords and tenants, between people competing for hard-to-find parking places, and the like. Writers such as Howard Bloom (1995) have argued that warfare and violence are normative behaviors among all species, so that stressful existence is universal and serenity is essentially ephemeral. Yet, despite the omnipresent potential for distress in urban life, many persons live in protective enclaves that they do not find so chaotic. Although there are many settings where people do feel endangered, many humans seem to live relatively predictable and safe lives. In fact, some of us are lucky enough not to suffer from violence or natural catastrophes most of the time. How is it that some persons can remain relatively free of violence or the fear of life-threatening events?

MEMBERSHIP IN SOCIAL GROUPS

When I was a member of a grant-reviewing study group under the aegis of the National Institutes of Mental Health in Washington, D.C., an incident occurred that provides some clues as to how we humans protect ourselves from potential violence from our fellow humans. At the end of each of three days of presentation and review of dozens of grant proposals, our entire group of about 15 psychologists would meander in a leisurely fashion toward some highly recommended restaurant in the Washington, D.C., area. Engaged in endless conversations, we were probably only half-aware of where we were during the perambulations that eventually led us to our chosen restaurant. I can recall that one such evening, as we wandered in the direction of that night's restaurant, we found ourselves in a dilapidated neighborhood where dissolute-looking adults and ominous-looking adolescents seemed to be watching us as predator lions might when confronted with a herd of gazelles that foolishly ventures into their territory. I'm not sure that any of us were completely aware of being in danger. Nevertheless, we began bumping into each other as we narrowed into a tighter cluster, stragglers and outliers drifting to the center of the "herd" that seemed to be hastening our arrival at the destination. We never panicked or broke into a run, but we jostled each other, tripped over each other's feet, talked more effusively and loudly, and had become a "tight little group" by the time we arrived at our restaurant. I don't recall anyone mentioning our behavior during that walk. It would have been embarassing to admit that we were frightened and sought to save our skins in favor of someone else's. However, our behavior was instructive. Like any other animal that can become prey to more aggressive and violent animals, we each tried to avert danger by not being on the periphery of our group. We sought physical proximity to others and widened the spaces between our group and the dilapidated fences and walls where our potential predators lounged.

In a similar sense, we can speak of humans' affiliative behavior, our desire to belong to our own personal groups and places, as deriving from a need for protection from the threats that surround us. These threats may be external, consisting of dangers that range from physical or social attack to financial ruin, or they may be internal, including fears that we might lose emotional control of ourselves or succumb to disintegrative diseases and death. In our social lives we find protection from these sources of threat and violence that surround us.

In a literature concerned with the ramifications of our awareness and dread of death, Solomon, Greenberg, and Pyszczynski (1991) outlined a theory of *terror management* derived from the writings of Ernest Becker (1973). They described the tendency of humans to increase adherence to their membership groups when they are in some way made aware of their mortality.

This literature, which has generated a considerable amount of supportive research, is based on the assumption that humans among all species are uniquely aware of their own mortality and that cultures and group identifications evolve as an antidote to the crippling fears and paralyses that such an awareness can produce.

Empirically, the terror management literature (Solomon, Greenberg, & Pyszczynski, 1990) has demonstrated that people become more adamant about their belonging to groups when they are made aware of their mortality. In two papers (Rosenblatt, Greenberg, Solomon, Pyszczynski, & Lyon, 1989; Greenberg et al., 1990) the writers have shown that subjects evaluate similar and dissimilar others in more polarized ways following exercises that promote sensing the immediacy of dying. This was produced in one study by having subjects write about their anticipated feelings about dying. Subjects were more apt to adjudge culture violators (prostitutes) harshly and heroes highly after death became salient.

In another study (Solomon et al., 1990) subjects had to "misuse" icons (a cross and a flag) that symbolized their group memberships if they were to deal correctly with assigned problem-solving tasks. The cross had to be used as a hammer and the flag as a strainer for water if the subjects were to succeed at tasks that presumedly reflected their ingenuity. After subjects had written about their feelings about dying, they were much less likely to "defile" their group icons than if they had not done so.

The consistency of the results found by the terror management researchers is impressive. Even political alliance seems to be strengthened when death becomes salient. During the 1988 presidential election campaign, supporters of George Bush were found to be more adamantly for him following the presentation in the Republican Party camp of the photograph of the criminal

Willie Horton. The release of such prisoners on probation had been blamed on the "revolving door" policies of governors like Democrat Michael Dukakis of Massachusetts (Pyszczynski, Becker, Gracey, Greenberg, & Solomon, 1989). This focus on violence and death seemed to evoke fears of mortality that served to enhance allegiance to Bush among people who might otherwise been lukewarm in their support of him.

That our adherence to groups somehow affirms our existence and protects us from threats seems self-evident. Most animals who become isolated from their packs, prides, gaggles, mobs, and so on are more liable to fall victim to violence and death. Even when a group of baboons, for example, does not welcome the arrival of a "stranger," the newcomer will risk life and limb to become part of that group. Recent writings by animal trainers have emphasized the affiliative natures of most creatures that must be respected if training is to be done without agony. Monty Roberts's (1997) well-received book *The Man Who Listens to Horses* is an excellent example of this genre. The social nature of animals is also attested to in a recent book about elephant behavior, *Silent Thunder* by Katy Boynton-Payne (1998), who found that elephants' behavior reveals that loyalty and communication in their family groups extends beyond death. To be isolated has always been threatening. Boardinghouse neighborhoods where people seem detached from others have always been described by sociologists as dangerous places where schizophrenics and other "lost souls" commonly fall prey to violence. Like all animals, people too need to belong to groups.

A voluminous literature attests to the role of social belonging in facilitating humans' ability to deal with stressful events. Humans become demoralized and withdrawn when they experience the loss of that sense of belonging to their own valued groups. Bruno Bettelheim (1943, 1960) described how the persons who retained their sense of well-being in the Nazi concentration camps were mostly those who believed that their incarceration was not incomprehensible because they belonged to underground resisters or the like. Those who suffered most seemed to be persons who felt themselves to be loyal Germans who did not oppose the Nazification of their country. It was as if they had been deposed, deprived of their group membership. The former, on the other hand, could take heart in being part of a movement or social organization in which they would be rewarded for the efforts that brought them to the camp. In essence, the former would be honored by their groups; the latter felt they had been defiled.

Another example of the importance of membership groups was reported by Robert Lifton (1967), who described the demoralization and personal decline of prisoners who were subjected to "brainwashing" in Korean and Chinese prisons. When some prisoners were bribed to become "snitches," the atmosphere became rife with distrust because gross punishment, torture, and possible execution would follow even if only discussions of potential insubordination were reported. The demoralization in such camps was most apparent following deaths and pathological withdrawal was commonly noted among prisoners referred to as "musselmanner" who were said to have surrendered to despair and hopelessness. The separation of potential leaders from those who were rank and file no doubt helped foster that withdrawal.

A beautiful example of how soldiers can be rescued from despair and ennui by adherence to their group was presented in the classic film *Bridge on the River Kwai*. Although "loyalty as folly" is a central theme, it showed that the men who were enlisted to build the bridge under the command of their own officer "came alive" as the feeling of membership in their group was revived despite the Japanese commandant's efforts to subvert the power of the British colonel. In sum, from anecdotal accounts to empirical research, humans have been found to benefit from closeness to others in their membership groups when they encounter difficulties in their lives.

SOCIAL SUPPORT AS A MODERATOR
OF STRESSFUL LIFE EXPERIENCES

The number of books and research studies concerned with the effects of social support is so great that it has become an onerous chore to keep up with the latest findings. We know that social support relieves us of emotional discomfort. However, it may depend on who offers the support, whether friends, parents, or peers of the same or opposite sex, and what the nature of the support is, whether verbal reassurance, material help, advice, and so on (Cohen, Mermelstein, Kamarck, & Hoberman, 1985).

One study that has always stood out for me as an example of the importance of social support was reported in a book by sociologists George Brown and Tirril Harris (1978). In this volume, *The Social Origins of Depression*, the authors focused on the development of depression among British women in London whom the authors repeatedly interviewed over a period of several years. The interviews were designed to explore the range of stressful events that were occurring in the womens' lives and to examine the personal characteristics that could account for the resilience that many of them displayed in confronting the effects of those events.

In studies summarized here the likelihood that a woman would show up at a mental health clinic looking for relief from depression could be predicted with confidence. The authors were able to isolate several characteristics that seemed to account for resilience as opposed to susceptibility to the detrimental effects of stress. The importance of each factor made sense, and many were of the sort that would elicit an "of course" from readers. Among those

characteristics that made the women seem more vulnerable to stress was social class; those from lower socioeconomic circumstances were the most likely
to approach clinics for help with depression. Second if the woman's mother
had died before she was 11 years of age she was more likely to become depressed, especially if she was now at home with three young children under
age 14 and did not work outside the home. But among all the characteristics,
the absence of a "confidante," someone with whom it was possible to share
the intimate details of her life, was the most salient variable among the host of
variables that allowed for the prediction of depression. If a woman had a confidante, whether her husband or another person, the likelihood of turning up
at a mental health clinic for help with depression was very low. This factor of
shared intimacy accounted for as much of the variance as the other factors
noted earlier, and was also highly related to social class. Women from lower
socioeconomic circumstances were far more likely to lack shared intimacy,
even if they were married, than were women from middle-class backgrounds.

Research like this inspired me and one of my graduate students, Rickey
Miller, to explore the role of intimacy in the lives of men and women (Miller &
Lefcourt, 1982, 1983; Lefcourt, 1985). We created a measure of intimacy using
a definition that appeals to common sense. We asked people to name the
person with whom they felt closest, that is, their best friend. We then asked
them to express how important it would be to share their experiences with
this friend, and how really close they felt to that person. For example, subjects
were asked how often they would confide in him or her about very personal
information, and how affectionate they felt toward that person. In essence,
we asked people how much they liked being with their closest friend and how
close they felt to that person to whom they were most attached. The higher
their scores, the more close or intimate they were with their best friends.

Among several samples of subjects, we found that people in troubled
marriages had lower than normative intimacy scores and that our measure of
intimacy was related to scores on other scales that reflect accessibility to social support, such as loneliness (Russell, Peplau, & Ferguson, 1978), interpersonal relationship scale (Shlien, Guerney, & Stover, as cited in Guerney, 1977)
and self-esteem (Fitts, 1965). Those who felt more distant from their closest
friends reported greater feelings of loneliness, distrust, and low self-esteem.
However, the most important of our findings pertained to the relationship
between stress and mood disturbance. It seemed that those who had more
intimate relations with others were less likely to become emotionally distraught
than those whose relationships were more distant, regardless of whether they
had undergone stressful circumstances or not. That is, intimacy along with
life stress could afford prediction of mood disturbance though not in an interactive sense.

Findings such as these indicating that social support is negatively related to mood disturbance have been reported with great consistency, though in many instances social support is also found to be a moderator of stressful events. That is, social closeness with others reduces the likelihood that mood disturbances will occur in response to stressful events, with the Brown and Harris research findings among those pointing to this relationship. In another study in my labs we found that social support had particular effects on mood disturbances among persons with an internal locus of control (Lefcourt, Martin, & Saleh, 1984). For those who believed that their achievement and affiliation experiences were due to their own actions (internals), social support was most important in allaying the emotional consequences of stress. More fatalistic persons (externals) did not seem to require social support as much for protection from the effects of stress. These findings suggest that social support might be most important for persons who tend to be autonomous, who rely on themselves more than others. Writers who spend large amounts of time working by themselves often do speak of the need to share aspects of their projects with their partners or valued friends, using them as sounding boards; without them they come to fear the possibility of being ignominious failures.

Some of the contrary results obtained by different investigators may derive from the various assessment tools used to measure stress, social support, and emotional upset. Nevertheless, the literature generally supports the proposition that social support moderates the impact of stressful experiences. Volumes such as those by the Sarasons (Sarason & Sarason, 1985; Sarason, Sarason, & Pierce, 1990) and others (Eckenrode, 1991; Gottlieb, 1988) are among many that have reinforced the assertion that we are social animals in need of closeness with others in order to weather inevitable stressful circumstances. In a review of human history and scientific literature concerned with the behavior of organisms up and down the phylogenetic scales, Howard Bloom (1995) has contended that this need for closeness and belonging to groups that we observe among humans is a basic principle of most life forms, from the very lowest of microorganisms. Suffering with stressful demands seems to require a togetherness with others if individual members of most species are to survive.

HUMOR AS AN ENHANCER OF SOCIAL BELONGING

In discussing the impact of humor with others, I have been impressed by the number of times that people have ended their stories about humorous events with unsolicited comments to the effect that the persons who shared the event felt much closer to each other after they had laughed together about it. One story that I heard recently eloquently attests to this effect. The author,

Derek Maitland, is a professional writer who has become interested in humor because of his own experiences with it.

> One of the blackest moments in my life occurred in my mid-40s, when my marriage irretrievably collapsed. There were children involved, and all the guilt, sense of failure, and helplessness that happens in these situations. At the final breakup, I went to stay with my parents for a couple of days before flying out of the country. It was while we were having supper that the grief suddenly hit me, and hit me hard, and I left the table and went into another room, where I broke down completely and bawled and sobbed. As I was weeping, I felt my father sit down beside me. He waited a while, as I sobbed and choked, and then he finally spoke. "I can't understand why you're tearing yourself apart like this, son," he said softly. "All I said was that you couldn't leave the table until you'd finished all your greens." I was dumbstruck for a moment. Then the sheer comic audacity of what he'd said turned all the grief and helplessness into an incredulous love for this man; and we both sat roaring with laughter. It didn't cure the grief, but it certainly resigned me to the essential frailty and absurdity of life, and at the right time.

In this wonderful story, the redemptive power of humor is clear. The writer's loneliness seemed palpable. He was with his parents, but he was also alone in his midyears, having lost his own immediate family with whom his meaningful social life was involved. His father's "audacity" was to cut through the distance that can form between parents and their adult children, making a joke that contrasts present role relationships between father and son with those that existed when the writer was a child, dependent on his father and family for social belonging. In a sense, his father was alluding to the "old" relationship, contrasting current feelings of aloneness and isolation with the family closeness that would have characterized a happy childhood. Pretending that the writer had left the table because he had been banished for a childish infraction rather than because he was overwhelmed with despair was a cover-up and a joke. The "audacity" of the joke rested on trust that the writer would not look askance at his father, regard him as crazy, and reject his solace. The joke was an offering that the son could have rejected. What his father provided was a reprise of the closeness and social support they had probably enjoyed when the son was young. Coming now at a time when the son felt bereft of closeness and belonging served to remind him of the social support that was still available to him. Of course, the earlier relationship between the father and son had to be close for this to have worked as it did.

Another story provided by one of my undergraduate students likewise shows how humor allows people to "be together," restoring relationships that are in jeopardy. In this case the relationship was less intimate than the previous one, being between a student and a high school teacher. To a child or adolescent a teacher can appear to be a gatekeeper, the person who shepherds the student to the next stages in her development and progress. Rejection by authority figures in the school years can signal an ousting from the expected pathways to success and trouble with other authorities like one's parents.

This event occurred when I was in 10th grade. We had just finished a test in my world politics class and were leaving the room when my teacher, Mr. Taylor, called my name and asked me to stay after class. Mr. Taylor projected a very stern, gruff image and possessed a very intimidating scowl that rarely left his face. He had a reputation for having a bad temper, and there had been rumors about chalk hitting students when he was pushed far enough.

Being a rather shy student, I immediately began to quiver in the face of an authority figure who might yell at me. I squirmed at the thought of a confrontation and knew that when he called my name in that loud, stern voice, I was definitely in trouble.

My friend Fred, who, to be kind, I will say was less than an enthusiastic student, always sat behind me in class. Knowing that I received good marks, Fred had decided that copying answers from my test paper was a good way to ensure a decent mark. Unfortunately, Mr. Taylor saw Fred looking at my paper, which, as I learned later, was not done in a terribly subtle manner.

After the others had left, Mr. Taylor stood at the front on the classroom, lording over me with grim eyes. He told me that he had seen Fred cheating during the test, that he was copying answers from my paper. As soon as he said this, panic gripped me like an iron glove and I could feel my heart pounding. He continued to say that he knew I was good student but regardless of the fact that I was not the one actually cheating, I was just as guilty if I had let him copy my answers. If I had been aware of what he was doing and allowed him to do it, I would receive a zero on the test, just as Fred would. At that moment, as my face was red with embarrassment and tears threatened to roll from my eyes, a mint that Mr. Taylor had been eating fell from his mouth and landed on the floor between us. Simultaneously, we looked down at the mint, lying lifeless on the floor, and then looked up at each other. Before I had a chance to suppress it, a giggle squeaked from my lips. My eyes widened in fear as I awaited his reaction. Seconds later, after a stunned moment, a smile appeared, which then turned into an embarrassed laugh. The two of us soon were giggling together at the silliness of the event.

Once we stopped laughing, I felt more relaxed and the intimidating authority figure disappeared into a simple man who, like me, could make a mistake. I then felt confident enough to tell him that I had not known that Fred was copying my answers. I was able to leave with just a mere suggestion that I sit far away from Fred the next time we had a test.

In this situation, where I was nervous, completely intimidated, and frightened of the serious consequences that could occur, humor allowed me to release my anxieties and decrease my arousal to a more manageable level. Mr. Taylor, whom I greatly respected yet feared, stood before me as a daunting, foreboding figure. With his steely grey eyes and towering height, he had the power to call me a cheater, give me a zero and possible detentions, and crush my self-esteem to the ground. But when the mint dropped from his mouth, his superior status dwindled. After laughing, I was able to see that he was just a man, concerned that cheating was going on and wanting to know about it. Once I saw him as a (relative) equal, I lost most of my nervousness and could defend myself, without blushing and stammering like a thief who got caught in the act.

I am sure that he was embarrassed by what happened and knew that the tension and fear I was feeling, which we had both created for different reasons, was lost. Knowing that, he laughed at his own foolishness, allowing me to release my heightened feelings of arousal that I had only been experiencing for minutes, although it felt like hours. After that day, Mr Taylor and I developed a wonderful rapport and I had even greater respect for him as a teacher and as a man.

Although this story lacks the intensity of the previous drama, it shares with it certain features that might not be immediately obvious. In this schoolroom drama we have the adolescent's view of isolation, failure, detention, and derision from the teacher. In essence, the respected teacher is in a position to make the young student feel different from and less than others—a form of isolation and rejection from the pack. The fear involved in this possible rejection was strong, but the alleviation of that fear by humor was complete, allowing the student to regain her sense of belonging and worth, expressed as regaining a "sense of equality." How were they equal? After all, he was the teacher and she the student, a substantial status difference. The flight of the mint did not have to result in humor. But it did, and the teacher's laugh in response to that of the student suggested that he was not going to reject her, that he already felt some sympathy for her.

Most importantly, the student noted at the end of her story that the result of their interaction was greater respect and rapport. In other words, their social contract was restored. She was not to be placed in academic limbo with all the attendant punishments from parents and other school officials. The threat of rejection was cancelled, resulting in positive affect and relief.

In both stories, the protagonists were rescued by sharing humor with other persons, a deliberate joke occurring in the first instance and a comic event occurring by chance in the second. In both cases, there was a rapid shifting of attention to a surprising intrusion—the father's comment and the teacher's expectorated mint—followed by a sharing of that altered moment with the other persons that resulted in feelings of communion, laughter, and warmth.

Norman Dixon (1980) asserted that humor probably evolved as an alternative to the experience and expression of anger, anger becoming less adaptive as humans came to live in less nomadic and more populous groups. As noted by Diamond (1997), anger and violence were simply not acceptable means for resolving conflicts if people had to live in proximity to each other in stable societies. As long as people were nomadic, following herds or continually seeking places with more clement weather and edible plants, violence could have a hit-and-run nature. Perpetrators did not have to remain in proximity to others who might seek revenge for a murdered family member, as would be the case in a stable food-producing society. As Dixon argued, the expression of anger and aggression would have become *nonadaptive* in settings where populations became stable. In such settings, humor may have evolved as an alternative response to the annoyances and irritations that could otherwise escalate into violence and murder. Today's epidemic of "road rage" is an example of the aggressive responses to strangers that are always possible in crowded urban settings.

If humor can be said to be a tool that averts the likelihood of violence between people, it can also be said to be a quality that enhances potential interactions in social groups. As Bonanno and Keltner (1997) found, bereaved persons who smile fully and laugh when they speak about their deceased spouses seem to be attractive and appealing to their interviewers even if they evoke less nurturance or caretaking from them. If people can laugh about what has been a difficult or even dreaded experience, they seem to be more approachable. Over the years, Ann Landers' columns have often contained references to the difficulties people have in interacting with bereaved persons. People are simply not well-practiced in offering condolences and they are prone to make comments that, in the minds of the bereaved, seem inappropriate. Laughter, smiling, and humor seem to be invitations to others, indicating that the mourners are ready to return to social interaction and making it that much easier for others to approach them. To this end, Keltner and Bonanno (1997) assert that laugher gives evidence that bereaved persons have become more involved in their ongoing experiences and less dedicated to reminiscence and involvement with their past. This involvement enhances the likelihood that they will engage in their social groups once again, a participation that serves to protect them from the ravages brought on by stressful life experiences.

An example of the way in which laughter and humor directed at oneself can invite positive affect and support from others is described by Webb Hubbell (1997) in his book about political life in the 1990's. Shortly after Bill Clinton had been jeered following his "failed" nomination speech for Michael Dukakis at the 1988 Democratic National Convention, several friends arranged for him to appear on the "Tonight" show, in order to undo the political harm it was thought he had done himself. In his comeback appearance, he was "funny, self-effacing, human," joining others in laughing at his failed speech (p. 145). Hubbell asserts that this appearance may have helped to save Clinton's political career. The use of self-directed humor was said to be atypical for Clinton, who felt he was on a "mission" and therefore could not readily admit that his failures were not grave. Apparently, after this "human" performance Clinton's reputation was to some degree restored, with people feeling more friendly and supportive of him. As an epilogue, Hubbell noted that "Washington would be a saner place if people there could laugh at themselves a little more" (p. 145). Clinton's display of self-directed humor may have signaled approach-ability, which, as was found in the research with bereaved spouses, can result in social support and enhanced social belonging.

As described in the previous chapter, Sapolsky (1994) examined the ef-fects of stress on male baboons and reported on the disastrous consequences that it can have on the physiological well-being of those animals. In observa-tions of the personality characteristics of baboons who were resilient, or less likely to give evidence of physiological arousal during stressful occasions, Sapolsky described their playful, affiliative behavior. Those baboons who chose to groom others without the promise of sex in return, who were playful with infants and young baboons, whose demeanor could be said to be "laid back," were the least likely to manifest chronic physiological arousal, as was deter-mined by cortisol levels in blood samples drawn by the investigator. In addi-tion, many baboons formed coalitions with others for mundane purposes, as in food procurement and simply in friendship. These animals who were more affiliative were also less likely to exhibit chronic arousal.

Although we are not privy to the jokes and humor that baboons may share with each other, the willingness to play with youngsters and the close-ness involved in "unselfish" grooming can be seen as rudimentary forms of humor. That such animals could then become "friends" or operate in coali-tions suggests that the relationship between humor and social support that we have been discussing as correlates in our species may be common to other species as well.

Humor has been found to have ameliorative effects on individuals who might otherwise have suffered from the effects of egregious violence. Anton Obrdlik (1942), a sociologist, described a fascinating set of events that took place in his native Czechoslovakia during World War II. Rather than dissolv-ing into depression and withdrawal during Nazi occupation, some Czechs took to telling jokes about the occupiers. Not content simply to tell jokes to a limited number, they often painted jokes on walls and fences so that they could spread throughout a good portion of the population. Humor seemed to bolster the resistance of the victims and at the same time undermined the morale of the oppressors. German soldiers were deployed each day to wash the walls and fences of jokes that were insulting to them and Hitler. Perpetra-tors were threatened with execution, attesting to the impact that humor was having on the occupiers and the occupied. Where German soldiers were becoming demoralized, the Czechs experienced increased social cohesion. The importance of this boost to the Czechs was evident in some responses to the Nazi death threats. One person described took to writing out jokes and burying them in bottles in the back of his garden. There are many other examples of humor sustaining individuals while promoting social cohesion. Elie Cohen (1953) described the use of humor in concentration camps, referring to its power to relieve victims of the seriousness with which all the menaces were regarded. In further discussion of concentration camp behavior, Cohen asserts the need for comradeship among inmates. Lone wolves did not survive; humor was one form of sharing that facilitated comradeship. Finally, Nevo and Levine (1994) presented evidence of an "outburst of humor" during the Gulf War. Citing a great number of jokes that were told during the dangerous days when Israelis were bunkered down to avoid incoming Scud missiles, Nevo and Levine were able to discern a trend among the soldiers to laugh at their plight by alluding to their own history and cultural traditions. The jokes were said to enhance cohesion in the group and foster ridicule of the attackers, similar to how the Czech's denigrated their Nazi occupiers while fostering their own solidarity.

Here, we can see the power of humor to unite people so that they do not feel isolated and forgotten and to reduce the morale of those who are the targets of humor. This power of humor to elicit friendliness from others brings with it the solace that belonging to social groups can offer, the closeness that can sustain people as they face suffering and terror, as in the examples offered by Bettelheim (1943, 1960) and Lifton (1967).

Is there some further benefit that people attain when we avoid the consequences of stress through social support? In the next chapter we will explore what happens to us physiologically when we do suffer the effects of stress.

CHAPTER 10

SENSE OF HUMOR
AND PHYSIOLOGICAL
STRESS RESPONSES

If humor can effectively reduce the magnitude of negative emotional responses that originate with uncontrollable stressful experiences, then its impact may be directly evident in reduced sympathetic nervous system and adrenal activity and, indirectly, in the disinhibition of immune system responsivity. In this chapter we will examine what evidence there is of that connection between humor and stress-related physiological responses.

HUMOR AND AUTONOMIC NERVOUS SYSTEM ACTIVITY

William Fry (1987, 1992), who was among the first to examine the physiological correlates of humor, has described what seem to be the paradoxical effects of laughter upon stress-related physiological processes. Rather than being an immediate antidote to increases in adrenal activation, Fry found that humor, or more specifically, laughter, was associated with signs of arousal. Fry found that laughter resulted in physiological changes including rapid increases in blood pressure, heart rate, and muscular spasms, each of which is commonly associated with anxiety arousal. Other investigators as well have corroborated this link between humor or laughter and sympathetic nervous system activation. Levi (1965) found increases in epinephrine and norepinephrine secretions with exposure to humor and Langevin and Day (1972) found skin conductance and heart rate changes indicating adrenal arousal among

their subjects when they were exposed to humor stimuli. As Fry noted, however, such changes rapidly dissipate with muscle relaxation quickly following
laughter along with decreases in blood pressure and heart rate. In other words,
the physiological changes occurring with laughter bear initial similarity to those
in evidence during stressful circumstances, but their duration is shorter and
the return to a relaxed state is very rapid. Laughter, then, allows one to experience the process described by Berlyne (1969, 1972) wherein pleasure is experienced with what he referred to as an *arousal boost* followed by an *arousal
jag*. Arousal boosts that accompany laughter activate the autonomic nervous
system without incurring untoward health effects because of the rapid dissi-
pation of activity.

Berk *et al.* (1989) studied the effects of humor on neuroendocrine hormones that are involved in classical stress responses. With a rather small sample
(five experimental and five control subjects) Berk et al. had their experimental subjects watch a 60-minute humorous videotape while blood samples were
taken every 10 minutes (three baseline samples, six samples during the presentation, and three during the recovery period). Control group subjects were
provided with an equivalent "quiet time" during which they were exposed to
neutral stimuli. Blood samples were later assayed for corticotropin (ACTH),
cortisol, beta-endorphin, dopac, epinephrine, norepinephrine, growth hormone, and prolactin, all of which usually change during stressful encounters.
Of these eight neuroendocrine hormones, five were found to have notably
decreased among experimental subjects while remaining stable among control subjects. Berk et al. (1989) concluded that mirthful laughter modifies or
attenuates some of the neuroendocrine and hormone levels that are associated with stress.

After failing to find differences in heart rate and blood pressure between
subjects who were in laughter or relaxation conditions, or in a control group
hearing lectures concerning health in one study (White & Camarena, 1989),
White and Winzelberg (1992) compared the effects of similar conditions in a
second study after the subjects had been engaged in a mildly stressful task.
Here, heart rate, skin temperature, and skin conductance were measured at
intervals during a mental arithmetic task and during and following "treatment" (laughter, relaxation, or distraction conditions). Subjects also completed
the CHS and SHRQ measures of humor and measures of state anxiety
(STAI).

The mental arithmetic task resulted in increased heart rates and skin
conductance, and decreased skin temperature and elevated STAI scores for
all subjects, indicating that the task was experienced as stressful for everyone
to some degree. Changes in the physiological effects during and following
"treatment" were inconsistent. The showing of one humorous film (two different comedies were used) resulted in increased skin conductance and the

other humorous film resulted in lower skin temperature, both possibly reflecting the momentary arousal that occurs with laughter as noted earlier. The CHS was consistently negative in its relationship with skin conductance changes following one of the two humorous films. That is, there were significant negative correlations between CHS and changes between the poststressor measurements (which served as prescores or baselines against which the treatment measurements were compared) and each of the three posttreatment measurements of skin conductance. Those scoring high on the CHS were less likely to show changes in skin conductance following one of the humorous treatments. This pattern occurred to a somewhat lesser degree with SHRQ as well.

When these data were examined for males and females separately, the findings improved in clarity. Among males, relationships between CHS and physiological variables (heart rate, skin conductance, and skin temperature) were negligible. Among females, CHS was positively related to ratings of the enjoyment of the humorous films and negatively related to heart rate at both the prestressor and posttreatment time periods. Although sex differences in the effects of humor were not obtained on all physiological measures, this pattern of results differing between the sexes bears similarity to findings that we have obtained in our labs, which will be discussed in some detail in the chapter to follow.

With an all-male sample, Newman and Stone (1996) used a similar procedure to that employed by Martin & Lefcourt (1983) in which subjects were asked to create a humorous monologue to accompany a stressful film. Where Martin and Lefcourt found that those who could create funny monologues were the least likely to report emotional duress after stressful life events, Newman and Stone found corroborating evidence with measures of physiological arousal that are indicative of stress. These investigators found that the act of creating a humorous monologue to accompany an industrial accident film used in lab studies of stress (Lazarus, 1966) had a marked effect on heart rate, skin conductance, and skin temperature. In contrast to subjects who were asked to create a serious monologue to accompany the film, those creating a humorous script evinced lower heart rates and skin conductance levels and higher skin temperatures than their "serious" counterparts. Therefore, active humor creation seemed to have an anxiety-reducing effect during the presentation of the stressful film.

The subjects had earlier completed the SHRQ and CHS measures of humor, and only those scoring one standard deviation above or below the normative means had been selected for further participation. Although the SHRQ was related to most self-report measures of tension, amusement in creating the humorous monologue, and dysphoria in the serious condition in predictable ways, the scale afforded little or no prediction of the physiological responses to this quasi-stressful film. That the film was stressful was evident in the main effects for time periods during the film. Heart rate and skin conductance both increased as the film progressed whereas skin temperature declined, all three returning gradually to baselines several minutes after the film ended.

Although this study failed to show a relationship between SHRQ and the effects of humorous monologue creation, the findings might have borne greater similarity to those in earlier work (Martin & Lefcourt, 1983) had Newman and Stone (1996) recorded and rated the monologues for funniness. In our earlier research, the ability to create humorous monologues during a stressful film presentation was correlated with SHRQ scores. If subjects' monologues had been recorded and rated in this more recent study, it is possible that both the success in creating funny monologues and the physiological indications of lesser distress would have been found to be greater among the high than the low SHRQ subjects. That is, the high SHRQ subjects might have produced funnier monologues than the low SHRQ subjects, and those who produced funnier responses in the humor monologue condition might have exhibited less physiological signs of distress than those creating less funny monologues.

Nevertheless, this investigation reveals something important—that the very instructions to create a humorous monologue to a distressing film eventuate in a lessening of physiological responses indicative of arousal. Whether or not subjects were able to create a funny script, the results suggest that the intention to do so served to alleviate distress.

In some recent work in our own labs (Lefcourt, Davidson, Prkachin, & Mills, 1997) we have found evidence with regard to humor as a stress moderator that may shed some light on the occasional variability of results and conclusions notable in this literature. Subjects in this study were engaged in a series of five tasks that have all been used previously to induce stress (type A interview, favorable impressions task, cold pressor task, mental arithmetic, and the Stroop test).

The type A interview is an irritating 12-minute structured interview to assess "Type A" behaviors (expressions of anger and impatience) during which subjects are interrupted and otherwise annoyed (Chesney, Eagleston, & Rosenman, 1980). The favorable impressions task (Borkovec, Stone, O'Brien, & Kaloupek, 1974) requires subjects to converse with a member of the opposite sex with the goal of creating a favorable impression. Frustration is aroused because the person who is the listener remains completely unresponsive. The cold pressor rask (Hilgard *et al.*, 1974) involves submersing an arm in a circulating bath of ice water, which is painful and distressing. The mental arithmetic task (Rose, Grim, & Miller, 1984) entails serial subtractions in one's head, without the aid of paper or calculators (e.g., 13 from 7683, 13 from 7670, etc.). This task is difficult, guaranteeing failure and often embarassment. The *Stroop Color-Word Test* (Jensen & Rohwer, 1966) causes "cognitive interference" when subjects have to name colors that are written in inks of conflicting colors (e.g., the word *red* written in blue). This readily causes subjects to become "tongue-tied," halting, and error-prone.

During each of these procedures subjects' blood pressure was measured at regular intervals by remote monitors. As anticipated, their systolic blood pressures increased above resting levels, reaching a peak toward the end of each task, and then receded toward resting levels after five minutes had elapsed. When each of the humor variables, which had been assessed during a previous session, was then examined opposite blood pressure scores, a similar pattern was found during the performance of each task.

Women who scored high on the CHS measure of humor invariably displayed lower mean blood pressures than women who scored low on the CHS, and lower than most male subjects regardless of their CHS scores. However, among males, those who scored high on the CHS exhibited higher mean systolic blood pressures than those who scored low on the CHS, and this obtained throughout the testing sessions, even when subjects were at rest. On the other hand, though the results were not as consistent as they were with the CHS, males who scored high on the SHRQ often manifested lower systolic blood pressures than did those who had scored low on the SHRQ. With regard to the scores of females on the SHRQ, there was some similarity to the pattern found with males. However, their pattern was rarely as strong. The SHRQ seemed particularly predictive of male blood pressures whereas the CHS seemed more predictive of female blood pressures. In addition, when the CHS was used with males the results were the opposite of those found with females: high coping-humor males evinced higher systolic blood pressures than low scorers throughout the stressful tasks. The consistency across tasks is evident in Figure 10-1.

These contrasting findings suggest that some of the variations in results that have been reported in the study of humor as a stress moderator may be attributable to the mistaken aggregation of data from males and females. Although sex of subjects often has been reported in the humor and stress moderator literature, it has not often been included as a predictor variable, usually being deleted from analyses after investigators found minimal differences in mean humor scores between males and females. In attempting to explain the sex differences we have found, we have reexamined some of our own previous research findings and consulted the literature concerning humor and sex. These new findings will be reported in the following chapter.

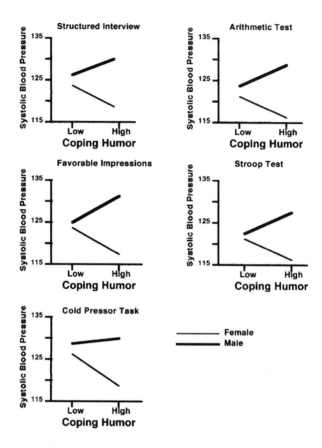

FIGURE 10-1. CHS scores are negatively related to systolic blood pressure among women, but positively related among men. Adapted from Lefcourt *et al.* (1997a).

HUMOR AND IMMUNE SYSTEM ACTIVITY

As noted in Chapter 7, immune system activity is inhibited when the organism sustains adrenergic stimulation over time. Chronic or prolonged stress can result in the inhibition of immune system activity, leaving the organism vulnerable to illnesses that, under more normal circumstances, it would more likely resist.

That immune system activity is diminished among humans with the occurrence of stressors is well-documented. In the literature concerning affect and immune system activity, several researchers have reported finding that stressful events and the associated negative affect commonly result in immunosuppression (Andersen, Kiecolt-Glaser, & Glaser, 1994; McClelland, Alexander, & Marks, 1982; Kiecolt-Glaser et al., 1987; Kiecolt-Glaser et al., 1998; O'Leary, 1990; Pennebaker, Kiecolt-Glaser, & Glaser, 1988; Vollhardt, 1991).

If stress and negative affect can result in immunosuppression, Dillon, Minchoff, & Baker (1985) hypothesized that humor, a positive emotional state, may be a natural "antidote" to immunosuppression or a potential immune system enhancer. Although humor had not been directly examined as a moderator of the stress–immunosuppression relationship in earlier research, the research by Dillon et al. has led to a spate of studies in which humor or positive affect has been found to be associated with enhanced immune system functioning.

Because of the simplicity and the economy of its collection, most of these studies have made use of salivary immunoglobulin A (S-IgA) as the measure of immune system activity. S-IgA is reputed to be the body's first line of defense against upper respiratory viral and bacterial infection (Tomasi, 1976; Goldblum, 1990). Looking specifically at humor as a potential enhancer of immune system functioning began with research by Dillon and her colleagues (Dillon et al., 1985) using a small sample of 10 subjects. Dillon et al. found that laughter induced by a humorous videotape led to a significant increase in concentrations of salivary immunoglobulin A (S-IgA). In addition, these investigators had their subjects complete the CHS and found that the CHS and S-IgA concentrations were positively correlated with an average $r = .75$, ($p < .02$) across four measurements of S-IgA. Such high magnitude relationships between biochemical changes and a paper-and-pencil measure, albeit with a very small sample, could not be ignored.

Dillon and Totten (1989) proceeded to replicate and expand upon these findings. From a small sample of 17 mothers who were breast-feeding their infants, these investigators found significant positive relationships between CHS and S-IgA ($r = .61$) and negative relationships between CHS and upper respiratory infections (URI, $r = -.58$). In addition, mothers' CHS scores were negatively related to their infants' URI incidence ($r = -.58$). When mothers' immunoglobulin A concentrations were assayed from breast milk, as opposed to saliva, however, it not only proved to be unrelated to salivary immunoglobulin A (S-IgA) but also to URI and CHS.

Other investigators have taken up the challenge of replicating these compelling findings. Martin and Dobbin (1988) found that the relationship between the daily hassles measure of stress (Kanner, Coyne, Schaeffer, & Lazarus, 1981) and changes in S-IgA concentrations obtained a month and a half later were moderated by scores on the CHS, SHRQ, and Svebak's (1974) SHQ (specifically the metamessage sensitivity subscale) measures of humor. In the analysis of each interaction, they found that low-humor subjects exhibited the greatest decline in S-IgA concentrations from baseline levels after they had experienced a significant number of stressful hassles. High-humor subjects, on the other hand, showed minimal change in S-IgA levels as a function of daily hassles. That there was a month-and-a-half delay between the measurements of hassles and S-IgA makes these findings both challenging and puzzling. By their very nature one might expect hassles to be short-term stressors that would not have long-lasting effects. However, in the stress literature evidence has been found to show that the effects of major stressors on distress are often mediated by minor stressors or hassles (Wagner, Compas, & Howell, 1988; Pillow, Zautra, & Sandler, 1996). Consequently, it is possible that subjects who reported a greater number of hassles had also earlier undergone serious life changes that had left them feeling irritable and thus more easily subject to daily annoyances. Conceivably, it is these major events that were ultimately responsible for the observed immune system changes.

Further linkage between humor and immune system functioning was established by Lefcourt, Davidson, and Kueneman (1990), who found that the presentation of humorous material resulted in increased concentrations of S-IgA. This investigation consisted of three separate studies in which the humor stimuli, the methods for deriving S-IgA assays, and the sex of the samples varied. The findings from these three studies are illustrated in Figure 10-2. When the humorous material was almost universally rated as being highly funny by our subjects ("Bill Cosby Live"), S-IgA concentrations of most subjects increased substantially. However, when the humorous material (Mel Brook's and Carl Reiner's 2000-year old man) was not universally appreciated, producing considerable variability in funniness ratings, large increases of S-IgA concentrations were found primarily among those who scored high on the CHS measure of humor in one all-female sample. In another sample, however, which contained an equal number of males and females, this interaction was not found, although the SHRQ produced a borderline interaction. Those who scored high on that measure were more likely to exhibit elevated S-IgA levels. These differences in results for samples differing in sex distribution may not have been chance variations, a point to which we will return in the next chapter. What this study demonstrated was that, despite complications, humorous stimuli and subjects' characteristic sense of humor do have positive implications for immune system functioning.

These findings have been replicated to some degree by McClelland and Cheriff (1997). In their three studies which, like our own, varied the humorous stimuli and used two different methods for assaying S-IgA, increases in concentrations of S-IgA were found following the presentation of the humorous material. In addition, when humor appreciation was assessed by a shortened version of the SHQ (Svebak, 1974), those who scored high were found to show greater increases in S-IgA concentrations and a lesser frequency and

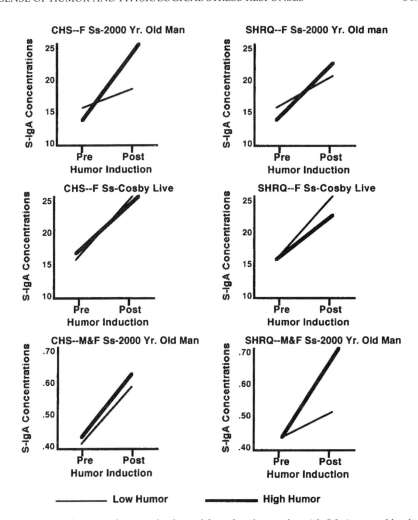

FIGURE 10-2. The upper four graphs derived from female samples with S-IgA assayed by the radial immunodiffusion method (RID). The lower two graphs reflect S-IgA data drawn from a sample balanced for sex. Assays were made by the enzyme-linked immunosorbent method (ELISA). Humor conditions always resulted in increased S-IgA concentrations. Adapted from Lefcourt et al. (1990).

magnitude of colds in the ensuing months. A measure of humor production, derived from the SHQ, and the CHS produced less definitive results especially with regard to the development and severity of colds.

Berk and his colleagues (Berk et al., 1988; 1989) have reported that mirthful laugher elicited during a humorous film was associated with increased spontaneous lymphocyte blastogenesis and natural killer-cell activity. This study is singular in not being restricted to the assessment of salivary immuno-globulin A concentrations as the marker of immune system activity.

Finally, in studies focusing on immune system activity and mood states, S-IgA has been found to increase with positive mood states (Stone, Cox, Valdimarsdottir, Jandorf, & Neale, 1987) and with listening to pleasant music (Rider *et al.*, 1990).

In each of these studies humor, along with other positive emotional states, has been found to be associated with enhanced immune system functioning. Since immunosuppression commonly occurs in stressful circumstances when negative affect is elicited and adrenal secretions are prolonged, these findings suggest that humor may serve to reduce negative affect or increase positive affect, which, in turn, disinhibits potential immune system activity.

CONCLUSIONS

Although it may be premature to draw conclusions from the work de-scribed here, because it is at such an early stage of development, the results obtained thus far are compelling. Their relative consistency in showing that humor is associated with a reduction of the known effects of stress should provide encouragement to future researchers interested in the connections between humor and health.

In studies concerned with autonomic nervous system activation and im-munosuppression, there is evidence that males and females differ with re-gard to the effects of humor. Females who assert that they use humor to ame-liorate stressful conditions seem to draw benefits from that predilection, showing fewer signs of physiological arousal and distress in those conditions than their less humor-prone peers. However, among males this finding is less clear, and if anything seems to be the reverse, with humor-prone males seem-ing to be more distressed than their less humor-using peers. In the next chap-ter I will explore this apparent sex difference, hoping to uncover the different meanings that humor may have for males and females and the ramifications for the ways in which they cope with stressful circumstances.

SEX AND HUMOR: INTERACTIVE PREDICTORS OF HEALTH?

For as long as we have been conducting research with regard to humor we have often been at least mildly confused when we have found higher-level interactions between humor and gender in the prediction of varied criteria. Upon finding that the CHS consistently predicted females' physiological responses to stressful tasks better than it did for males, we felt compelled to reexamine the findings in some of our earlier research. In doing so, we discovered other seemingly enigmatic data suggesting that humor had different implications for males and females.

In one study (Miller, Lefcourt, Holmes, Ware, & Saleh, 1986) in which we observed interactions between spouses (N = 88) as they role-played conflict situations common to many marriages (Gottman, 1979), we came across a number of striking differences between husbands' and wives' use of humor, assessed by paper-and-pencil measures of humor and live observations. Among wives, the CHS was positively associated with self-reported marital satisfaction (r = .20, p < .06) and happiness (r = .22, p < .05). Although these are not high magnitude relationships, they contrasted markedly with the equivalent correlations from among their husbands (rs = –.15 and .04, respectively). These differences could easily have been dismissed were it not for the additional data. Similar differences were found among the subjects' observed and rated behaviors in their acting out of conflicts involved in the role-playing exercises. Each couple had been observed as they went about solving conflicts about "mandatory" visits with the husbands' families at holiday time, budgetary problems resulting from impulsive purchases, and communications problems when one partner wanted to talk and the other did not feel ready to listen.

In each role enactment, spouses were rated for the degree to which they actively listened to each other and participated in resolving their conflicts. The resulting dimension ranged from "engagement" to "avoidance"; the former indicating high involvement with evidence of active listening to the partner while the latter indicated attempts to withdraw, not listen, or avoid eye contact with spouses.

Among wives, the CHS proved to be positively related to engagement (r = .26, p < .02), but it was of no pertinence to the husbands' engagement behavior (r = .02). However, when spouses' behaviors were rated for destructiveness, defined as the sum of negative affect and hostility displayed during the enactments, female behavior was unpredictable (r = .03), whereas husbands' behavior tended to be positively associated with CHS scores (r = .21, p < .06). That is, destructiveness during interactions with their wives was positively associated with coping humor scores of husbands. In turn, destructiveness was negatively associated with both spouses' ratings of their own marital satisfaction (r = −.35, p < .001).

When we examined the frequency and duration of laughter during role enactments, both measures were found to be negatively related to destructiveness (r = −.30, p < .01; r = −.23, p < .05, respectively) among husbands but not among wives (rs = −.06, −.01). Interestingly enough, these displays of laughter were unrelated to CHS scores for all spouses, indicating that laughter and self-reported use of humor measured by the CHS were independent. Among husbands, however, laughter seemed to counterindicate destructiveness whereas self-reported use of humor suggested a tendency toward destructiveness. Although most of these relationships are not of a high magnitude, their consistency suggests that humor has different implications for males and females and that further attention is warranted. The following are a sample of findings from our own and others' investigations that support our suspicions that humor may have different meaning and implications for men and women.

In one recent investigation into the joint effects of stressful life events and interpersonal behaviors on depression and marital stability among newlyweds, humor, anger, and sadness were found to have some paradoxical effects on spouses. Cohan and Bradbury (1997) examined the effects of negative life events and marital communication on changes in depressive symptoms and marital adjustment over an 18-month period. Spouses interacted in problem-solving tasks similar to those that we had used in our research, and their behaviors were coded as verbal content (labeled as positive and negative behaviors) and expressions of affect (anger, sadness, and humor). Verbal expressions, categorized as positive or negative, and affective expressions were related to one another in a coherent fashion, humor being negatively related to anger ($r = -.73$, $p < .001$) and negative behavior ($r = -.23$, $p < .05$) among males. Among females as well humor was negatively related to anger ($r = -.75$, $p < .001$) and negative behavior ($r = -.40$, $p < .01$). In addition, among wives humor was negatively related to expressions of sadness ($r = -.31$, $p < .01$) and positively associated with marital satisfaction ($r = .26$, $p < .05$). Beyond these anticipated relationships, however, there were major divergences between men and women.

Women who revealed anger during laboratory problem-solving interactions with their husbands seemed to fare better with regard to avoiding depression and enjoying marital satisfaction if they were to experience major life stresses in the ensuing 18 months. That is, if stressed in the interim between visits to the lab, those women who had expressed anger in laboratory interactions with their husbands before the occurrence of stressful events, exhibited less depressiveness and marital dissatisfaction following stressful experiences than did those who did not display anger as readily in their lab interactions. As an interesting contrast, husbands whose wives had expressed anger were more likely to manifest increases in depresssive symptoms following stressful interpersonal events over the 18-month period, though their marital satisfaction seemed to have been unaffected.

On examining the impact of humor, the investigators found that depression and marital satisfaction were less affected than was marital stability. That is, if husbands exhibited humor during the problem-solving interactions with their wives and then went on to experience major stresses during the following 18-months, there was greater likelihood that their marriages dissolved or went into "limbo" during that ensuing time period. This finding appeared regardless of whether it was the husband or the wife who had undergone stressful experiences in that 18-month interim between lab sessions.

Cohan and Bradbury concluded that the wife's anger had proven to be beneficial with regard to personal and marital adjustment in the context of stressful events, but that couples were at risk for divorce following stressful experiences if husbands had readily expressed humor in the problem-solving task.

To make sense of these findings, the authors suggest that the wife's expression of anger, even if it can eventuate in the husband's becoming depressed, may serve to promote constructive problem solving, relieve marital strains, and be associated with a greater sense of efficacy in marriage. On the other hand, the husband's humor may reflect "disengagement from marital problem solving" and an avoidance of problem confrontation. Given that the subjects were newlyweds, humor may have also indicated discomfort or disaffection between the spouses at a time when they were in the process of becoming more familiar with each other. Husbands' laughter may have been more directed *at* their wives' rather than *with* them. Unfortunately, the authors do not provide examples of when and how humor occurred. If laughter followed upon serious problem-solving attempts by the wife, it may have been more a sign of condescension and disdain on the part of the husband than a show of sympathy, a situation that would bode ill for marital stability.

For whatever reasons, humor proved to be a mixed blessing in this study. For both spouses humor appeared to be the opposite of characteristics such as anger and negative behavior. However, the husband's humor held ill portents for marital stability under stressful conditions, whereas the wife's anger was associated with positive outcomes for herself.

It may seem puzzling to some that marital satisfaction and marital stability were not associated in the same ways with humor expression. The relationship between these variables, however, may be powerfully affected by the desire of couples to maintain the positive impressions others may have of their marriages. It may be too difficult for young couples in particular to admit to marital dissatisfaction early in their marriages. Feelings of inadequacy and self-recriminations may be so hard to accept that spouses may be unable to admit negative feelings to themselves, let alone to a psychological investigator.

In one other study focusing on marital interaction, Gottman and Krokoff (1989) found that positive verbal expressions, which included humor, made during marital problem-solving tasks similar to those noted in the previous example, were positively related to marital satisfaction, especially for wives. The wives' positive verbal expressions were significantly related to their own marital satisfaction ($r = .51$, $p < .01$) and to that of their husbands ($r = .58$ $p < .01$). Although in the same direction, the husbands' positive verbal expressions failed to reach significance in the relationship with marital satisfaction ($rs = .33$ and $.27$ for themselves and their wives, respectively). In interesting contrast, positive nonverbal expressions, which included smiles and laughter, were primarily related to their exhibitors' marital satisfaction. That is, husbands' positive nonverbal expressions were related significantly to their own marital satisfaction ($r = .27$, $p < .05$) but less so to their wives' ($r = .18$); wives' positive nonverbal expressions were also more predictive of their own marital satisfaction ($r = .27$) than of their spouses ($r = .17$).

In addition, husbands' positive verbal expressions in the laboratory problem-solving task afforded prediction of their own negative expressions in a recorded interaction in their homes ($r = -.50$, $p < .01$) though they failed to have a consistent effect on their wives' negativity ($r = -.01$). On the other hand, the wives' positive verbal expressions were related at borderline significance to both their own ($r = -.25$) and their husbands' negativity ($r = -.23$) in the home interaction. Similar patterns were obtained with nonverbal expressions, husbands' positivity being negatively related to their own negativity during the home interaction ($r = -.39$, $p < .05$) but not their wives' ($r = -.00$). Similarly, the wives' nonverbal positivity predicted their own negativity at the home task ($r = -.26$) but not their husbands' ($r = .07$).

Some of these results in the Cohan and Bradbury (1997) and in Gottman and Krokoff (1989) investigations bear similarity to those in our research. A husband's manifestation of humor may often be associated with destructive behavior in his interaction with his wife. However, humor displayed by wives seems to have a fairly consistent positive impact on their own and their spouses' marital satisfaction, more so than does humor displayed by husbands. That the effects of humor can differ when the emitter and the recipient is male or female underlines an issue that we will look at in some detail: It is possible that there may be different kinds of humor that express different intentions, and males may more often indulge in the kinds of humor that can prove to be destructive to the maintenance of relationships.

Before we began to search through the psychological literature for further evidence and possible explanations of sex differences in the meaning and use of humor, we returned to some of our own earliest investigations, when we were trying to establish the reliability and validity of our measures of humor. In some of these original validity studies (Martin & Lefcourt, 1983, 1984) we had occasionally found sex differences that we chose to ignore or at least failed to emphasize in subsequent research. This was due to the fact that the differences were rarely of a high magnitude, and also because we could not make much sense of them at the time.

For example, we had found the SHRQ to be somewhat more strongly related to laughter frequency and duration among males ($rs = .52, p < .05; .62, p < .001$) than among females ($rs = .39, p < .05; .40, p < .05$) while our subjects were telling us their "life stories." We had also asked our subjects to provide the names of close friends who could be queried about the subjects' characteristic behaviors. Among the ratings obtained by telephone from the friends, we asked how often the subjects were likely to laugh in a wide variety of situations. These ratings were then correlated with subjects' SHRQ scores. The correlations were found to be significant for males ($r = .40, p < .05$) and negligible among females ($r = .15$). In addition, when we compared the friends' ratings to the laughter we observed in the laboratory, the relationships were in the same direction but were only significant for males ($r = .50, p < .05$) and not for females ($r = .31$).

In a second study with a larger sample of subjects, the differences in predictability between males and females were most stark when the subjects' friends were asked how likely the subject would be to find humor in problematic situations. In this case, males' scores on the SHRQ were highly related to friends' ratings ($r = .56, p < .001$) whereas females' scores were not ($r = .11$). On the other hand, CHS scores predicted friends' ratings of females' ($r = .48, p < .01$) as well as males' ($r = .52, p < .01$) humor responses during difficult circumstances. And when we asked the subjects' friends whether the subject was apt to take himself or herself too seriously, the CHS was highly related to friends' ratings for both sexes but more so for females ($r = -.78$, $p < .001$) than for males ($r = -.58$, $p < .001$). A similar pattern was obtained between the SHRQ and seriousness, though males ($r = -.39$, $p < .05$) and females ($r = -.48$, $p < .01$) did not differ as strongly as they did with the CHS. It would seem that females were more predictable in their humor-related behavior from the CHS than they were from the SHRQ. One final observation of note in our second validity study concerns the relationship between humor and self-esteem. Among females, both SHRQ and the CHS were related to a measure of self-esteem ($rs =.$ 40, $p < .05$; .49, $p < .01$), whereas for males the equivalent relationships were insignificant ($rs = .23$ and .15, respectively).

In one other of our original validity studies, when we examined witty comments made by subjects as they attempted to create funny stories about a table full of props, females proved to be less predictable than males. Correlations between the SHRQ and witty comments were significant for males ($r = .33$, $p < .05$) but not for females ($r = .06$).

Other researchers who have included sex as a variable in their analyses have found variations between the sexes similar to ours, suggesting that the meaning of humor may differ for males and females. In two studies (Labott & Martin, 1987; Overholser, 1992) the interactions between CHS and sex revealed differences demanding further attention. Labott and Martin (1987) began their investigations with an interest in the way in which people who are more likely to weep during stressful situations might differ from those less likely to weep. In their first study, they found that people who are more likely to weep exhibited stronger relationships between stressful events and mood disturbances than did those less likely to be weepers. In a second study, they included the CHS measure of humor to ascertain whether humor might provide some moderation of the stress–mood disturbance relationship among weepers. Interestingly enough, among all subjects characterizable as nonweepers, those who were less likely to use humor as a coping strategy manifested stronger relationships between stress and mood disturbances. However, when examining the equivalent relationships among weepers, there was an interaction between sex and the CHS. Where the CHS moderated the effects of stress on mood disturbance for weeper females in the same way as it did for nonweeper females, among males only those who were non-weepers exhibited the moderating effect of humor. For males who were likely to weep during distressing circumstances, the CHS proved to have little positive value. Conceivably, weeping among males may be more pathogenic than it is among females, and it may have more implications for depressiveness regardless of propensities toward humor. If female weeping is less sex-role incompatible than male weeping, it is possible that humor may be "too little, too late" to be protective for males whose tendency to weep may have more serious implications, such as indicating greater vulnerability to the effects of stressful circumstances than humor can ameliorate.

Overholser (1992) likewise has found CHS and sex interactions in the prediction of affect measures, though his results were not uniform and were often perplexing. For example, the CHS allowed for the prediction of depression among females, though in the opposite direction from what had been predicted. That is, females who scored high on the CHS exhibited a strong relationship between stressful events and depression ($r = .55$), whereas those who had scored low on the CHS evinced a zero order relationship between stress and depression ($r = .03$). Among males there were no such interactions between humor and stress in the prediction of affective responses, though humor was directly related to loneliness; that is, the higher the humor score, the less loneliness. In addition, humor was positively related to self-esteem among both males and females.

Although it seems that scores on measures like the CHS have different meaning for males and females, explanations for those differences are not readily apparent in the data that have been reported by experimenters thus far. In fact, perusal of the differences and the directions of the obtained relationships that have been found are mind-boggling and could be simply attributed to sample differences, measurement errors, and the like. However, there is enough consistency in the data we have scrutinized to at least suggest that the CHS may have more relevance for the prediction of females' behavior, whereas the SHRQ seems to afford more prediction of behavior manifested by males. At this point, we will turn our attention to psychological literature that may help us to interpret some of the differences in humor use between males and females.

POSSIBLE SOURCES OF SEX DIFFERENCES IN HUMOR USAGE

In the greater literature on humor there have been some contributions that may illuminate a number of the sex diffences that we have been discussing. In his longitudinal study of Harvard men entitled *Adaptation to Life* (1997), when Vaillant described humor as a "mature defense mechanism" he differentiated between "self-deprecating" humor and wit or tendentious humor. The former was described as adaptive, allowing us to laugh at ourselves while undergoing stress, which in turn would lessen the impact of that stressful event. Wit or hostile humor, on the other hand, was thought to be an aggressive means for controlling others and therefore less likely to afford relief when a person is on the receiving end of stressful experiences. There is no acceptance of the inevitable, no relief from taking oneself too seriously in humor that is characterized by competition and aggression. Only in self-directed humor in which people laugh at their own disappointments and failings was relief to be expected.

In the literature on humor differences of males and females there is a strong suggestion that women are more likely to engage in and appreciate self-deprecating humor, whereas males seem more apt to manifest wit and appreciation of jokes. For example, in content analyses of the routines of stand-up comedians, Levine (1976) found that the females' object of derision was most often themselves (64% of all jokes), whereas among males self-deprecation occurred least often (7% of jokes). For jokes where the objects of derision were other persons of the same sex, male comedians exhibited a much higher frequency (26% of jokes) than females (6% of jokes). In contrast to assertions that joking is more often directed at the opposite sex, Levine found little difference in the frequency of such joking for females (3%) and males (9%).

In an examination of humor preferences and practices, Crawford and Gressley (1991) asked subjects how likely they were to engage in different kinds of humor. Whereas males were most apt to enjoy hostile humor (e.g., jokes making fun of racial groups), to tell jokes, and to appreciate slapstick humor, females were found most likely to engage in what the authors refer to as *anecdotal humor*—telling funny stories about things that happened to themselves and their acquaintances. In essence, the humor of the males, characteristically, is directed at others, whereas the females humor more often focuses upon herself.

In a study of "put-down humor," Zillmann and Stocking (1976) had subjects listen to taped renditions of an original disparaging humorous routine. Subjects were asked to provide their reactions to the disparager and his humor. When the narrator was a male college student disparaging either himself, a friend, or an enemy, males found the disparagement of the enemy to be the funniest and the disparagement of self to be the least funny. Females showed the reverse preference, enjoying self-disparaging humor over humor that consists of disparagement of an enemy. As an interesting point, neither males nor females found the disparagement of a friend to be funny. In a second study the taped narration was performed by a female college student. Female subjects again enjoyed the self-disparaging version most highly whereas males found it to be the least funny. In both studies, then, females were found to prefer self-disparaging humor whether of a male or female. Males, on the other hand, displayed a relative dislike of such humor, and seemed to dislike it particularly when it was engaged in by females. However, it should also be noted that males commonly seem to enjoy females' disparagement of other females.

In a recent study by Janes and Olson (2000) disparaging humor was found to be intimidating to both males and females. Their subjects were asked to complete a number of tasks in which conformity, fear of failure, creativity, and vulnerability to rejection were assessed after they had watched a video-taped presentation in which a person engaged in self-directed or other-directed ridiculing humor. A third group that was not subjected to a humorous presentation served as a control group. With the exception of the creativity task, subjects were found to exhibit negative effects from the ridiculing humor. If subjects observed the ridiculing comic, they became more conforming, fearful, and sensitive to rejection than those who had observed self-disparaging humor by the comic. No differences were found between subjects in the self-directed humor and those in the nonhumor control group. Self-disparagement humor evidently does not have the dampening effects on the well-being of observers that humor that ridicules others does. Conceivably, the comic who uses others as targets for his or her humorous jibes will be less well accepted and liked by observers because of the observers' fear of becoming a subsequent target for the ridiculing comic. Disparaging humor may therefore result in social isolation of the comic even if the expression of dislike for his ridiculing behavior is not made obvious by "fearful" observers. On the other hand, self-disparaging comics, who are more often female, may continue to enjoy the pleasure of social engagement because their humor does not arouse fear or rejection among observers.

If self-disparagement humor comprises what Vaillant (1977) termed a mature defense mechanism with beneficial properties, then it would seem that females are more apt to be the possessors of this mature strategy with its attendant benefits. If when females respond to the questions in the CHS they are alluding to their use of self-directed humor, then our positive findings for high CHS females in our study of systolic blood pressure responses during stressful tasks (Lefcourt et al., 1997a) may become explainable.

If elevated CHS scores reflected womens' tendency to laugh at themselves as they fumbled through our stressful tasks, they may have been better able to accept their failures, inabilities, and frustrations more easily than men. Conceivably, female subjects with a propensity to use humor as a coping strategy, may have begun to think of the experiment as something to share and laugh at with their friends, anticipating social support in the process. If males, on the other hand, mean that they engage in wit and joking that is derisive toward others when they score highly on the CHS, then we might not expect to find the surcease of distress, indicated by lowered systolic blood pressure that was found among women. That is, humor associated with competition and attempts at control should be less helpful for minimizing distress when one is engaged in circumstances where wit or other-directed humor will not gain one social support or provoke laughter from others.

That we found the same pattern of results between sex and CHS scores in each of the five stress tasks that had been administered (Lefcourt et al.,

1997a) indicates its importance for studies that purport to examine the role of humor as a stress-moderating variable. The results with the SHRQ were less clear, though it would seem that this variable was more closely related to levels of SBP among males. That is, males scoring high on the SHRQ are apt to manifest lower blood pressure than those who scored low on this measure, which stands in marked contrast to relationships found with CHS scores among males. Because the SHRQ measures the likelihood that one would respond with amusement rather than create humor (as is the case with the CHS) in potentially irritating situations, it may be particularly germane to males, for whom anger and aggression may be more common responses to irritations than they are for females. Dixon (1980) has suggested that humor may have evolved as an alternative to anger, allowing humans to live with each other without engaging in continuous battle. Finding amusement in irritating circumstances may be an important form of humor for males who are apt to become emotionally aroused when irritated. On the other hand, the use of humor as a coping device may have evolved among females as an effective tool to help reduce the anger of their physically stronger male partners and therefore to increase their own safety. Each form of humor, then, may reflect mechanisms designed to deal with each sex's own "adaptive challenges" (Buss, 1995).

Finally, Rim (1988) and Thorson and Powell (1996) have each found age to be negatively related to humor scores on the CHS and SHRQ for males but positively associated with humor among females. Although these data were cross-sectional, it would seem possible that as men age they become less likely to display and use humor whereas for women the reverse may be true. Whether this is due to transformations that are concomitant with hormonal developments or to role and status changes, it is evident that humor involves different properties and functions for males and females which may shift and change throughout the life span.

CONCLUSION

Much of the evidence presented in this chapter is based on low-magnitude but somewhat consistent and statistically significant findings. Some of the studies offer contradictory data and many not discussed in this chapter offer no support for assumed sex differences in the use and effects of humor. In a recent review of this literature, Martin Lampert and Susan Ervin-Tripp (1998) offer some illuminating evidence that may help to reduce some of the confusion and uncertainties that abound in the literature on humor and gender. After reviewing findings derived from the use of self-report measures and ratings by acquaintances and observers, the authors turned their attention to evidence deriving from observations of interactions between persons in lab and field situations.

In reviewing earlier research, Lampert and Ervin-Tripp reported findings that seem contradictory to many of the studies noted in this chapter. For example, the authors cite a study by Bryant, Comisky, and Zillman (1979), in which the lectures given by faculty at their university were recorded and content-analyzed for, among other things, the use and direction of humor. Contrary to expectation, male instructors were more likely to use themselves as the objects of their jokes and humorous stories whereas female instructors were more likely to engage in the disparagement of others in their joking. Another surprise was that the female instructors were also more apt to make sexual jokes than were males.

To make sense of these findings, Lampert and Ervin-Tripp conjecture that female instructors in the late 1970s may have had a greater concern than their male counterparts with maintaining their position with their students in the classroom and therefore avoided any signs of vulnerability that could arise with self-deprecating humor. They carefully note that this behavior may be confined to the situation in which it was observed and might not serve as an indication of humor behavior to be observed in other situations.

Likewise, after discussing the findings by Levine (1976) on self-directed humor among male and female comedians, Lampert and Ervin-Tripp note that with the changing roles of women in the last two decades, audiences have shifted in what they have come to expect from comedians. In consequence, Fraiberg (1994) and Sheppard (1985) have contended, female comedians have become more successful in using humor that lampoons others, which is evident in their satirizing of political figures and the social roles of men and women. Quite possibly, then, the earlier differences between males and females may have reflected the demands of social situations more than humorous styles or personality characteristics.

On the other hand, the authors describe a study by Foot, Chapman, and Smith (1977), who found that boys laughed more while watching a cartoon after they engaged in an "intimate" interaction: drawing portraits of each other while sitting face-to-face. In direct opposition, girls laughed more while watching a cartoon if they had been separated from one another, coloring pictures in separate cubicles. These findings led Lampert and Ervin-Tripp to conjecture that for boys laughter serves to reduce arousal whereas for girls it helps to reestablish intimacy.

In these lab observations, then, there is some mixed evidence in support of observed differences between males and females, though the differences may have been at odds with results in previous studies and attributable to perceived acceptability and transitory demands rather than characteristic traits.

At this point, we may wonder whether there might be some facile way to deal with these further enigmatic findings.

In turning to field observations, Lampert and Ervin-Tripp do manage to make some sense of these seeming complexities and paradoxes. With the assumption that humor expression should match conversational style, Lampert and Ervin-Tripp hypothesized that men's humor is more apt to be competitive and focused on self-enhancement. Womens' humor, on the other hand, is more apt to be supportive and concerned with the sharing of experiences. Men could therefore be expected to engage in joke-telling and comedic routines that denigrate others. Women, in contrast, "should be more likely to share funny and personal stories, intended to establish closeness between the themselves and their listeners" (p. 262).

In an early test of their hypotheses, Lampert and Ervin-Tripp addressed the question of whether these hypothesized differences may have faded with the changing roles of women in the last few decades. The authors had made use of the University of California at Berkeley's Cognitive Science Database of Natural Language, where conversations between same sex, opposite sex, and mixed group members have been preserved.

In their sample of European-American conversants, they found that women were more likely to joke, tease, or tell funny stories in mixed groups than were men, though this was not the case for Latino and Asian men and women. European-American men and women were both highly jocular and near-equals. When interactions were coded for the direction of humor targeting, they found a further surprise: in mixed company, European-American women were the most likely to joke about persons not in their own groups, and European-American men produced the greatest number of self-directed humorous remarks.

These results would seem at odds with those of previous investigations noted earlier in this chapter. However, when conversations between same-sex individuals were analyzed, women were found to engage in more self-directed humor than men. It seemed that men were more likely to make self-directed humorous remarks in mixed groups than they were in all-male groups. In the latter circumstance, median frequencies of self-directed humor approached zero. To risk looking foolish in an all-male group may have seemed too high a price to pay for males who feel vulnerable while attempting to protect their position in a status hierarchy. In mixed company, on the other hand, the authors conjecture that men may joke about their own behavior to "offset possible criticism from women for being too egotistical, crude, or cocky" (p. 266). Further evidence of feminine proclivities in humor derived from a larger sample in which the authors found that self-directed humor emerged among women primarily in same-sex interactions "as part of a self-disclosing narrative." Another way of discussing these results is to conclude that self-directed humor occurs primarily when either men or women interact with women. The absence of women in social groups may preclude self-deprecating humor, which would leave a would-be joker vulnerable to confirming put-downs by other men. Women could be said to be more charitable in such circumstances, being more ready to commiserate rather than engage in competitive jousting.

These findings, then, bring us back to the discussion at the end of the previous chapter. Although there are commonalities between men and women in their tendencies to be funny, and in their types of joking on given occasions, humor can be said to have more positive effects for women than for men as they encounter stressful situations. The greater tendency of women to use self-deprecating humor when speaking with other women may serve to make them feel closer to one another. Such closeness and social support, as noted in Chapter 9, may effectively serve as a defense against stress. Although men can engage in this kind of humor, they are less apt to do so when with other men. Whether they would obtain sympathetic responses if they were to do so is the point at issue. Perhaps men are less able to secure support from other men by use of self-deprecating humor and by other means as well. The well-known findings that men suffer more prolonged distress than women after being widowed or separated from their spouses may be attributable to the role that social support and sympathy, which are more often displayed by women, play in helping to protect us from the stresses of daily life.

SUMMING UP

For readers who believed that there is a voluminous literature about humor in psychology I hope that I have been able to show that the subject matter is more in its early stages than at maturity. There is much to be added and more to be challenged than in many areas of study. Although humor and laughter have provoked the interest of philosophers and biologists for a long time, empirical research, especially by psychologists, is not lengthy and potential examiners of the phenomena can apprise themselves of research in the area in relatively short order.

As I noted in the opening chapter of this book, psychology has not engaged in the study of positive human assets for very long. The economics of research funding have always favored work directed at the solution of immediate and pressing problems. This is understandable, even admirable. Until the evidence is presented that a phenomenon is linked in some vital way to a pressing problem, it will most likely be ignored. Humor and laughter are such phenomena.

Even if recent evidence revealing the health relevance of humor had not become generally available to the public, the popularity of humor in the mass media would eventually have provoked curiosity. Why, people were bound to ask, are comedians paid so much to entertain us? Why are comic films so popular?

In our earlier book on humor research (Lefcourt & Martin, 1986), I alluded to the novel *Zorba the Greek* (Kazantzakis, 1953). At the end of the story, Zorba, a buoyant and earthy native of Greece, cajoles his depressed and guilt-ridden "boss" into simply accepting his sad experiences and not prolonging his feelings of failed responsibility. This is not easy for the young poetic intellectual, because his behavior in a little village on a Greek island has led inexorably to death and mayhem. But Zorba teaches him to dance and indulge in good humor in spite of these disasters. The vibrant, joyous notes of the dance that ends the film version of the story still reverberate in my mind as I type these words.

Other writers have given us the same message with similar eloquence. Fans of Federicko Fellini will never forget the wild, ecstatic dancing at the end of the classic film *8½* when Guido, the film director, gives up his obsessive quest to find some binding theme to his life and simply participates in it. The characters portraying the figures of his past cease pestering him about their roles and join in the festivities. In essence, the writer stops trying to make meaning and allows these figures to breathe on their own, finding joy in being alive.

A quieter deliberation on the search for pleasure in life through storytelling and fun inheres in a stage play by Herb Gardner entitled *I'm Not Rappaport* (1986), which, incidentally, was made into a memorable film. In it, an elderly Jewish man and an elderly black man engage in a series of fanciful, funny adventures, some of which are also quite perilous. The Jewish man, in railing against society's treatment of the elderly, becomes mentor to the black man by encouraging him to protest his treatment by others even if it proves costly. Although both of them end up battered and bruised and in somewhat worse shape as a result of their efforts to protest, they regain their desire to carry on. The black man, whose role is that of a sort of Sancho Panza to the Jewish man's Don Quixote, is at first naive and gullible and later skeptical and disbelieving. However, at the end, when he faces a choice between skepticism and belief, he shelves his doubts and comes to relish his friend's fantasies of greatness and activism. As he urges the storyteller on to create more visions the film comes to a close, much like *Zorba* or *8½*, with the sharing of joy in participation and laughter at life.

In light of these cultural treasures as exemplars of humor, how is it that humor can also sometimes be cruel and hostile? Most things can be put to diverse purposes. Where the authors of these three works view a humorous vantage point as life-saving and invigorating, others can point to the hostile purposes of humiliation and torment to which humor can be applied. The Nazi slogan "Arbeit Macht Frei" (Work Makes for Freedom), which was emblazoned on the entrances to certain concentration camps, was nothing but a cruel joke, a trick to make incoming victims think they were entering work camps where the probability of their survival would be increased through their exertions. One can imagine how the perpetrators may have laughed while constructing this duplicity. Humor can be as ugly as delightful. Knowing this two-sided nature of humor, what can we conclude from our review of this psychological study that goes beyond our literary cousins' offerings?

Among the issues this book discussed are the origins of humor and their relationship to other familiar personality characteristics. The previously unreported data from the Blocks' longitudinal personality investigation that Nat Kogan shared with me provides an interesting convergence with the early work that I conducted linking humor to locus of control.

In the two studies that were published over two decades ago (Lefcourt et al., 1974a; Lefcourt et al., 1974b) locus of control and field independence were both found to be predictors of humor in certain situations that we created in our labs. In the first study, we deceived our subjects about the purposes of our experiment, lulling them into a dull torpor from which they had to emerge if they were to recognize that the last portion of the study was anything but dull. The administration of a word association test that included a gradually increasing number of sexual double entendres represented a real change and a challenge, because the test administrator was a rather attractive young woman. Perhaps today it would not be as trying for a young man to acknowledge or utter sex words to a young woman in a psychology experiment. But at that time to speak of "cunt" and the like was certain to arouse consternation.

In that first task, internals (locus of control) who were also field-independent were the first to show long delays in response times, indicating that they were aware of the alternative meanings of the words being presented and were thinking about what to say. They were also the first to show facial expressions revealing their quandary (judged from videorecordings of their facial expressions). Moreover, some of their verbal responses were themselves double entendres, Thus we found that internal-field independent subjects were more aware of what was going on than their peers and were more apt to exhibit laughter and knowing smiles, and occasionally to provide us with funny retorts.

In our second study we found that internal-field independent subjects manifested more humor and laughter while role-playing situations involving successes or failures in achievement and affiliation-relevant interactions.

Given these early findings, it was exciting to peruse the longitudinal data that Kogan and Block (1991) had obtained linking field independence to humor. That parental humor and playfulness should be associated with the development of field independence, and that field independence should eventually prove to be related to humor during young adulthood, suggested that our early findings were not due to chance.

Nevertheless, there is a caveat. Differences between men and women should prove provocative to future researchers. Women have almost always scored as more field dependent than men, making errors in the judgment of the vertical in the direction of contextual backgrounds and failing to disembed figures from within patterns. Because field independence has long been associated with the development of mathematical skills, women were often thought to be disadvantaged in mathematics because of the lesser perceptual skills evident in research with field dependence. However, the negative characteristics associated with field dependence have not often been found among women. Humor and laughter, for instance, have not been associated with field independence among women as they have been among men.

Why should internal-field independence be associated with humor appreciation and production among males? Both an internal locus of control and field independence are thought to indicate a more highly developed sense of self as separate from one's surroundings. Persons with more sharply defined identities have often seemed readier than others to assimilate information about what is happening around them, allowing them to act more effectively in their milieus. In essence, an internal locus of control and field independence would be more likely to be associated with activity, participation, assertiveness, and the like among males—and are the very correlates of humor that have been found in children's behavior at home and at school.

The locus of control and field-dependence-independence constructs have also been used in the study of stress, the former being among the first personality characteristics identified as a stress moderator. That is, persons with an internal locus of control were found to be less likely than externals to evince dysphoric affects in response to stressful events.

Only in the waning years of the 20th century did we become more aware psychologically of the stressful effects that—simply put—daily living exacts from us. When we suffer the loss of loved ones, the loss of our work and purpose, the loss of our friends and the familiar ways of doing things, we are confronting stressors. When such stress is experienced for any length of time, the somatic responses involved leave us vulnerable to the development of illnesses that could be prodromal to death. Agonizing over losses or anticipated losses can cost us our health. Our immune systems are put on hold when our hearts are busily pumping nutrients throughout our bloodstreams to energize us to fight the agonies that are challenging us. Accepting our failures and losses, so poetically advocated in the three theatrical stories mentioned, is a prescription for health. Ending the arousal accompanying those losses allows the organism to return to revitalizing activities.

With persistent physiological arousal those processes, which normally rebuild and heal us, weaken. We become less well defended against aberrant growths that threaten to interfere with our body's healthy functioning, and we become less capable of enjoying the natural sources of pleasure that we are heir to as humans: competence, instrumentality, sex, procreation, and close intimacy with others.

It is the awareness of the price to be paid for continued arousal that has led to some of the current interest in humor among psychological researchers. Norman Cousins's writings about his use of humor to undo the agonies of his stress-related illness and his subsequent books about lifestyle and health have had a profound impact on the reading public. Although some have argued that humor may have had less effect than Cousins's active participation in and control of his medical treatment, and others have questioned whether the diagnosis of ankylosing spondylitis was accurate, the results of his writing have made salient the role that affect can have on health and well-being. When Cousins observed that laughter seemed to have an analgesic effect that allowed him to sleep, humor suddenly became a real object of interest. That laughter and humor could be associated with physiological processes suddenly gave them more weight.

If positive processes were still regarded as a peripheral concern in psychology, I doubt that we would even have progressed the little bit that we have. But the promise of significance from studies concerned with positive affect has played a vital role in readying us to respond with interest to the research initiatives that occurred in the last decade.

After completing the first book, *Humor and Life Stress*, with my graduate student at that time, Rod Martin (Lefcourt & Martin, 1986) I was quite prepared to abandon my work with humor and return to the study of locus of control, to which most of my research career has been dedicated. But fate then intervened in the form of a note from a young psychological investigator who, to date, does not know how she altered my research career. Kathy Dillon (Dillon et al., 1985; Dillon & Totten, 1989), whose work was described in an earlier chapter, reported such high-magnitude correlations between laughter, one of our measures of humor (CHS), and concentrations of salivary immunoglobulin A (S-IgA) that I was left dumbfounded by the possible implications. I wrestled with whether I wanted to pursue these findings, which necessitated learning new technologies and acquainting myself with what had been an alien literature for me. If my earliest proclivities had not been so strongly in favor of physiological psychology, inspired by a brief stint as an assistant to John Lacey at the Fel's Research Institute, I might not have yielded. But the convergence of Dillon's data, my interest in physiological processes, and my tendency to become tantalized by oddities, may have prodded me to continue on that path.

In the years since receiving those findings from Kathy Dillon, I have engaged in a number of studies involving humor and physiological processes that are relevant to health and illness. Had I known how argumentative and territorial were the pioneers in the budding field of psychoneuroimmunology I might never have undertaken three years of research that resulted in merely one paper concerned with humor and concentrations of S-IgA (Lefcourt et al., 1990). Although during personal encounters, I received encouragement from certain immunologists, I did not know that the field was so rife with conflict that novices are quite apt to be overwhelmed in a quagmire of criticisms. Other colleagues have shared similar experiences with me, explaining why they made only one research sortie into this area despite what seemed to be exciting findings. One hopes that this will become a more welcoming area of investigation in future.

Despite these considerations, the very magnitude of the relationships between seemingly different realms of data such as scales pertaining to the use of humor (CHS) and concentrations of S-IgA would be enough to provoke many investigators into research activity if they were driven by curiosity, let alone an interest in health. I was delighted when my colleague and former graduate student seemed to have been similarly enticed (Martin & Dobbin, 1988). The result of all the ensuing research activity linking humor to health has yet to produce definitive data that would assure us of the value of humor and laughter. However, if we expand our interests into all of those activities that can alter our moods and emotions, our expectations for humor should become more secure.

Humor, along with beliefs about control (Lefcourt, 1982), the establishment of meaning for our experiences (Frankl, 1969; Baumeister, 1991), and the accessibility of social support (Sarason & Sarason, 1985) are agents of change for our emotional well-being. Physiological arousal experienced as anger, anxiety, depression, and the like serve to diminish us. Humor, control, meaning, social support, and optimism, along with other as yet unnamed characteristics, seem to be life-affirming not simply in terms of our affections but in actual physiological processes that support our vitality. Again, however, differences between the sexes can draw the attention of researchers. The humor expressed by females seems more conducive to social cohesion than that of males; the latter more often joke about others, the former more often laugh at themselves. That these different forms of humor may have different health consequences needs to be studied further to see if suggestive findings obtained thus far are reliable.

On many occasions I have been asked how—if humor is so useful for our well-being—we can improve it. My response has never been very satisfying, because although there is evidence and much anecdotal lore about the beneficial effects of humor for health and well-being there is a surprising dearth of literature about how people can improve their sense of humor. Several programs have been designed to encourage the development of humor (Goodman, 1983; McGhee, 1994; Salameh, 1987; Ziv, 1988). However, with the exception of McGhee's efforts there has been little attempt to subject these programs to any form of rigorous evaluation or empirical testing; and even McGhee's assessment of change consisted only of a self-report follow-up questionnaire. Given the social desirability issues in the assessment of humor, it would seem highly problematic to obtain validity data in this fashion.

A few volumes have reviewed the use of humor in various psychotherapeutic enterprises (Fry & Salameh, 1987, 1993), but these have mostly contained descriptive accounts of humor use rather than focusing on the improvement of humor itself. Recently, Nevo, Aharonson, and Klingman (1998) attempted to evaluate a more systematically designed program to increase humor use among a sample of schoolteachers in Israel. These authors admitted, however, that their failure to find definitive results revealed more about how difficult it was to conduct suitable outcome research than it was about the substance of their results. Good-naturedly, they admitted to several flaws in their investigations. Nevertheless, they did present a useful model for a program to improve one's sense of humor based on Ziv's (1981) distinctions between appreciation, production, and disposition toward humor. Nevo et al. (1998) expanded the dispositional element to include motivational, emotional, social, and behavioral components of humor, which became targets for instruction in their program. In essence, they sought to alter their subjects' desire to improve their humor and to enhance the cognitive skills associated with humor, such as rapid shifting of cognitions, tolerance of childishness, playfulness, and the like. Ultimately, they sought to alter their subjects' abilities to produce and appreciate humor but failed to demonstrate such changes. Aside from basic sampling problems, the very measures of outcomes such as ratings by peers or completion of cartoons or creativity tasks were difficult and unlikely to change in the 20-hour time period during which the programs were completed. Nevertheless, the authors' description of their plans of operation could be a good starting point for anyone wishing to conduct such research.

If one did little else, encouraging flexible thinking and learning to generate multiple responses to singular stimuli, and lessening the fear of rejection for attempts at comedy or laughter, could be good starting points for those wishing to enhance the humor abilities of their subjects.

As a final example of the power of humor, I would like to draw on another personal experience in which it played a role in making life bearable. As in the experience described by Brian Keenan (1992), a zany joke served to rescue me from feelings of misery. But because this event was more pedestrian and the joking less dramatic, it may prove more accessible and familiar to readers.

My wife and I were vacationing with our son, daughter-in-law, and 3-year-old grandson in a tropical region of Australia. We had arranged to spend three nights at a resort where wild animals wandered about freely and the hot nights would be cooled in our air-conditioned cabins. As it turned out, the temperature was well over 30° Celsius (above 90° Fahrenheit) and the humidity was as high as 95%—and it did not lessen at night. The air conditioners in the cabins were barely adequate, lowering the temperature only slightly. But we settled in and hoped for the best. Others at the park were camping in tents or staying in unair-conditioned recreation vehicles that had to be worse than anything we were experiencing; and as far as we knew they did not seem to be complaining.

The heat was so oppressive and the humidity so high that nothing dried. When we showered for the umpteenth time, trying to cool off each day, the futility of the exercise became evident because the water from the cold taps seemed to be hotter than body temperature. Amid swarms of flies curiously exploring our faces, we had to amass firewood for the barbecue pit near our cabins so as to cook dinner quickly before sunset. And then the peacocks came running, attracted by the aromas. On other occasions, the sight of the peacocks would surely have been a delight, their colorful plumage providing aesthetic pleasure. To our dismay, however, we found that the birds defecate freely and plentifully as they wander about, and their bounty is less birdlike and more akin to dog poop. The rickety tables we had set up in front of our cabins to enjoy the tropical outdoors and spare our air conditioners from over-work were soon surrounded by mounds of odiferous manure. As those regal, nonchalant birds continued their evening strolls around us we furiously tried to sweep away their mess while yelling and throwing tropical tree debris at them to hold them at bay. I vividly recall the sweat, the stench, the unbearable anticipation of long nights of tossing and turning in our cramped quarters with sweat-soaked sheets, and the despair of hot showers taken late at night in the wistful hope of a slight cooling before bedtime.

It was while walking back from the showers one night that my son, look-ing at the recreation vehicles and tents where steam and smoke rose thickly from the barbecues, said, "Well, here we go back to the Taj Mahal of Outback Heaven." Just like Derek Maitland's father's response to his son's agony, this zany comment that encompassed the agony of all the campers at the park and expressed commiseration with my palpable misery, bred a wonderful feeling of closeness with my son, to whom I'll always be grateful. In that one remark, humor coupled with social support rescued us from the despair that so often accompanies the experience of absurdity in our lives. I like to think that this little joke not only made that moment more bearable but also enhanced the pleasure of our time together, leaving us feeling healthier and happier than we otherwise would have felt.

THE COPING HUMOR SCALE (CHS)

Please indicate the extent to which you agree or disagree with each statement by circling the appropriate number.

1. I often lose my sense of humor when I am having problems.

1	2	3	4
(strongly)	(mildly)	(mildly)	(strongly)
(disagree)	(disagree)	(agree)	(agree)

2. I have often found that my problems have been greatly reduced when I try to find something funny in them.

1   2   3   4

3. I usually look for something comical to say when I am in tense situations.

1   2   3   4

4. I must admit my life would probably be a lot easier if I had more of a sense of humor.

1   2   3   4

5. I have often felt that if I am in a situation where I have to either cry or laugh, it's better to laugh.

1   2   3   4

6. I can usually find something to laugh or joke about even in trying situations.

1   2   3   4

7. It has been my experience that humor is often a very effective way of coping with problems.

1   2   3   4

GUIDE FOR SCORING OF THE CHS

1. All questions are scored positively with the exceptions of questions 1 and 4, which are scored in reversed direction:

   a = 1, b = 2, c = 3, d = 4:
   a = 4, b = 3, c = 2, d = 1 (for questions 1 and 4)

2. Omitted response is coded as 2.

3. Add scores for 7 items to get total CHS score.

TABLE A-1. Norms for CHS

Total sample	Mean	20.2
	S.D.	3.56
	N	244
Males	Mean	19.9
	S.D.	3.87
	N	120
Females	Mean	20.5
	S.D.	3.27
	N	124

THE SITUATIONAL HUMOR RESPONSE QUESTIONNAIRE (SHRQ)

Humor and laughter mean different things to different people. Each of us has our own conceptions of what situations are funny, our own notions of the appropriateness of humor in various situations, and our own sense of the importance of humor in our lives. In this questionnaire you will find descriptions of a number of situations in which you may have found yourself from time to time. For each question, please take a moment to recall a time when you were actually in such a situation. If you cannot remember such an experience, try to imagine yourself in such a situation, filling in the details in ways that reflect your own experience. Then indicate the phrase that best describes the way you have responded or would respond in such a situation.

1. If you were shopping by yourself in a distant city and you unexpectedly saw an acquaintance from school (or work), how have you responded or how would you respond?
   a. I would probably not have bothered to speak to that person.
   b. I would have talked to the person but wouldn't have shown much humor.
   c. I would have found something to smile about in talking with him/her.
   d. I would have found something to laugh about with the person.
   e. I would have laughed heartily with the person.
2. If you were awakened from a deep sleep in the middle of the night by the ringing of the telephone, and it was an old friend who was just passing through town and decided to call and say hello . . .
   a. I wouldn't have been particularly amused.
   b. I would have felt somewhat amused but would not have laughed.
   c. I would have been able to laugh at something funny my friend said.
   d. I would have been able to laugh and say something funny to my friend.
   e. I would have laughed heartily with my friend.
3. You had accidently hurt yourself and had to spend a few days in bed. During that time in bed, how would you have responded?
   a. I would not have found anything particularly amusing.
   b. I would have smiled occasionally.
   c. I would have smiled a lot and laughed from time to time.
   d. I would have found quite a lot to laugh about.
   e. I would have laughed heartily much of the time.

4. When you have been engaged in some lengthy physical activity (e.g., swimming, hiking, skiing) and you and your friends found yourselves to be completely exhausted . . .
   a. I wouldn't have found it particularly amusing.
   b. I would have been amused, but wouldn't have shown it outwardly.
   c. I would have smiled a lot and laughed from time to time.
   d. I would have laughed.
   e. I would have laughed heartily.

5. If you arrived at a party and found that someone else was wearing a piece of clothing identical to yours . . .
   a. I wouldn't have found it particularly amusing.
   b. I would have been amused, but wouldn't have shown it outwardly.
   c. I would have smiled.
   d. I would have laughed.
   e. I would have laughed heartily.

6. If a friend gave you a puzzle to solve and you found, much to your friend's surprise, that you were able to solve it very quickly,
   a. I wouldn't have found it particularly amusing.
   b. I would have been amused, but wouldn't have shown it outwardly.
   c. I would have smiled.
   d. I would have laughed.
   e. I would have laughed heartily.

7. On days when you've had absolutely no responsibilities or engagements, and you've decided to do something you really enjoy with some friends to what extent would you have responded with humor during the day?
   a. The activity we were engaged in would not have involved much smiling or laughter.
   b. I would have been smiling from time to time, but wouldn't have had much occasion to laugh aloud.
   c. I would have smiled frequently and laughed from time to time.
   d. I would have laughed aloud quite frequently.
   e. I would have laughed heartily much of the time.

8. You were travelling in a car in the winter and suddenly the car spun around on an ice patch and came to rest facing the wrong way on the opposite side of the highway. You were relieved to find that no one was hurt and no damage had been done to the car . . .
   a. I wouldn't have found it particularly amusing.
   b. I would have been amused, but wouldn't have shown it outwardly.
   c. I would have smiled.
   d. I would have laughed.
   e. I would have laughed heartily.

9. If you were watching a movie or T.V. program with some friends and you found one scene particularly funny, but no one else appeared to find it humorous, how would you have reacted most commonly?
   a. I would have concluded that I must have misunderstood something or that it wasn't really funny.
   b. I would have "smiled to myself," but wouldn't have shown my amusement outwardly.
   c. I would have smiled visibly.
   d. I would have laughed aloud.
   e. I would have laughed heartily.

10. If you were having a romantic evening alone with someone you really liked (girlfriend, boyfriend, spouse, etc.) . . .
    a. I probably would have tended to be quite serious in my conversation.
    b. I'd have smiled occasionally, but probably wouldn't have laughed aloud much.
    c. I'd have smiled frequently and laughed aloud from time to time.
    d. I'd have laughed aloud quite frequently.
    e. I'd have laughed heartily much of the time.

11. If you got an unexpectedly low mark on an exam and later that evening you were telling a friend about it . . .
    a. I would not have been amused.
    b. I would have been amused but wouldn't have shown it outwardly.
    c. I would have been able to smile.
    d. I would have been able to laugh.
    e. I would have laughed heartily.
12. You thought you recognized a friend in a crowded room. You attracted the person's attention and hurried over to him/her, but when you got there you discovered you had made a mistake and the person was a total stranger . . .
    a. I would not have been particularly amused.
    b. I would have been amused, but wouldn't have shown it outwardly.
    c. I would have smiled.
    d. I would have laughed.
    e. I would have laughed heartily.
13. If you were eating in a restaurant with some friends and the waiter accidently spilled a drink on you . . .
    a. I would not have been particularly amused.
    b. I would have been amused, but wouldn't have shown it outwardly.
    c. I would have smiled.
    d. I would have laughed.
    e. I would have laughed heartily.
14. If you were crossing a street at a crosswalk and an impatient car driver, who had to stop for you, honked the horn . . .
    a. I would not have been particularly amused.
    b. I would have been amused, but wouldn't have shown it outwardly.
    c. I would have smiled.
    d. I would have laughed.
    e. I would have laughed heartily.
15. If there had been a computer error and you had spent all morning standing in line at various offices to get the problem sorted out . . .
    a. I wouldn't have found it particularly amusing.
    b. I would have been able to experience some amusement, but wouldn't have shown it.
    c. I would have smiled a lot.
    d. I would have laughed a lot.
    e. I would have laughed heartily.
16. If the teacher announced that she or he would hand back the exams in order of grade, beginning with the highest mark in the class, and your name was one of the first to be called . . .
    a. I would not have been particularly amused.
    b. I would have been amused, but wouldn't have shown it outwardly.
    c. I would have smiled.
    d. I would have laughed.
    e. I would have laughed heartily.
17. In the past, if your girlfriend (or boyfriend) decided to break up with you because she or he had found someone else, and a few days later you were telling a good friend about it . . .
    a. I wouldn't have found any humor in the situation.
    b. I would have been able to experience some amusement, but wouldn't have shown it.
    c. I would have been able to smile.
    d. I would have been able to laugh.
    e. I would have laughed quite a lot.

18. If you were eating in a restaurant with some friends and the waiter accidently spilled some soup on one of your friends . . .
   a. I would not have been particularly amused.
   b. I would have been amused, but wouldn't have shown it outwardly.
   c. I would have smiled.
   d. I would have laughed.
   e. I would have laughed heartily.

19. In choosing your friends, how desirable to you feel it is for them to be easily amused and able to laugh in a wide variety of situations?
   a. The most important characteristic I look for in a friend
   b. Very desirable, but not the most important characteristic
   c. Quite desirable
   d. Neither desirable nor undesirable
   e. Not very desirable

20. How would you rate yourself in terms of your likelihood of being amused and of laughing in a variety of situations?
   a. My most outstanding characteristic
   b. Above average
   c. About average
   d. Less than average
   e. Very little

21. How much do you vary from one situation to another in the extent to which you laugh or otherwise respond with humor (i.e., how much does it depend on who you are with, where you are, how you feel, etc.)
   a. Not at all
   b. Not very much
   c. To some extent
   d. Quite a lot
   e. Very much so

GUIDE FOR SCORING OF THE SITUATIONAL HUMOR RESPONSE QUESTIONNAIRE (SHRQ)

1. For questions 1 to 18, give numeric scores as follows:
   a = 1, b = 2, c = 3, d = 4, e = 5.
2. Questions 19 to 21 are scored in reverse:
   a = 5, b = 4, c = 3, d = 2, e = 1
3. Omitted response is coded as 3.
4. Add scores for 21 items to get total SHRQ score.

TABLE B-1. Norms for SHRQ

Total sample	Mean	59.6
	S.D.	9.06
	N	497
Males	Mean	60.0
	S.D.	9.60
	N	282
Females	Mean	59.1
	S.D	8.31
	N	215

BIBLIOGRAPHY OF RESEARCH WITH THE CHS AND SHRQ

Abel, M. H. (1998). Interaction of humor and gender in moderating relationships between stress and outcomes. *Journal of Psychology, 132,* 267–276.

Anderson, C. A., & Arnoult, L. H. (1989). An examination of perceived control, humor, irrational beliefs, and positive stress as moderators of the relation between negative stress and health. *Basic and Applied Social Psychology, 10*(2), 101–117.

Carroll, J. L., & Shmidt, J. L. (1992). Correlation between humorous coping style and health. *Psychological Reports, 72,* 402.

Deaner, S. L., & McConatha, J. T. (1993). The relation of humor to depression and personality. *Psychological Reports, 72,* 755–763.

Deckers, L., & Ruch, W. (1992), Sensation seeking and the Situational Humor Response Questionnaire: Its relationship in American and German samples. *Personality and Individual Differences, 13,* 1051–054.

Dillon, K. M., Minchoff, B., & Baker, K. H. (1985). Positive emotional states and enhancement of the immune system. *International Journal of Psychiatry in Medicine, 15,* 13–17.

Dillon, K. M., & Totten, M. C. (1989). Psychological factors, immunocompetence, and health of breast-feeding mothers and their infants. *Journal of Genetic Psychology, 150*(2), 155–162.

Graham, E. E., Papa, M. J., & Brooks, G. P. (1992). Functions of humor in conversation: Conceptualization and measurement. *Western Journal of Communication, 56,* 161–183.

Gruner, C. R. (1996). Appreciation and understanding of satire: Another quasi-experiment. *Psychological Reports, 78,* 194.

Hampes, W. P. (1992). Relation between intimacy and humor. *Psychological Reports, 71,* 127–130.

Hudak, D. A., Dale, J. A., Hudak, M. A., & DeGood, D. A. (1991). Effects of humorous stimuli and sense of humor on discomfort. *Psychological Reports, 69*(3), 779–786.

Korotkov, D. (1991). An exploratory factor analysis of the sense of humor personality construct: A pilot project. *Personality and Individual Differences, 12,* 395–397.

Korotkov, D., & Hannah, T. E. (1994). Extraversion and emotionality as proposed superordinate stress moderators: a prospective analysis. *Personality and Individual Differences, 16,* 787–792

Kuiper, N. A., Martin, R. A., & Dance, K. A. (1992). Sense of humor and enhanced quality of life. *Personality and Individual Differences, 13*(12), 1273–1283.

Kuiper, N. A., Martin, R. A., & Olinger, L. J. (1993). Coping humor, stress, and cognitive appraisals. *Canadian Journal of Behavioral Science, 25*(1), 81–96.

Kuiper, N. A., & Martin, R. A. (1993). Humor and self-concept. *Humor: International Journal of Humor Research, 6*(3), 251–270.

Kuiper, N. A., McKenzie, S. D., & Belanger, K. A. (1995). Cognitive appraisals and individual differences in sense of humor: motivational and affective implication. *Personality and Individual Differences, 19*(3), 359–372.

Labott, S. M., & Martin, R. B. (1987). The stress-moderating effects of weeping and humor. *Journal of Human Stress, 13*(4), 159–164.

Labott, S. M., & Martin, R. B. (1990). Emotional coping, age, and physical disorder. *Behavioral Medicine, 16*(2), 53–61.

Labott, S. M., Ahleman, B. A., Wolever, M. E., & Martin, R. B. (1990). The physiological and psychological effects of the expression and inhibition of emotion. *Behavioral Medicine, 16*(4), 182–189.

Lefcourt, H. M. (1996). Perspective-taking humor and authoritarianism as predictors of anthropocentrism. *Humor: International Journal of Humor Research, 9*(1), 61–75.

Lefcourt, H. M. (2000). The humor solution. In C. R. Snyder (Ed.), *Coping and Copers: Adaptive processes and people.* New York: Oxford University Press.

Lefcourt, H. M., & Davidson, K. (1991). The role of humor and the self. In C, R. Snyder & R. F. Donelson (Eds.) *Handbook of social and clinical psychology: The health perspective* (pp 41–56). New York: Pergamon.

Lefcourt, H. M., Davidson, K., & Kueneman, K. (1990). Humor and immune system functioning. *Humor: International Journal of Humor Research, 3*(3), 305–322.

Lefcourt, H. M., Davidson, K., Prkachin, K. M., & Mills, D. E. (1997a). Humor as a stress moderator in the prediction of blood pressure obtained during five stressful tasks. *Journal of Research in Personality, 31*, 523–542.

Lefcourt, H. M., Davidson, K., Shepherd, R. S., Phillips, M., Prkachin, K. M., & Mills, D. (1995). Perspective-taking in humor: Accounting for stress moderation. *Journal of Social and Clinical Psychology, 14*(4), 373–391.

Lefcourt, H. M., Davidson, K., Shepherd, R. S., & Phillips, M. (1997b). Who likes "Far Side" humor? *Humor: International Journal of Humor Research,10*(4), 439–452.

Lefcourt, H. M., & Martin, R. A (1986). *Humor and life stress.* New York: Springer-Verlag.

Lefcourt, H. M., & Shepherd, R. S, (1995), Organ donation, authoritarianism, and perspective-taking humor. *Journal of Research in Personality, 29*, 121–138.

Lefcourt, H. M., & Thomas, S, (1998), Humor and stress revisited. In W. Ruch (Ed.), *The sense of humor* (pp. 179–202). Berlin: Mouton de Gruyter.

Martin, R, A., & Dobbin, J. P. (1988). Sense of humor, hassles, and immunoglobulin A: Evidence for a stress-moderating effect of humor. *International Journal of Psychiatry in Medicine, 18*, 93–105.

Martin, R. A., Kuiper, N. A., Olinger, L. J., & Dance, D. A. (1993). Humor, coping with stress, self-concept, and psychological well-being. *Humor: International Journal of Humor Research, 6*(1), 89–104.

Martin, R. A., & Lefcourt, H. M. (1983). Sense of humor as a moderator of the relation between stressors and moods. *Journal of Personality and Social Psychology, 45*, 1313–1324.

Martin, R. A., & Lefcourt, H. M. (1984). The Situational Humor Response Questionnaire: A quantitative measure of the sense of humor. *Journal of Personality and Social Psychology, 47*, 145–155.

Moran, C. C. (1996). Short-term mood change, perceived funniness, and the effect of humor stimuli. *Behavioral Medicine, 22*(1), 32–38.

Newman, M. G., & Stone, A. A. (1996). Does humor moderate the effects of experimentally-induced stress? *Annals of Behavioral Medicine, 18*(2), 101–109.

Nezu, A. M., Nezu, C. M., & Blissett, S. E. (1988). Sense of humor as a moderator of the relation between stressful events and psychological distress: A prospective analysis. *Journal of Personality and Social Psychology, 54*, 520–525.

Overholser, J. C. (1992). Sense of humor when coping with life stress. *Personality and Individual Differences, 13*(7), 799–804.

Porterfield, A. L. (1987). Does sense of humor moderate the impact of life stress on psychological and physical well-being? *Journal of Research in Personality, 21,* 306–317.

Rim, Y. (1988). Sense of humor and coping styles. *Personality and Individual Differences, 9,* 559–564.

Rim, Y. (1990). Optimism and coping styles. *Personality and Individual Differences, 11,* 89–90.

Rotten, J., & Shats, M. (1996). Effects of state humor, expectancies, and choice on postsurgical mood and self-medication: A field experiment. *Journal of Applied Social Psychology, 26,* 1775–1794.

Shepherd, R. & Lefcourt, H. M. (1990). What's so funny about death? Sense of humor, mood disturbance, and beliefs as predictors of willingness to confront mortality. In J. Shanteau & R. J. Harris (Eds.), *Organ donation and transplantation: Psychological and behavioral factors.* Hyattsville, Md.: APA.

Thorson, J. A., & Powell, F. C. (1991). Measurement of sense of humor. *Psychological Reports, 69,* 691–702.

Trice, A. D., & Price-Greathouse, J. (1986). Joking under the drill: A validity study of the CHS. *Journal of Social Behavior and Personality, 1,* 265–266.

White, S. & Winzelberg, A. (1992). Laughter and stress. *Humor: International Journal of Humor Research, 5*(4), 343–355.

Yovetich, N. A., Dale, J. A., & Hudak, M. A. (1990). Benefits of humor in reduction of threat-induced anxiety. *Psychological Reports, 66,* 51–58.

REFERENCES

Aldis, O. (1975). *Play Fighting*. New York: Academic Press.

Alexander, C. (1998). *The Endurance: Shackleton's Legendary Antarctic Expedition*. New York: Knopf.

Allport, G. W. (1950). *The Individual and His Religion*. New York: Macmillan.

Als, H. (Sept. 13, 1999). A Pryor love. *The New Yorker*, pp. 68–81.

Andersen, B. L., Kiecolt-Glaser, J. K., & Glaser, R. (1994). A behavioral model of cancer stress and disease course. *American Psychologist, 49*, 389–404.

Anderson, C. A., & Arnoult, L. H. (1989). An examination of perceived control, humor, irrational beliefs, and positive stress as moderators of the relation between negative stress and health. *Basic and Applied Social Psychology, 10*(2), 101–117.

Andrews, G., Franz, C. P., & Stuard, G. (1989). The determination of defense style by questionnaire. *Archives of General Psychiatry, 46*, 455–460.

Ansbacher, H., & Ansbacher, R. (1956). *The Individual Psychology of Alfred Adler*. New York: Basic Books.

Apter, M. J. (1982). *The Experience of Motivation*. London: Academic Press.

Bandura, A. (1977). Self-efficacy: Toward a unifying theory of behavioral change. *Psychological Review, 84*(2), 191–215.

Barth, K. (1981). *Ethics*. New York: Seabury Press. (Original work published 1928)

Baumeister, R. (1991). *Meanings of Life*. New York: Guilford Press.

Beattie, J. (1776). On laughter and ludicrous composition. In *Essays*. Edinburgh: Creech.

Beck, A. T., Ward, C. H., Mendelson, M., Mock, J., & Erbaugh, J. (1961). An inventory for measuring depression. *Archives of General Psychiatry, 4*, 561–571.

Becker, E. (1973). *The Denial of Death*. New York: Free Press.

Bell, N. J., McGhee, P. E., & Duffey, N. S. (1986). Interpersonal competence, social assertiveness, and the development of humor. *British Journal of Developmental Psychology, 4*, 51–55.

Berger, P. L. (1997). *Redeeming Laughter: The Comic Dimension of Human Experience*. New York: Walter de Gruyter.

Bergson, H. (1911). *Laughter: An Essay on the Meaning of the Comic.* New York: Macmillan.

Berk, L. S., Tan, S. A., Nehlsen-Cannarella, S., Napier, B. J., Lewis, J. E., Lee, J. W., & Eby, W. C. (1988). Humor associated laughter decreases cortisol and increases spontaneous lymphocyte blastogenesis. *Clinical Research, 36,* 435A.

Berk, L. S., Tan, S. A., Fry, W. F., Napier, B. J., Lee, J. W., Hubbard, R. W., Lewis, E., & Eby, W. C. (1989). Neuroendocrine and stress hormone changes during mirthful laughter. *American Journal of Medical Sciences, 298,* 390–396.

Berkowitz, L. (1970). Aggressive humor as a stimulus to aggressive responses. *Journal of Personality and Social Psychology, 16,* 710–717.

Berlyne, D. E. (1969). Laughter, humor, and play. In G. Lindsey & E. Aronson (Eds.), *Handbook of Social Psychology* (2nd ed., Vol. 3, pp. 795–852). Reading, MA: Addison-Wesley.

Berlyne, D. E. (1972). Humor and Its kin. In J. H. Goldstein & P. E. McGhee (Eds.), *The Psychology of Humor* (pp. 43–60). New York: Academic Press.

Bettelheim, B. (1943). Individual and mass behavior in extreme situations. *Journal of Abnormal & Social Psychology, 38,* 417–452.

Bettelheim, B. (1960). *The Informed Heart.* Glencoe, IL: Free Press.

Bloom, H. (1995). *The Lucifer Principle: A Scientific Expedition into the Forces of History.* New York: Atlantic Monthly Press.

Bonanno, G. A., & Keltner, D. (1997). Facial expressions of emotion and the course of conjugal bereavement. *Journal of Abnormal Psychology, 106*(1), 126–137.

Borkovec, T. D., Stone, N. M., O'Brien, G. T., & Kaloupek, D. (1974). Evaluation of a clinically relevant target behavior for analog outcome research. *Behavior Therapy, 5,* 503–513.

Bowen, E. S. (1954). *Return to Laughter.* New York: Harper & Bros.

Boynton-Payne, K. (1998). *Silent Thunder: In the Presence of Elephants.* New York: Simon & Schuster.

Brown, G. W., & Harris, T. (1978). *Social Origins of Depression: A Study of Psychiatric Disorder in Women.* New York: Free Press.

Brownell, H. H., & Gardner, H. (1988). Neuropsychological insights into humour. In J. Durant & J. Miller (Eds.), *Laughing Matters: A Serious Look at Humour* (pp. 17–34). Essex, England: Longman House.

Bryant, J., Comiskey, P. W., & Zillman, D. (1979). Teacher's humor in the college classroom. *Communication Education, 28,* 110–118.

Buss, D. M. (1995). Psychological sex differences: Origins through sexual selection. *American Psychologist, 50,* 164–168.

Cannon, W. (1931). *The Wisdom of the Body.* New York: Norton.

Cantor, J. R., & Zillmann, D. (1973). Resentment toward victimized protagonists and severity of misfortune they suffer as factors in humor appreciation. *Journal of Experimental Research in Personality, 6,* 321–329.

Carson, D. K., Skarpness, L. R., Shultz, N. W., & McGhee, P. E. (1986). Temperament and communicative competence as predictors of young children's humor. *Merrill-Palmer Quarterly, 32,* 413–426.

Carver, C. S., & Gaines, J. G. (1987). Optimism, pessimism, and postpartum depression. *Cognitive Therapy and Research, 11,* 449–462.

Carver, C. S., Pozo, C., Harris, S. D., Noriega, V., Scheier, M. F., Robinson, D. S., Ketcham, A. S., Moffat, F. L., & Clark, K. C. (1993). How coping mediates the effect of optimism on distress: A study of women with early stage breast cancer. *Journal of Personality and Social Psychology, 63*(2), 375–390.

Chesney, M. A., Eagleston, T., Rosenman, R. H. (1980). The Type A Structured Interview: A behavioral assessment in the rough. *Journal of Behavioral Assessment, 2,* 255–272.

Coan, R. (1974). *The Optimal Personality: An Empirical and Theoretical Analysis.* New York: Columbia University Press.

Coelho, G. V., & Ahmed, P. I. (1980). *Uprooting and Development: Dilemmas of Coping with Modernization.* New York: Plenum.

Cogan, B., Cogan, D., Waltz, W., & McCue, M. (1987). Effects of laughter and relaxation on discomfort thresholds. *Journal of Behavioral Medicine, 10*(2), 139–144.

Cohan, C. L., & Bradbury, T. N. (1997). Negative life events, marital interaction, and the longitudinal course of newlywed marriage. *Journal of Personality and Social Psychology, 73*(1), 114–128.

Cohen, E. A. (1953). *Human Behavior in the Concentration Camp.* New York: Grosset & Dunlap.

Cohen, S., & Edwards, J. R, (1988). Personality characteristics as moderators of the relationship between stress and disorder. In R. W. J. Neufeld (Ed.), *Advances in the Investigation of Psychological Stress* (pp. 235–283). New York: Wiley.

Cohen, S., Mermelstein, R., Kamarck, T., & Hoberman, H. M. (1985). Measuring the functional components of social support. In I. G. Sarason & B. R. Sarason (Eds.), *Social Support: Theory, Research and Applications* (pp. 73–94). Boston: Martinus Nijhoff.

Cousins, N. (1979). *Anatomy of an Illness.* New York: W.W. Norton.

Cousins, N. (1983). *The Healing Heart.* New York: W.W. Norton.

Cousins, N. (1989). *Head First: The Biology of Hope.* New York: Dutton.

Crawford, M., & Gressley, D. (1991). Creativity, caring, and context: Women's and men's accounts of humor preferences and practices. *Psychology of Women Quarterly, 15,* 217–231.

Danzer, A., Dale, J. A., & Klions, H. L. (1990). Effect of exposure to humorous stimuli on induced depression. *Psychological Reports, 66*(3), 1027–1036.

Darwin, C. (1872). *The Expression of Emotions in Man and Animals.* London: William Pickering.

Davies, R. (1975). *World of Wonders.* Toronto: Macmillan.

Dawidowicz, L. (1975). *The War against the Jews.* New York: Holt, Rinehart, & Winston.

deCharms, R. (1968). *Personal Causation: The Internal Affective Determinants of Behavior.* New York: Academic Press.

Denby, D. (Mar. 15, 1999). In the eye of the beholder. *The New Yorker,* pp. 96–99.

Denby, D. (Nov. 16, 1998). Film Review: Life Is Beautiful. *The New Yorker,* pp. 96–99.

Descartes, R. (1649). *A Discourse of a Method for the Well Guiding of Reason and the Discovery of Truth on the Sciences.* London: T. Necombe.

Diamond, J. (1997). *Guns, Germs, and Steel: The Fates of Human Societies.* New York: Norton.

Dillon, K. M., & Totten, M. C. (1989). Psychological factors, immunocompetence, and health of breast-feeding mothers and their infants. *Journal of Genetic Psychology, 150*(2), 155–62.

Dillon, K., M., Minchoff, B., & Baker, K. H. (1985). Positive emotional states and enhancement of the immune system. *International Journal of Psychiatry in Medicine, 15,* 13–18.

Dixon, N. F. (1980). Humor: A cognitive alternative to stress? In I. G. Sarason & C. D. Spielberger (Eds.), *Stress and Anxiety* (Vol. 7, pp. 281–289). Washington, DC: Hemisphere.

Dorfman, A. (1992). *Death and the Maiden.* New York: Penguin.

Duncker, K. (1945). On problem solving. *Psychological Monographs, 58*(5 Whole No. 270).

Dweck, C. S. (1975). The role of expectations and attributions on the alleviation of learned helplessness. *Journal of Personality and Social Psychology, 31,* 674–685.

Dworkin, E., & Efran, J. (1967). The angered: Their susceptibility to varieties of humor. *Journal of Personality and Social Psychology, 6,* 233–236.

Eco, U. (1980). *The Name of the Rose.* New York: Harcourt, Brace, Jovanovich.

Eckenrode, J. (1991). *The Social Context of Coping.* New York: Plenum.

Ekman, P. (1973). *Darwin and Facial Expression.* New York: Academic Press.

Ekman, P. (1984). Expression and the nature of emotion. In K. R. Scherer & P. Ekman (Eds.), *Approaches to Emotion.* Hillsdale, NJ: Erlbaum.

Fisher, S., & Fisher, R. L. (1981). *Pretend the World is Funny and Forever.* Hillsdale, NJ: Erlbaum.

Fitts, W. H. (1965). *Tennessee Self-Concept Scale.* Nashville: Counselor Recordings and Tests.

Flugel, J. C. (1954). Humor and laughter. In G. Lindsey (Ed.), *Handbook of Social Psychology* (1st ed., Vol. 2, pp. 709–734). Reading, MA: Addison-Wesley.

Foot, H. C., Chapman, A. J., & Smith, J. R. (1977). Friendship and social responsiveness in boys and girls. *Journal of Personality and Social Psychology, 35,* 401–411.

Fraiberg, A. (1994). Between the laughter: Bridging feminist studies through women's stand-up comedy. In G. Finney (Ed.), *Look Who's Laughing: Gender and Comedy* (pp. 315–364). New York: Gordon & Breach.

Frankl, V. (1969). *The Will to Meaning.* New York: World Publishing.

Freud, S. (1905). *Jokes and Their Relation to the Unconscious.* Leipzig: Deuticke.

Freud, S. (1928). Humor. *International Journal of Psychoanalysis, 9,* 1–6.

Friedman, H. S., Tucker, J. S., Tomlinson-Keasey, C., Schwartz, J. E., Wingard, D. L., & Criqui, M. H. (1993). Does childhood personality predict longevity? *Journal of Personality and Social Psychology, 65,* 176–185.

Fry, W. F. (1987). Humor and paradox. *American Behavioral Scientist, 30*(3), 42–71.

Fry, W. F. (1992). Physiologic effects of humor, mirth, and laughter. *Journal of the American Medical Association, 267*(13), 1857–1858.

Fry, W. F., & Allen, M. (1975). *Make 'em Laugh.* Palo Alto, CA: Pacific Books.

Fry, W. F., & Salameh, W. A. (1987). *Handbook of Humor and Psychotherapy: Advances in the Clinical use of Humor.* Sarasota, FL: Professional Resource Exchange.

Fry, W. F., & Salameh, W. A. (1993). *Advances in Humor and Psychotherapy.* Sarasota, FL: Professional Resource Exchange.

Gallup, C. G. (1977). Self-recognition in primates: A comparative approach to the bidirectional properties of consciousness. *American Psychologist, 32,* 329–338.

Gardner, H. (1986). *I'm Not Rappaport*. Garden City, NY: Doubleday.

Garmezy, N., & Tellegen, A. (1984). Studies of stress-resistant children: Methods, variables, and preliminary findings. In F. Morrison, D. Keating, & C. Lord (Eds.), *Applied Developmental Psychology* (Vol. 1, pp. 231–287). New York: Academic Press.

Garmezy, N., Masten, A. S., & Tellegen, A. (1984). The study of stress and competence in children: A building block for developmental psychopathology. *Child Development, 55*, 97–111.

Glass, D. G., & Singer, J. E. (1972). *Urban Stress: Experiments on Noise and Social Stressors*. New York: Academic Press.

Goldblum, R. M. (1990). The role of IgA in local immune protection. *Journal of Clinical Immunology, 10*, 64S–70S.

Goldstein, J. (1982). A laugh a day. *The Sciences, 22*, 21–25.

Goodall, J. (1968). The behavior of free-living chimpanzees in the Gombe Stream Reserve. *Animal Behavior Monographs, 1*, 165–311.

Goodman, J, (1983). How to get more smileage out of your life: Making sense of humor, then serving it. In P. E. McGhee & J. H. Goldstein (Eds.), *Handbook of humor research* (Vol. 2, pp. 1–21). New York: Springer-Verlag.

Goodwin, D. K. (1997). *Wait Till Next Year: A Memoir*. New York: Simon & Schuster.

Gottlieb, B. H. (1988). *Marshalling Social Support: Formats, Processes, and Effects*. Newbury Park: Sage.

Gottman, J. M. (1979). *Marital Interaction: Experimental Investigations*. New York: Academic Press.

Gottman, J. M., & Krokoff, L. J. (1989). Marital interaction and satisfaction: A longitudinal view. *Journal of Consulting and Clinical Psychology, 57*(1), 47–52.

Greenberg, J., Pyszczynski, T., Solomon, S., Rosenblatt, A., Veeder, M., Kirkland, S., & Lyon, D. (1990). Evidence for terror management theory II: The effects of mortality salience on reactions to those who threaten or bolster the cultural worldview. *Journal of Personality and Social Psychology, 58*, 308–318.

Grziwok, R., & Scodel, A. (1956). Some psychological correlates of humor preferences. *Journal of Consulting Psychology, 20*, 42.

Guerney, B. G. (1977). *Relationship Enhancement*. San Francisco: Jossey-Bass.

Hartley, D. (1971). *Observations on Man, His Frame, His Duty, and His Expectations*. New York: Garland. (Original work published 1749)

Hilgard, E. R., Ruch, J. C., Lange, A. F., Lenox, J. R., Morgan, A. H., & Sachs, L. B. (1974). The psychophysics of cold pressor pain and its modification through hypnotic suggestion. *American Journal of Psychology, 87*, 17–31.

Hobbes, T. (1651). *Leviathan or, the Matter, Forms, and Power of a Commonwealth Ecclesiastical and Civil*. London: Crooke.

Hobden, K. L., & Olson, J. M. (1994). From jest to antipathy: Disparagement humor as a source of dissonance-motivated attitude change. *Basic and Applied Social Psychology, 15*, 239–249.

Holmes, T. H., & Rahe, R. H. (1967). The social readjustment rating scale. *Journal of Psychosomatic Research, 11*, 213–218.

Horne, J. (1996). *Mysticism and Vocation*. Waterloo, Ontario: Wilfred Laurier University Press.

Hubbell, W. (1997). *Friends in High Places*. New York: Morrow.

Hudak, D. A., Dale, J. A., & Hudak, M. A., & DeGood, D. E. (1991). Effects of humorous stimuli and sense of humor on discomfort. *Psychological Reports, 69*(3), 779–786.

Isen, A. M., Daubman, K. A., & Nowicki, G. P. (1987). Positive affect facilitates creative problem solving. *Journal of Personality and Social Psychology, 52,* 1122–1131.

Jahoda, M. (1958). *Current Concepts of Positive Mental Health.* New York: Basic Books.

Janes, L. M., & Olson, J. M. (2000). Jeer pressure: The behavioral effects of observing ridicule of others. *Personality and Social Psychology Bulletin, 26*(4), 474–485.

Janis, I. L. (1958). *Psychological Stress.* New York: Wiley.

Janis, I. L. (1965). Effects of fear arousal on attitude change: Recent developments in theory and experimental research. In L. Berkowitz (Ed.), *Advances in Experimental Social Psychology* (pp. 167–225). New York: Academic Press.

Janus, S. S. (1975). The great comedians: Personality and other factors. *Journal of Psychoanalysis, 35,* 169–174.

Jensen, A. R., & Rohwer, W. D. (1966). The Stroop Color-Word Test: A review. *Acta Psychologica, 25,* 36–93.

Johnson, J. H., & Sarason, I. G. (1979). Moderator variables in life stress research. In I. G. Sarason & C. D. Spielberger (Eds.), *Stress and anxiety* (Vol. 6, pp. 151–167). Washington, DC: Hemisphere.

Joubert, L. (1579). *Treatise on Laughter.* Paris: Chez Nicolas Chesneav.

Kanner, A. D., Coyne, J. C., Schaeffer, C., & Lazarus, R. S. (1981). Comparison of two modes of stress measurement: Daily hassles and uplifts versus major life events. *Journal of Behavioral Medicine 4,* 1–39.

Kasl, S. V., & Cobb, S. (1980). The experience of losing a job: Some effects on cardiovascular functioning. *Psychotherapy and Psychosomatics, 34*(2), 88–109.

Kazantzakis, N. (1953). *Zorba the Greek.* New York: Simon & Schuster.

Keenan, B. (1992). *An Evil Cradling.* New York: Viking-Penguin.

Kelly, G. A. (1955). *The Psychology of Personal Constructs.* New York: W. W. Norton.

Keith-Spiegel, P. (1972). Early conceptions of humor: Varieties and issues. In J. H. Goldstein & P. E. McGhee (Eds.), *The Psychology of Humor* (pp. 3–39). New York: Academic Press.

Keltner, D., & Bonanno, G. A. (1997). A study of laughter and dissociation: Distinct correlates of laughter and smiling during bereavement. *Journal of Personality and Social Psychology, 73*(4), 687–702.

Keltner, D., & Ekman, P. (1994). Facial expressions of emotion: Old questions and new findings. *Encyclopedia of Human Behavior* (Vol. 2, pp. 361–369). New York: Academic Press.

Kiecolt-Glaser, J. K., Fisher, L., Ogrocki, P., Stout, J. C., Speicher, C. E., & Glaser, R. (1987). Marital quality, marital disruption, and immune function. *Psychosomatic Medicine, 49,* 13–34.

Klecolt-Glaser, J. K., Page, G. G., Marucha, P. T., MacCallum, R. C., & Glaser, R. (1998). Psychological influences on surgical recovery: Perspectives from psychoneuroimmunology. *American Psychologist, 53*(11), 1209–1218.

Kimmins, C. W. (1928). *The Springs of Laughter.* London: Methuen.

Kline, L. W. (1907). The psychology of humor. *American Journal of Psychology, 18,* 421–441.

Kobasa, S. C. (1979). Stressful life events, personality, and health: An inquiry into hardiness. *Journal of Personality and Social Psychology, 37,* 1–11.

Kobasa, S. C., Maddi, S. R., & Kahn, S. (1982). Hardiness and health: A prospective study. *Journal of Personality and Social Psychology, 42,* 168–177.

Kobler, A. L., & Stotland, E. (1964). *The End of Hope: A Socioclinical Study of Suicide.* New York: Free Press.

Koestler, A. (1964). *The Act of Creation.* London: Hutchinson.

Kogan, N., & Block, J. (1991). Field dependence from early childhood through adolescence: Personality and socialization aspects. In S. Wapner & J. Demick (Eds.), *Field Dependence–Independence: Cognitive Style across the Life Span* (pp. 177–207). Hillsdale, NJ: Erlbaum.

Kuiper, N. A., Martin, R. A., & Dance, K. A. (1992). Sense of humor and enhanced quality of life. *Personality and Individual Differences, 13*(12), 1273–1283.

Labott, S. M., & Martin, R. B. (1987). Stress-moderating effects of weeping and humor. *Journal of Human Stress, 13*(4), 159–164.

LaFave, L., Haddad, J., & Marshall, N. (1974). Humor judgments as a function of identification classes. *Sociology and Social Research, 58,* 184–194.

Lampert, M. D., & Ervin-Tripp, S. M. (1998). Exploring paradigms: The study of gender and sense of humor near the end of the 20th century. In W. Ruch (Ed.), *The Sense of Humor: Explorations of a Personality Characteristic* (pp. 231–270). New York: Mouton de Gruyter.

Langer, E. J. (1983). *The Psychology of Control.* Beverly Hills, CA: Sage.

Langer, E. J., & Rodin, J. (1976). The effects of choice and enhanced personal responsibility for the aged: A field experiment in an institutional setting. *Journal of Personality and Social Psychology, 34,* 191–198.

Langevin, R., & Day, H. I. (1972). Physiological correlates of humor. In J. H. Goldstein & P. E. McGhee (Eds.), *The Psychology of Humor* (pp. 129–142). New York: Academic Press.

Larson, G. (1988). *The Far Side Gallery 3.* Kansas City, MO: Andrews & McMeel.

Laumann, E. O., Paik, A., & Rosen, R. C. (1999). Sexual dysfunction in the United States. *Journal of the American Medical Association, 281*(6), 537–544.

Lauter, P. (1964). *Theories of Comedy.* New York: Doubleday.

Lazarus, R. S. (1966). *Psychological Stress and the Coping Process.* New York: McGraw-Hill.

Lazarus, R. S., & Folkman, S. (1984). *Stress, Appraisal, and Coping.* New York: Springer.

Le Bon, G. (1895). *The Crowd.* London: T. Fisher Unwin.

Lefcourt, H. M. (1966). Internal–external control of reinforcement: A review. *Psychological Bulletin, 265,* 206–220.

Lefcourt, H. M. (1976). *Locus of Control* (1st ed.). Hillsdale, NJ: Erlbaum.

Lefcourt, H. M. (1982). *Locus of Control* (2nd ed.). Hillsdale, NJ: Erlbaum.

Lefcourt, H. M. (1985). Intimacy, social support, and locus of control as moderators of stress. In I. G. Sarason & B. R. Sarason (Eds.), *Social Support: Theory, Research, and Application* (pp. 155–172). The Hague: Martinus Nijhof.

Lefcourt, H. M., & Davidson, K. (1991). The role of humor and the self. In C. R. Snyder & R. F. Donelson (Eds.), *Handbook of Social and Clinical Psychology: The Health Perspective* (pp. 41–56). New York: Pergamon.

Lefcourt, H. M., & Martin, R. A. (1986). *Humor and Life Stress.* New York: Springer-Verlag.

Lefcourt, H. M., & Shepherd, R. (1995). Organ donation, authoritarianism, and perspective-taking humor. *Journal of Research in Personality, 29,* 121–138.

Lefcourt, H. M., Gronnerud, P., & McDonald, P. (1973). Cognitive activity and hypothesis formation during a double entendre word association test as a function of locus of control and field dependence. *Canadian Journal of Behavioral Science, 5,* 161–173.

Lefcourt, H. M., Antrobus, P., & Hogg, E. (1974b). Humor response and humor production as a function of locus of control, field dependence, and type of reinforcements. *Journal of Personality, 42,* 632–651.

Lefcourt, H. M., Sordoni, C., & Sordoni, C. (1974a). Locus of control and the expression of humor. *Journal of Personality, 42,* 130–143.

Lefcourt, H. M., Miller, R. S., Ware, E. E., & Sherk, D. (1981). Locus of control as a modifier of the relationship between stressors and moods. *Journal of Personality and Social Psychology, 41,* 357–369.

Lefcourt, H. M., Martin, R. A., & Saleh, W. E. (1984). Locus of control and social support: Interactive moderators of stress. *Journal of Personality and Social Psychology, 47,* 378–389.

Lefcourt, H. M., & Davidson, K., & Kueneman, K. (1990). Humor and immune system functioning. *Humor: International Journal of Humor Research, 3,* 305-321.

Lefcourt, H. M., Davidson, K., Shepherd, R. S., Phillips, M., Prkachin, K. M., & Mills, D. E. (1995). Perspective-taking humor: Accounting for stress moderation. *Journal of Social and Clinical Psychology, 14,* 373–391.

Lefcourt, H. M., Davidson, K., Prkachin, K. M., & Mills, D. E. (1997a). Humor as a stress moderator in the prediction of blood pressure obtained during five stressful tasks. *Journal of Research in Personality, 31,* 523–542.

Lefcourt, H. M., Davidson, K., Shepherd, R., & Phillips, M. (1997b). Who likes "Far Side" humor? *Humor: International Journal of Humor Research, 10*(4), 439–452.

Leuba, C. (1955). Toward some integration of learning theories: The concept of optimal stimulation. *Psychological Reports, 1,* 27–33.

Levi, L. (1965). The urinary output of adrenalin and noradrenalin during pleasant and unpleasant emotional states: A preliminary report. *Psychosomatic Medicine, 27,* 80–85.

Levine, J. (1969). *Motivation in Humor.* New York: Atherton Press.

Levine, J. B. (1976). The feminine routine. *Journal of Communication, 26,* 173–175.

Lief, A. (1948). *The Commonsense Psychiatry of Dr. Adolph Meyer: Fifty-two Selected Papers.* New York: McGraw Hill.

Lifton, R. (1967). *Death in Life: Survivors of Hiroshima.* New York: Random House.

Maio, G. R., Olson, J. M., & Bush, J. (1997). Telling jokes that disparage social groups: Effects on the joke teller's stereotypes. *Journal of Applied Social Psychology, 27*(22), 1986–2000.

Mannell, R. C., & McMahon, L. (1982). Humor as play: Its relationship to psychological well-being during the course of the day. *Leisure Sciences, 5,* 143–155.

Martin, J. P. (1950). Fits of laughter (sham mirth) in organic cerebral disease. *Brain, 73,* 453–464.

Martin, R. A., & Dobbin, J. P. (1988). Sense of humor, hassles, and Immunoglobulin

A: Evidence for a stress-moderating effect of humor. *International Journal of Psychiatry in Medicine, 18,* 93–105.

Martin, R. A., & Lefcourt, H. M. (1983). Sense of humor as a moderator of the relation between stressors and mood. *Journal of Personality and Social Psychology, 45,* 1313–1324.

Martin, R. A., & Lefcourt, H, M. (1984). The Situational Humor Response Questionnaire: A quantitative measure of the sense of humor. *Journal of Personality and Social Psychology, 47,* 145–155.

Masten, A. S. (1986), Humor and competence in school-aged children. *Child Development, 57,* 461–473.

May, R. (1953). *Man's Search for Himself.* New York: Random House.

McClelland, D. C., & Cheriff, A. D. (1997). The immunoenhancing effects of humor on secretory IgA and resistance to respiratory infections. *Psychology and Health, 12,* 329–344.

McClelland, D. C., Alexander, C., & Marks, E. (1982). The need for power, stress, immune function, and illness among male prisoners. *Journal of Abnormal Psychology, 91,* 61–70.

McDougall, W. (1903). The nature of laughter. *Nature, 67,* 318–319.

McDougall, W. (1908). *Introduction to Social Psychology.* London: Methuen.

McDougall, W. (1922). A new theory of laughter. *Psyche, 2,* 292–303.

McGhee, P. E. (1979). *Humor: Its Origins and Development.* San Francisco: Freeman.

McGhee, P. E. (1980). Development of the sense of humor in childhood: A longitudinal study. In P. E. McGhee & A. J. Chapman (Eds.), *Children's Humor* (pp. 213–236). Chichester, UK: Wiley.

McGhee, P. E. (1994). *How to Develop Your Sense of Humor.* Dubuque, IA: Kendal & Hunt.

McNair, D. M., Lorr, M., & Droppleman, L. F. (1971). *The Profile of Mood States.* San Diego, CA: EDITS.

Mednick, M. T., Mednick, S. A., & Mednick, E. V. (1964). Incubation of creative performance and specific associative priming. *Journal of Abnormal and Social Psychology, 69,* 84–88.

Menninger, K. (1963). *The Vital Balance.* New York: Viking.

Mikes, G. (1954). *Eight Humorists.* London: Allan Wingate.

Miller, R. S., & Lefcourt, H. M. (1982). The assessment of social intimacy. *Journal of Personality Assessment, 46,* 514–518.

Miller, R. S., & Lefcourt, H. M. (1983). The stress-buffering function of social intimacy. *American Journal of Community Psychology, 11,* 127–139.

Miller, P. E., Lefcourt, H. M., Holmes, J., Ware, E. E., & Saleh, W. E. (1986). Marital locus of control and marital problem-solving. *Journal of Personality and Social Psychology, 51,* 161–169.

Mischel, W. (1968). *Personality Assessment.* New York: Wiley.

Monro, D. H. (1963). *Argument of Laughter.* Notre Dame, IN: University of Notre Dame Press.

Moody, R. (1978). *Laugh after Laugh: The Healing Power of Humor.* Jacksonville, FL: Headwaters Press.

Morreall, J. (1987). *The Philosophy of Laughter and Humor.* Albany: State University of New York Press.

Morreall, J. (1999). The comic and tragic visions of life. *Humor: International Journal of Humor Research, 11*(4), 333–355.

Mowrer, O. H., & Viek, P. (1948). An experimental analog of fear from a sense of helplessness. *Journal of Abnormal and Social Psychology, 43,* 193–200.

Murphy, L. B., & Moriarity, A. E. (1976). *Vulnerability, Coping and Growth: From Infancy to Adolescence.* New Haven, CT: Yale University Press.

Murray, H. A. (1934). Mirth response to aggressive jokes as a manifestation of aggressive disposition. *Journal of Abnormal and Social Psychology, 24,* 560–572.

Newman, M. G., & Stone, A. A. (1996). Does humor moderate the effects of experimentally-induced stress? *Annals of Behavioral Medicine, 18*(2), 101–109.

Nevo, O., & Levine, J. (1994). Jewish humor strikes again: The outburst of humor in Israel during the Gulf War. *Western Folklore, 53,* 125–146.

Nevo, O., Keinan, G., & Teshimovsky-Arditi, M. (1993). Humor and pain tolerance. *Humor: International Journal of Humor Research, 6*(1), 71–88.

Nevo, O., Aharonson, H., & Klingman, A. (1998). The development and evaluation of a systematic program for improving sense of humor. In W. Ruch (Ed.), *The Sense of Humor* (pp. 385–404). New York: Mouton de Gruyter.

Nezu, A. M., Nezu, C. M., & Blissett, S. E. (1988). Sense of humor as a moderator of the relation between stressful events and psychological distress: A prospective analysis. *Journal of Personality and Social Psychology, 54*(3), 520–525.

Niebuhr, R. (1946). *Discerning the Signs of the Times.* New York: Scribner.

Nowlis, V. (1965). Research with the mood adjective check list. In S. S. Tomkins & C. Izard (Eds.), *Affect, Cognition, and Personality* (pp. 352–389). New York: Springer.

Obrdlik, A. J. (1942). "Gallows humor:" A sociological phenomenon. *American Journal of Sociology, 47,* 709–716.

O'Leary, A. (1990). Stress, emotion, and human immune function. *Psychological Bulletin, 108,* 363–362.

Olson, J. M., Male, G. R., & Hobden, K. L. (1999). The (null) effects of exposure to disparagement humor on stereotypes and attitudes. *Humor: International Journal of Humor Research, 12*(2), 195–219.

Overholser, J. C. (1992). Sense of humor when coping with life stress. *Personality and Individual Differences, 13*(7), 799–804.

Pearlin, L. I. (1983). Role strains and personal stress. In H. B. Kaplan (Ed.), *Psychological Stress* (pp. 1–30). New York: Academic Press.

Pelligrini, D. S., Masten, A. S., Garmezy, N., & Ferrarese, M. J. (1987). Correlates of social and academic competence in middle childhood. *Journal of Child Psychology and Psychiatry, 28,* 699–714.

Pennebaker, J. W., Kiecolt-Glaser, J. K., & Glaser, R. (1988). Disclosure of traumas and Immune function: Health implications for psychotherapy. *Journal of Consulting and Clinical Psychology, 56*(2), 239–245.

Phares, E. J. (1976). *Locus of Control in Personality.* Morristown, NJ: General Learning Press.

Piaget, J. (1952). *The Origins of Intelligence in Children.* New York: International Universities Press.

Piaget, J. (1962). *Play, Dreams, and Imitation in Childhood.* New York: Norton.

Piddington, R. (1963). *The Psychology of Laughter: A Study in Social Adaptation.* New York: Gamut Press.

Pillow, D. R., Zautra, A. J., & Sandler, I. (1996). Major life events and minor stressors: Identifying mediational links in the stress process. *Journal of Personality and Social Psychology, 70*(2), 381–394.

Porterfleld, A. L. (1987). Does sense of humor moderate the impact of life stress on psychological and physical well-being? *Journal of Research in Personality, 21,* 306–317.

Premack, D., & Woodruff, D. (1978). Does a chimpanzee have a theory of mind? *Behavior and Brain Sciences, 1,* 512–526.

Provine, R. R. (1991). Laughter: A stereotyped human vocalization. *Ethology, 89,* 115–124.

Provine, R. R. (1993). Laughter punctuates speech: Linguistic, social, and gender contexts of laughter. *Ethnology, 95,* 291–298.

Provine, R. R. (1996). Laughter. *American Scientist, 84,* 38–45.

Provine, R. R., & Fischer, K. R. (1989). Laughing, smiling, and talking: Relation to sleeping and social context in humans. *Ethology, 83,* 295–305.

Pyszczynski, T., Becker, L., Gracey, L., Greenberg, J., & Solomon, S. (1989). *The terror management function of political attitudes: The effect of mortality salience on reactions to the 1988 presidential debates.* Accepted for publication, University of Colorado, Colorado Springs.

Rabkin, J. G., & Struening, E. L. (1976). Life events, stress, and illness. *Science, 194,* 1013–1020.

Radloff, L. S. (1977). The CES-D scale: A self-report depression scale for research in the general population. *Applied Psychological Measurement, 1,* 385–401.

Rider, M. S., Achterberg, J., Lawlis, G. F., Coven, A., Toledo, R., & Butler, J. R. (1990). Effect of immune system imagery on secretory IgA. *Biofeedback and Self-Regulation, 15,* 317–333.

Rim, Y. (1988). Sense of humor and coping styles. *Personality and Individual Differences, 9,* 559–564.

Roberts, M. (1997). *The Man Who Listens to Horses.* New York: Random House.

Rose, R. J., Grim, B., & Miller, B. (1984). Familial influences on cardiovascular stress reactivity: Studies of normotensive twins. *Behavioral Medicine Update, 6,* 21–24.

Rosenbaum, R. (1998). *Explaining Hitler.* New York: Random House.

Rosenberg, M. (1965). *Society and the Adolescent Self-image.* Princeton, NJ: Princeton University Press.

Rosenblatt, A., Greenberg, J., Solomon, S., Pyszczynski, T., & Lyon, D. (1989). Evidence for terror management theory I: The effects of mortality salience on reactions to those who violate or uphold cultural values. *Journal of Personality and Social Psychology, 57,* 681–690.

Rotter, J. B. (1954). *Social Learning and Clinical Psychology.* Englewood Cliffs, NJ: Prentice-Hall.

Rotter, J. B. (1966). Generalized expectancies for internal versus external control of reinforcement [whole issue]. *Psychological Monographs, 80*(609).

Rotton, J. (1992). Trait humor and longevity: Do comics have the last laugh? *Health Psychology, 11*(4), 262–266.

Rotton, J., & Shats, M. (1996). Effects of state humor, expectancies, and choice on postsurgical mood and self-medication: A field experiment. *Journal of Applied Social Psychology, 26,* 1775–1794.

Ruch, W. (1999). The sense of nonsense lies in the nonsense of sense. Comment on Paolillo's (1998) Gary Larsen's Far Side: Nonsense? Nonsense! *Humor: International Journal of Humor Research, 12*(1), 71–93.

Rumbaugh, D. M. (1990). Comparative psychology and the great apes: Their competence in learning language and numbers. *The Psychological Record, 40,* 15–39.

Rushdie, S. (1988). *The Satanic Verses.* New York: Viking-Penguin.

Russell, D., Peplau, L., & Ferguson, M. L. (1978). Developing a measure of loneliness. *Journal of Personality Assessment, 42,* 290–294.

Russell, D., Peplau, L., & Cutrona, C. (1980). The revised UCLA Loneliness Scale: Concurrent and discriminant validity evidence. *Journal of Personality and Social Psychology, 39,* 472–480.

Sagan, C., & Druyan, A. (1992). *Shadows of Forgotten Ancestors: A Search for Who We Are.* New York: Random House.

Salameh, W. A. (1987). Humor in integrative short-term psychotherapy. In W. F. Fry & W. A. Salameh (Eds.), *Handbook of Humor and Psychotherapy: Advances in the Clinical Use of Humor* (pp. 195–240). Sarasota, FL: Professional Resource Exchange.

Sandler, I. N., & Lakey, B. (1982). Locus of control as a stress moderator: The role of control perceptions and social support. *American Journal of Community Psychology, 10,* 65–80.

Sapolsky, R. M. (1994). *Why Zebras Don't Get Ulcers: A Guide to Stress, Stress-related Diseases, and Coping.* New York: Freeman.

Sarason, I. G., & Sarason, B. R. (1985). *Social Support: Theory, Research, and Application.* Boston: Martinus Nijhoff.

Sarason, I. G., Johnson, J. H., & Siegel, J. M. (1978). Assessing the impact of life changes: Development of the life experiences survey. *Journal of Consulting and Clinical Psychology, 46,* 932–946.

Sarason, B. R., Sarason, I. G., & Pierce, G. R. (1990). *Social Support: An International Review.* New York: Wiley.

Savage-Rumbaugh, S., & Lewin, R. (1994). *Kanzi: The Ape at the Brink of the Human Mind.* New York: Wiley.

Savage-Rumbaugh, S., Murphy, J., Sevcik, R., Williams, S., Brakke, K., & Rumbaugh, D. M. (1993). Language comprehension in ape and child. *Monographs of the Society for Research in Child Development, 58*(3–4), 1–221.

Scheier, M. F., & Carver, C. S. (1985). Optimism, coping, and health: Assessment and implications of generalized outcome expectancies. *Health Psychology, 4,* 219–247.

Scheier, M. F., & Carver, C. S. (1992). Effects of optimism on psychological and physical well-being: Theoretical review and empirical update. *Cognitive Therapy and Research, 16,* 201–228.

Schopenhauer, A. (1819). *Die Welt als Willie und Vorstellung.* Leipzig: Brockhaus.

Seligman, M. E. P. (1975). *Helplessness.* San Francisco: Freeman.

Seligman, M. E. P. (1991). *Learned Optimism.* New York: Knopf.

Seligman, M. E. P. (1998). Positive social science. *American Psychological Association Monitor, 29*(4), 1.

Seligman, M. E. P., Maier, S. F., & Geer, J. (1968). The alleviation of learned helplessness in the dog. *Journal of Abnormal and Social Psychology, 73,* 256–262.

Selye, H. (1936). A syndrome produced by diverse noxious agents. *Nature, 138,* 32.

Selye, H. (1956). *The Stress of Life.* New York: McGraw-Hill.

Shammi, P., & Stuss, D. T. (1999). Humour appreciation: A role of the right frontal lobe. *Brain, 122,* 657–666.

Sheppard. A (1985). Funny women: Social change and audience response to female comedians. *Empirical Studies of the Arts, 3,* 179–195.

Sherman, L. W. (1988). Humor and social distance in elementary school children. *Humor: International Journal of Humor Research, 1,* 389–404.

Singer, D. L. (1968). Aggression arousal, hostile humor, catharsis. [monograph supplement]. *Journal of Personality and Social Psychology, 8*(1).

Sklar, L., & Anisman, H. (1979). Stress and coping factors influence tumor growth. *Science, 205,* 513–515.

Sklar, L., & Anisman, H. (1981). Stress and cancer. *Psychological Bulletin, 89*(3), 369–406.

Solomon, S., Greenberg, J., & Pyszczynski, T. (1990). A terror management theory of self-esteem and its role in social behavior. In M.. Zanna (Ed.), *Advances in Experimental Social Psychology* (Vol. 24, pp. 93–159). New York: Academic Press.

Solomon, S., Greenberg, J., & Pyszczynski, T. (1991). Terror management of self-esteem. In C. R. Snyder & D. R. Forsyth (Eds.), *Handbook of Clinical and Social Psychology* (pp. 21–40). New York: Pergamon.

Spencer, H. (1891). Physiology of laughter. In *Essays, Scientific, Political, and Speculative* (Vol. 2). New York: Appleton. (Original work published 1860)

Spielberger, C. D., Gorsuch, R. L., & Lushene, R. E. (1970). *The State-Trait Anxiety Inventory.* Palo Alto, CA: Consulting Psychologists Press.

Sroufe, L. A., & Waters, E. (1976). The ontogenesis of smiling and laughter: A perspective on the organization of development in infancy. *Psychological Review, 83,* 173–189.

Stone, A. A., Cox, D. S., Valdimarsdottir, H., Jandorf, J., and Neale, J. M. (1987). Evidence that secretory IgA is associated with daily mood. *Journal of Personality and Social Psychology, 52,* 988–993.

Stotland, E. (1969). *The Psychology of Hope.* San Francisco: Jossey-Bass.

Stroebe, W., & Stroebe, M. S. (1987). *Bereavement and Health.* Cambridge: Cambridge University Press.

Sullivan, H. S. (1953). *The Interpersonal Theory of Psychiatry.* New York: W. W. Norton.

Sully, J. (1903). *Essay on Laughter.* London: Longmans, Green.

Svebak, S. (1974). Revised questionnaire on the sense of humor. *Scandinavian Journal of Psychology, 15,* 328–331,

Terman, L. M., & Oden, M. H. (1947). *Genetic Studies of Genius: IV. The Gifted Child Grows Up: Twenty-five Year Follow-up of a Superior Group.* Stanford, CA: Stanford University Press.

Thorson, J. A., & Powell, F. C. (1996). Women, aging, and sense of humor. *Humor: International Journal of Humor Research, 9*(2), 160–186.

Tomasi, T. B. (1976). *The Immune System of Secretions.* Englewood Cliffs, NJ: Prentice Hall.

Tomkins, S. S., & Demos, E. V. (1995). *Exploring Affect: The Selected Writings of S. S. Tomkins.* New York: Cambridge University Press.

Trice, A. D., & Price-Greathouse, J. (1986). Joking under the drill: A validity study of the CHS. *Journal of Social Behavior and Personality, 1,* 265–266.

Tsigos, C., & Chrousos, G. P. (1996). Stress, endocrine manifestations, and diseases. In C. L. Cooper (Ed.), *Handbook of Stress, Medicine, and Health* (pp. 61–85). New York: CRC Press.

Turnbull, C. M. (1972). *The Mountain People.* New York: Touchstone.

Turner, R. G. (1980). Self-monitoring and humor production. *Journal of Personality, 48,* 163–172.

Vaillant, C. E. (1977). *Adaptation to Life.* Toronto: Little Brown.

Velten, E. J. (1968). A laboratory task for the induction of mood states. *Behavior Research & Therapy, 6,* 473–482.

Visintainer, M., Volpicelli, J., & Seligman, M. E. P. (1982). Tumor rejection in rats after inescapable or escapable shock. *Science, 216,* 437–439.

Vollhardt, L. T. (1991). Psychoneuroimmunology: A literature review. *American Journal of Orthopsychiatry, 61,* 35–47.

Wagner, B. M., Compas, B. E., & Howell, D. C. (1988). Daily and major life events: A test of an integrative model of psychological stress. *American Journal of Community Psychology, 16,* 189–205 .

Walsh, J. J. (1928). *Laughter and Health.* New York: Appleton.

Watson, D., Clark, L. A., & Tellegen, A. (1988). Development and validation of brief measures of positive and negative affect: The PANAS scales. *Journal of Personality and Social Psychology, 54,* 1063–1070.

Weisfeld, G. E. (1993). The adaptive value of humor and laughter. *Ethology and Sociobiology, 14,* 141–169.

Weiss, J. M. (1977). Psychological and behavioral influences on gastrointestinal lesions in animal models. In J. D. Maser & M. E. P. Seligman (Eds.), *Psychopathology: Experimental Models* (pp. 232–269). San Francisco: Freeman.

White, R. W. (1959). Motivation reconsidered: The concept of competence. *Psychological Review, 66,* 297–333.

White, S., & Camarena, P. (1989). Laughter as a stress reducer in small groups. *Humor: International Journal of Humor Research* 2(1), 73–80.

White, S., & Winzelberg, A. (1992). Laughter and stress. *Humor: International Journal of Humor Research,* 5(4), 343–356.

Wicker, F. W., Baron, W. L., & Willis, A. C. (1980). Disparagement humor: Dispositions and resolutions. *Journal of Personality and Social Psychology, 39,* 701–709.

Witkin, H. A., Dyk, R. B., Faterson, H. F., Goodenough, D. R., & Karp, S. A. (1962). *Psychological Differentiation.* New York: Wiley.

Yovetich, N. A., Dale, J. A., & Hudak, M. A. (1990). Benefits of humor in reduction of threat-induced anxiety. *Psychological Reports,* 66(1), 51–58.

Young, P. T. (1973). *Emotion in Man and Animal.* Huntington, NY: Krieger.

Zillman, D. (1983). Disparagement humor. In P. E. McGhee & J. H. Goldstein (Eds.), *Handbook of Humor Research* (Vol. 1, pp. 85–108). New York: Springer-Verlag.

Zillman, D., & Cantor, J. R. (1976). Dispositional theory of humor and mirth. In A. J.

Chapman & H. C. Foot (Eds.), *Humor and Laughter: Theory, Research, and Applications* (pp. 93–115). London: Wiley.

Zillmann, D., & Stocking, S. H. (1976). Put-down humor. *Journal of Communication, 26*, 154–163.

Ziv, A. (1981). *Psychology of Humor.* Tel Aviv: Yachdav.

Ziv, A. (1984). *Personality and Sense of Humor.* New York: Springer.

Ziv, A. (1988). Teaching and learning with humor: Experiment and replication. *Journal of Experimental Education, 57*, 5–15.

Zuckerman, M. (1960). The development of an affect adjective checklist for the measurement of anxiety. *Journal of Consulting Psychology, 24*, 457–462.

AUTHOR INDEX

SUBJECT INDEX